LEARI S

DATE D

F

The Testing Trap

The Testing Trap

Andrew J. Strenio, Jr.

Rawson, Wade Publishers, Inc.
New York

Library of Congress Cataloging in Publication Data
Strenio, Andrew J
The testing trap.
Includes index.
1. Examination—United States—Evaluation.
I. Title.
LB3051.S87   371.2′6′013   80–51254
ISBN 0–89256–146–7

Published simultaneously in Canada by McClelland
and Stewart, Ltd.
Manufactured in the United States of America
Composition by American–Stratford Graphic Services, Inc.
Brattleboro, Vermont
Designed by Gene Siegel
First Edition

Grateful acknowledgment is made for permission to reprint excerpts from the following previously published material:

Reprinted by permission of Lawrence Erlbaum Associates, Inc., Hillsdale, New Jersey, from *The Science and Politics of I.Q.*, by Leon J. Kamin, published 1974. Buros, Oscar K., "Fifty Years in Testing: Some Reminiscences, Criticisms, and Suggestions;" *Educational Researcher,* July–August 1977, 6(7), pp. 9–14, Copyright © 1977, American Educational Research Association, Washington, D.C. Jacques Barzun, from his preface to *The Tyranny of Testing* by Banesh Hoffmann, 1962. Banesh Hoffmann (1962) *The Tyranny of Testing.* New York: Crowell-Collier; reissued 1978 by Greenwood Press, Westport, Conn. *Hurdles: The Admissions Dilemma in American Higher Education* by Herbert S. Sacks and Associates, New York: Atheneum Publishers, 1978. *Time* Magazine, "Getting Testy," November 26, 1979. "The American Class System and How to End It," James Fallows, February 1978. Reprinted with permission from *The Washington Monthly.* Copyright © 1978 by the Washington Monthly Co., 1611 Connecticut Avenue, N.W., Washington, D.C. 20009. "SAT cramming: Dead end or road to success," by Judith Weitzman, March 16, 1978, and "Testing the test-makers," editorial, July 19, 1979, reprinted courtesy of The Boston *Globe.* "Five Myths About Your IQ," by Christopher Jencks and Mary Jo Bane, Copyright © 1973 by *Harper's* Magazine. All rights reserved. Reprinted from the February 1973 issue by special permission. Preface reprinted from *The Sixth Mental Measurements Yearbook,* Oscar Krisen Buros,

*To my parents, my siblings, my relatives and
Aunt Essie, my friends and colleagues,
and to Judith.*

*For all those who have been trapped by standardized
tests, and in the hope that their experiences
will be the stimulus for reform.*

Acknowledgments

There are many people who deserve my thanks for their help and encouragement over the years that this book has been in the works. Not all will be mentioned by name because of their own wishes or due to an oversight on my part, yet I am deeply grateful to all of them for their contributions.

Scott Turow supplied encouragement and contacts when the project was getting under way in late 1977. Ned Chase was the first member of the publishing world to show interest in the idea, and Robin Rue was my first editor on the book with Rawson, Wade.

My colleagues and friends at the Huron Institute and the National Consortium on Testing provided support and information generously as I prepared a report on open testing. At Huron, Walt Haney was a source of direction, a diligent editor, and more. Norma Robbins and Barbara van Fossen had a high tolerance for scribbled notes and pleas for help. Emily Cahan dug up some obscure footnotes when the crunch was on. Some of the others at Huron who were of assistance at various times include: Rick Apling, David Cohen, Peter Cowden, Jack DeSanctis, Mike Garet, Mariellen McNicholas, Mark McQuillan, Gene Radwin, Maria Sachs, Laurie Scott, and Elinor Woods. Some of the people I met through the NCT whose advice proved helpful are Vito

ix

Perrone, Judah Schwartz, Frances Quinto, and Banesh Hoffmann, to name but a few.

There are numerous people working to reform standardized tests. I was fortunate enough to meet some of them and benefit from their experiences. John Weiss opened his files to me while in the midst of his own energetic efforts. Steve Solomon is one of the organizational wizards responsible for the passage of the New York Truth-in-Testing law. Mary Ann McLean is a dedicated staff counsel for the State of New York who made a copy of the hearing testimony available. Her boss, State Senator Kenneth LaValle, was one of the cosponsors of the law, along with Senator Donald Halperin and Assemblyman Albert Vann. Reid Edwards of the staff of Congressman George Miller of California supplied copies of testimony on H.R. 4949, cosponsored by Congressman Ted Weiss and Congresswoman Shirley Chisholm of New York. A *few* of the others concerned with the role of standardized tests in this country who offered information are: Steve Cary, Bob Chlopak, William Corbett, Paul Jacobs, Greg Kelley, Peter Liacouras, Carlyle Maw, Susan Mileff, Kimathi Mohammed, Allan Nairn, Lewis Pike, Jerry Schechter, and David White.

The law firm of Wald, Harkrader & Ross was most patient in allowing me time to work on this book before joining their ranks. Linda Kearney's skill as a secretary in keeping me organized, Judy Marwell's talent as a critical reviewer, and Susan Kassell's sincerity as my official welcomer, have eased the transition from writing to writs. The entire staff has been understanding while I've been typing up loose ends on the book.

Stanley Kaplan was open and responsive on a wide range of topics, as were several representatives of various testing organizations. They will go unnamed (despite my appreciation) on the chance that public thanks might not be universally well-received. My thanks also go to all those who granted me permission to reprint excerpts from their previously published material.

Friends and family were a constant source of comfort when they weren't supplying much-needed exhortations to get back to work. *Some* of the friends whose help springs to mind include: Greg Conderacci, Jim Cuno and Sarah Stewart, Jay Darby and Susan Lowy, Lonka and Zhenya Fogelman, Tom Kinsock,

Corky and Chris Plews, Father Tom Powers, Doug and Becky Rees, Sister Evelyn Ronan, Joel Smith, Steve and Lisa Simpson, Gregg Stone, Reid Stuntz, Cuneyt and Buket and Eren Ulsever, and Jeff Vinnik and Joanie Lieberman. This leaves out a lot of help from a lot of people.

Some special people have been with me for the long haul. Michael Civitello not only revived my enthusiasm when it ran low, but went through about a year's worth of old newspapers in search of clippings. Gail Hochman has done wonders as an agent, while her belief in this project has provided steady reassurance. Lisa Healy and James Wade have made me feel at home with the publishing company, while Lisa's editing and suggestions have made the book much better than the first version of the manuscript. Rollin Stearns did a thorough job of copy editing.

I can't say enough about all that my family has done for me. So I'll just thank Mom (who always knew I would write), Dad, Scott and Barbara, Susan and Arthur, Amy, Marie, Tom, and Esther. Judith helped with everything.

Of course, I am solely responsible for any errors of commission and omission which may be found in this book.

Washington, D.C.
May 5, 1980

Table of Contents

Introduction

What's all the fuss about anyway? If you've been following the news, you know that there has been a definite change in attitudes about standardized tests in America. There has always been a trickle of criticism directed at overstated claims regarding the accuracy of these tests, but lately that trickle seems to be turning into a raging torrent of skeptical words. Why are these tests under sustained attack? Don't they help us achieve the goal of using a fair, scientific, and objective method of selection whenever there are more people who want a job or admission to a particular school than there are openings for that job or school? Why are so many people so upset about this type of testing? If there are some problems with the tests, how can you protect yourself and your children? Do we really need to reform tests, and if so, how should we do it? That's what this book is about.

These are not just academic questions. Standardized tests play a significant part in your life, in the lives of your children, from the day you start school until your last try for a new job or promotion. Standardized tests have become a modern obsession. The scores you receive on these tests at various stages of your life will be used by officials such as teachers, admissions officers, and employers to make decisions about your prospects and your life. Equally important, these test scores influence the way many people think of themselves. The impact can be especially severe for impressionable children. If they are told by supposedly scientific tests that despite their satisfactory work in school they are really "slow" or below normal in intelligence, some of them sadly will take that message to heart. Whenever children or adults are convinced that they will fail, they are well on the way to making that prophecy a reality.

Low test scores can stigmatize fully competent boys and girls, women and men. This happens because we as a nation have come to believe in the accuracy and impartiality of standardized tests beyond all reasonable bounds. There is a kind of wishful thinking at work here. We see the supposed power these tests have to predict our lives and the lives of our friends and family. So we reason backward. If tests are this accurate in predicting our destinies, it must be because they are perfect for that purpose, and so this kind of reliance must be fully justified. This assumption about the predictive powers of standardized tests is made by many people who sincerely want a fair chance for everyone in our country. But as we will discuss, many of the justifications for the standardized tests that glut our schools, universities, and offices are far less scientific and unchallengeable than many would assume. While these tests can serve a valuable and constructive purpose when used properly, it is vital that we understand and respect their limits as well as their virtues. Otherwise, the way lies open to labeling children and adults, ethnic groups and whole races with false and harmful numbers.

You cannot avoid this threat of test abuse just by leaving the problem in the hands of the experts and hoping that they will come up with a solution. The decision of where, when, and how to use standardized tests reflects our values and priorities as a people. It is a decision that we all must participate in, for we will all surely feel its consequences. And it is a decision that we all are *capable* of participating in, for the basic ideas behind the theory of standardized testing are just that: basic. When you strip away the jargon and some of the statistical embellishments, what remains are some fundamentals which are easily understood and dealt with. We are not talking about nuclear physics or quantum mechanics here. If you can add, subtract, multiply, and divide, with or without the help of calculators, you will be able to follow everything said in this book and reach your own conclusions. If you decide to avoid this subject because of the "mystique" of numbers or an excessive deference to professional testers, you will be making a mistake. And you or your children may end up paying a price for that mistake someday. Your ability to handle standardized tests is becoming at least as important a survival skill as balancing a checkbook, filing tax returns, and making change at the grocery store.

Let's be clear about the kinds of tests discussed in this book. Standardized tests are usually written by a national testing company for use on thousands, hundreds of thousands, sometimes even millions of people all across the country. Commonly used standardized tests would include such things as IQ tests, reading readiness tests, reading achievement tests, prep school, college, graduate school, and professional school admission tests, Civil Service exams, licensing tests, and business and personality tests. You know the type—if it's time to break out the number 2 pencils and to break the seal of the exam booklet when told, to fill in completely and darkly the bubble on the answer sheet, to be sure when you erase that you don't leave any smudge because the computer will read that as an intended answer and mark it wrong, and you have to pick the right response out of four or five alternatives, then the odds are you are in the presence of a standardized test. If the name of the test includes the words "intelligence" or "aptitude" or "achievement" or "battery," then there is a good chance it's a standardized test.

When I use the word "test," I am most definitely not talking about teacher-made tests. Teacher-made tests are something we all grew up with. They are written and graded by the teacher, and then usually handed back to the students for educational purposes. Teacher-made tests have been staples of the American educational system for years, and they are very different in design, function, and scope from standardized tests. Teacher-made tests are not perfect; indeed, one of the virtues of standardized tests is that when used properly they can help correct the weaknesses in teacher-made tests to some extent. Be that as it may, in this book we will focus our attention on standardized tests.

Why is it that the problems of standardized tests suddenly seem to be receiving so much attention? I think there are two main reasons. First, the tests themselves have become more visible and pervasive in recent years. Because the "baby boom" children of the late 1940s and early 1950s started pushing and shoving for relatively scarce slots in the choicest schools and businesses, many admissions people and employers turned to the tests for quick and easy decisions. The stakes, then, of doing well or poorly on the tests went up. Sooner or later people were sure to look at the way those tests influence opportunities. Second, many members of the baby boom generation, grizzled veterans of years of taking standardized tests, are now in a position where they can look back on what they went through and ask if that is what they want for the generations to come. These people who have had to run the testing gamut in full force are very sensitive to perceived abuses. Many have memories of inequitable treatment dished out to them or classmates based at least partly on standardized tests. In discussing this subject, I have found that interest has largely centered in two age brackets. The first is the group I've just mentioned—baby boom adults who have recently been through the testing maze, as well as the teenagers who are just now entering it. The other group is older and consists of parents worried about how the tests affect their children, as well as the teachers and counselors and others who must cope with these exams as part of their professional work.

There is no question that these tests have a continuing emotional impact on students who have endured them. Many of my friends remember several of the days spent on crucial standardized tests more vividly than the years of schooling which surrounded them. Some still have nightmares about the test situation. Others recall the days and weeks of fear and tension waiting to get that envelope in the mail that would set the outer boundaries on what type of school was worth applying to. Word would spread quickly once the results were in, and it was not hard to tell the winners from the losers. Words of sympathy or congratulations would be passed out to the appropriate people. The winners would try not to be thought of as gloating while checking to see who they had bested. The losers would try to be gracious without conceding inferiority, while full of hurt, anger, and self-doubt.

I suspect that somewhere along the line someone will charge

that this book is biased because of my emotions about the tests. In reply, I would quote what writer and columnist Walter Lippmann said almost sixty years ago when he was accused of being emotionally involved in his criticisms of standardized tests. "Finally, a word about . . . [the] notion that I have an 'emotional complex' about this business. Well, I have. I admit it. I hate the impudence of a claim that in fifty minutes you can judge and classify a human being's predestined fitness in life. I hate the pretentiousness of that claim. I hate the abuse of scientific method which it involves. I hate the sense of superiority which it creates, and the sense of inferiority which it imposes."[1]

The main criticisms of these tests center on four areas: test quality, test use, the behavior of the test industry, and the consequences for society of test misuse. We will explore all these areas at length, but here's a sneak preview. In terms of test quality, we need to think about whether the questions are clear and unbiased; whether the multiple choice format is the most desirable; whether the tests are coachable and how this affects their fairness; and whether the tests really measure those qualities of mind they claim to assess. Test use is important to the extent that there is an overreliance on tests when other factors (interview skills, honesty, determination) should be considered as well. Misbehavior by the test industry may be a contributing cause of widespread misunderstanding about the weaknesses of the tests and the unaccountability and monopoly-like arrogance exhibited by some testers. Finally, the consequences for society of addiction to these tests may be devastating. These consequences range from the trauma inflicted upon test-takers, to discriminatory impacts which make the system less accessible for various groups, to the way tests can control what is taught in our classrooms. These are some of the broad concerns that have been expressed about the standardized tests. For the time being, I'd like to talk about the three S's connected to standardized tests: "science," secrecy, and scarcity.

"Science" refers to the mistaken notion many people have that standardized tests tell us the same sort of information about an individual's mental size as scales do about his weight or a yardstick about his height. We trust the numbers we get from a scale or yardstick absolutely, which is fine for most purposes, but we also put that same trust in numbers from IQ tests or SATs or achievement tests, and that is not acceptable. The simple truth is that the human mind, human intelligence, is much too complex ever to be measured with the precision of height or weight, no matter how elaborate the instrument. There's something more here. Whenever we measure a person's weight or height, but especially that of children, we expect those measurements to change over time. We know from everyday experience that a six-year-old is likely to grow taller, and that a person who eats too much food is going to gain weight. But when a youngster is assigned an IQ of 80 or 120, there is a tendency to think of that measurement as fixed, scientific, unchangeable. This is wrong. People's mental abilities change over time, in addition to the fact that standardized tests can be inaccurate in their readings of a person's abilities on any given day.

When standardized test scores are thought to be exact and unchanging pronouncements, terrible things can happen. We are all conscious of what people think of us, and of the roles we are expected to play. We don't always succumb to these expectations, but even the most mature adults are aware of strong pressures. If a standardized test brands a child as "dumb," that child may end up having to fight against the expectation that he is dumb, both in his dealings with others and in what he thinks about himself. What's more, it may be the test that is really dumb—either because it didn't measure the child's abilities well on a given day, or because the child is a slow starter who will improve in performance if given a fair chance. When adults in authority try to make a child conform to the test results instead of using those test results to help the child grow, something tragic is going on. It's as if we measured a kid's height and found that he was an even four feet tall. Then when he starts to grow we beat him over the head with a plank to try to keep him at four feet, because that's what the test told us his height is.

Secrecy has been inseparable from standardized tests, at least until recently. This secrecy about the questions asked on the tests may have made it easier to write the tests, but it also contributed to the public's misunderstanding of the tests by hiding them from view. In this atmosphere the idea of tests as omnipotent gods took hold. The work of test writers was seen as remote and mysterious and forever beyond the understanding of mere mortals whose function was to take the tests and accept the results without question. In a way it reminds me of the scene in *The Wizard of Oz* when Dorothy finally makes it to the Wizard's palace and discovers that all the bluster and majesty was just a front for the man behind the curtain. Secrecy is the curtain which has shielded the workings of these tests from public view for years. We must disregard the booming voice of authority telling us to "pay no attention to the man behind the curtain." It's time we got a look at the inner world of testing.

Scarcity refers to the limited amount of information that standardized tests give to us. Even the very best of these tests does little more than measure a set of specific skills thought to be related to school or job performance and then equate these skills with broader competencies we really care about. For example, a standardized test of writing ability may ask us to pick out some grammatical mistakes and punctuation errors. The testers then make the leap of faith based on their own studies— often prepared by their employees at company expense—that the ability to spot these sorts of mistakes is equivalent to the ability to write well. That's a big leap, and there are many who think those who make that leap don't quite make it to the other side. But even if they do get over the chasm in one piece, they've still left out an awful lot about a person that we would like to know. If you were in charge of picking people to attend your school or to work for you, you'd insist upon knowing more about them than just whether they had the sorts of talents measured on a standardized test. You'd want to know if these people had common sense, if they were motivated, if they could talk with and listen to others, if they had respect for the rights of their neighbors, and if they were worthy as human beings.

You wouldn't find out any of these things by relying only on standardized test scores to fill your school or staff your business. In a sense, these tests measure everything there is to know about a person except the important things. No test publisher claims the tests even attempt to measure these qualities of character and determination and stamina. They say, rightly, that the people in charge of making decisions of this sort should consider carefully the other variables in an applicant's portfolio. The trouble is that this message from testers tends to be overlooked in the barrage of promotional efforts designed to expand the market for tests. If nothing else, we must keep in mind that the ability to take tests well is not the same thing as the ability to perform well in those areas the tests try to predict. Let's say you are the owner of a professional basketball team, and I am the coach. We both agree that a team composed of smarter players would have an important edge because they would have the ability to adapt quickly to changes in game conditions. If I were then to select the players by giving a standardized test on the rules of basketball and choosing the top scorers, you'd find a new coach pronto. You evaluate basketball players by how well they play basketball—that's the skill we care about. Shouldn't we then be very careful to see that we are evaluating our students and workers on the basis of their actual performance, in preference to their scores on tests that only attempt to predict that performance?

Please notice that I tend to be harsh at times with various standardized tests and their publishers. I am doing this in order to drive home points about the problems inherent in the current crop of tests. But I am emphatically not out to "get" particular tests or testing companies. My quarrel is with the way test scores are abused and the failure of testers to take actions that would cut back on this potential for misuse. My quarrel is not with the men and women of the testing industry who are doing their best, and who share a goal of maximum quality in tests and fairness in selection. They pursue means that seem inadvisable to me, but I do not question their integrity and dedication. However, I do criticize the testing companies, and the bulk of my criticism is directed at some of the higher-quality companies. There are two reasons for this. One, since they hold themselves out as being higher-quality businesses, they should be judged on the basis of the level of expertise they claim. Two, if the best companies in the testing industry are making tests that fall short of what we would consider the minimum acceptable standards, how much worse must the tests produced by the lower-quality testers be?

One of the reasons I've been so interested in tests is that my paternal grandparents emigrated to the U.S. from what is now Czechoslovakia around the turn of this century. Family lore has it that my grandparents entered America a few years before Henry Goddard and others started giving IQ tests in English to immigrants arriving at Ellis Island, New York. My grandparents did not speak English when they first came here, so if they had arrived a few years later, they might have been refused admission to this country because a supposedly scientific test called them feebleminded. You will read more about Ellis Island shortly, but the point is that my grandparents narrowly missed becoming victims of flagrant test abuse. They were very intelligent people, yet they could have been turned away on the basis of a misunderstanding of what a standardized test can and cannot measure. Here is my nightmare: that seventy years after Ellis Island my brother and sister Americans are still subject to false and arbitrary labeling due to flaws in standardized tests and their application. The flaws today may be more subtle and no longer the product of actual malice toward certain groups, but they still lurk and they still harm.

My father did not learn English until he started public school. If he had been given IQ and aptitude tests in English in the first several grades, he could have been shunted into a tracking system which would have relegated him to the bottom of the barrel and done its best to see that he stayed there. And this would have been justified in the name of scientific accuracy, in the name of fairness and efficiency. Here is my nightmare: that forty years after my father was spared that fate because of the concern, dedication, and autonomy of his teachers, other Americans who start off speaking literally or figuratively a different language are branded and sorted to dead-end programs through the misuse of standardized tests. David Stratman, the director of the Campaign for the Future, testified in Congress that, "As it was with immigrants in the 1910s and 1920s, so it is now with the children of the working class: standardized testing is constructed to justify the advancement of the children of the middle class, and to assign to working class children a low status and a diminished future. The tests justify in terms of 'aptitude,' 'ability,' or even 'intelligence,' what is in fact a clash of values and family background."[2]

Don't get me wrong. I do not oppose fair competition. I am not "anti-test." I believe that these tests do have positive merits that support their proper use. I realize the need for some types of standardized tests to supplement other information we can obtain about individuals, to be used as one of many diagnostic, remedial, and selection tools. I freely acknowledge the contributions to the general good made by the arduous process of thorough research and the employment of statistical methods. Yet we should not accept it when the careful and painstaking work of scholars and scientists is perverted into some sort of national palm-reading sideshow with many mistakes made and many people hurt. It is true that life is unfair, but it is not necessary for us to make it more unfair and then say it was all the product of impartial science.

I'd also like to say that I am not out to "slay the messenger who brings the bad news." You will hear the argument that people who point out the problems with tests shouldn't be listened to because all they really want to do is abolish all tests to protect their selfish interests. I reject that. Most critics want better tests, and want them used in the correct manner. But to do that, what is desperately needed is a chance to cross-examine these messengers. Have they been tampering with the messages that are sent or only delivering ones that reflect their inclinations? Are they the ones responsible for writing many of the messages in the first place? Until we are able to ask the messengers some hard questions and get answers to them, we will remain unconvinced that much faith can be placed in the truthfulness of the messages received.

This book is not motivated by sour grapes on my part about the tests. I have been fortunate in getting very high scores on the standardized tests I've had to take. I have noticed, though, that some of the people around me whom I considered to be more talented or more suited for particular schools or jobs did not always fare as well. A good friend in college did not get into a top law school the first year he applied; his good but not outstanding scores on the Law School Admission Test (LSAT) were the reason as far as I could tell. Yet this friend's drive, integrity, empathy, and bone-deep desire to be a great lawyer will make him outshine many a "three-hour prodigy" on the LSATs. The more I've been exposed to these tests, and the more research I've done on them, the more astonished I've become that they could have captured such a firm hold on the public imagination. Much has already been written regarding the problems which abound in the use of standardized tests. The surprising thing is not the existence of a chorus of complaints, but rather the way that the sound of this chorus seems to be smothered within the massive walls of the cathedral of testing.

One explanation for this may be that the debate over standardized tests is to some extent an echo of some louder debates reverberating through all of American society. There's the whole matter of accommodating diversity of cultures and values without fragmenting into a mere collection of totally unrelated groups. The question of how we can be fair to all the groups in our American melting pot involves more than the type of tests used for schools and employment. Then there is the tension between treating everyone as equals before the law, yet ranking them according to skills society finds valuable. This is the idea of a meritocracy in action. The concern, though, is whether all the competitors enter the race on even terms, or whether some start fifteen yards in front and others ten yards behind. Add in our national love for the underdog, and a recognition that this country was built and founded by people considered failures in their old countries (misfits, religious heretics, paupers, and convicts among them), and you have a fascinating stew set to simmer. We have always hated the idea of artificial restraints, of judging ability on the basis of extraneous measures, rather than performance. We ask, "Can she or he do the job?" If someone can overcome a handicap, we say, "Congratulations," not, "You shouldn't have been able to do that job and we don't intend to see you do it again." These thoughts all have a bearing on the way we build tests and the flexibility we show in interpreting test results.

Finally, there is the attitude we take toward science. Science has been called the religion of a secular America. In this regard, decisions on standardized tests, as on other "scientific" matters, have often been made by a kind of secular priesthood, by a few who don the mantle of "expert." It is natural that "experts" would want to protect their turf, but it is not always a good thing to submit to that instinct. N. J. Block and Gerald Dworkin put it well when writing about criticisms of IQ tests: ". . . this controversy is a concrete example of an issue that is becoming more acute with the rapid advance of science and technology—the use and abuse of science in the formation of public opinion and the promotion of public policy. A crucial task facing the educational system is that of teaching people to understand and assess the findings of scientists and their policy implications. A healthy and democratic society must bear in mind that although not all can make social policy, all may judge it."[3]

This book is intended to help you judge the social policy of relying heavily on standardized tests when making important judgments about individuals. I have tried to avoid jargon and the more complex refinements of testing theory in order to concentrate on the fundamentals. While I sometimes go easy on the statistical frosting, the cake is all here. You will find the book is arranged in four sections. Part I tells what is wrong with standardized tests and why you should care. Part II shows in depth how large a part tests play in our lives, from nursery school to job licensing boards. Part III explores some reasons for the explosive growth of testing and why we have allowed it to happen. Part IV lays out a number of steps you can take to help yourself do well on the tests and to help reform the tests themselves.

Reforming the tests and our manner of using them will not be achieved quickly or easily. But it is a task of enormous importance. As Jacques Barzun has written: "Given the widespread use of tests built on these shaky foundations, their evils affect every literate person, directly or through his children. More abstractly, but no less truly, the fate of the nation is affected by what tests do, first, to the powers of those who are learning, and, second, to the selection the tests make among the potential leaders of thought and discoverers of new knowledge."[4]

One has only to read around in the literature of the subject . . . to see how easily the intelligence test can be turned into an engine of cruelty, how easily in the hands of blundering or prejudiced men it could turn into a method of stamping a permanent sense of inferiority upon the soul of a child.

Walter Lippmann
1922

But even if we are fully aware of the narrow and transitory significance of the IQ and how tenuously it is related to what we usually think of as intelligence . . . does it not seem somehow to brand the child?

Banesh Hoffmann
1962

We must recognize at the outset that the history of the IQ test, and of special education classes built on IQ testing, is not the history of neutral scientific discoveries translated into educational reform. It is, at least in the early years, a history of racial prejudice, of Social Darwinism, and of the use of the scientific "mystique" to legitimate such prejudices.

Judge Robert Peckham
1979

PART ONE

What's Wrong with Standardized Testing?

CHAPTER ONE

You May Be the Next Victim of "Scientific" Testing

Standardized tests are crucial to your future and that of your children, and will be for many years to come. Some of you will benefit from your familiarity with, and skill at taking, these tests. But others will be victims of the national cult of standardized testing. You may be more intelligent, more skilled, more decent than the next person, but if you can't handle the challenge of these tests, the chances are the next person who is favored by the tests will pass you by. If you want to reduce the odds of falling prey to the trap of test abuse, and help your children escape that fate, the first step is to learn about the tests. Once you understand the history and theory of standardized testing—and contrary to myth it is not that difficult—you will be better able to protect yourself and your family from being branded as less capable than you and they truly are. You will be better able to build on the strengths of these tests and compensate for their weaknesses. And you may choose to join a movement that is seeking to change tests so that they are more accurate and dependable. We need to stop relying so heavily on tests that predict future performance and start evaluating people more on their actual performance.

Why are these tests so crucial? Look at some facts. It has been estimated that somewhere between 400 and 500 million standardized tests are given every year in the United States alone.[1] Another source estimates that 90 percent of all American adults have taken at least one standardized test.[2] Sales of standardized tests are thought to run around $200 to $300 million a year, for the tests alone.[3] The total cost of testing is many times higher when the income of coaching schools, test preparation textbook publishers, and test administrators is added. There are standardized tests for admission to kindergarten, to become an auto mechanic, to become a CIA agent, to become a real estate or life insurance broker, to become a doctor, nurse, lawyer, teacher, social worker, police officer, fire fighter, or school principal, to obtain a high school diploma or admission to college, graduate school, or even the fifth grade, to become a superintendent of schools or a foreign diplomat, to become a stockbroker or urban planner or an actuary, and the list goes on.

These tests begin early in life. A child may be required to take in the first grade or earlier one of a number of standardized tests that purport to measure readiness to begin learning to read. Next comes a barrage of intelligence tests and achievement tests and aptitude tests. There are tests to see if a kid is ready to be promoted to the next grade, to put a child on a "fast" or "slow" or "average" track in school. Minimum competency tests are now required in approximately forty states either to diagnose problems or to determine who gets a high school diploma and who does not. Teachers, schools, and school districts are increasingly judged on the basis of student performance on these tests. Standardized tests play a large role in sorting out the "admits" from the "rejects" at colleges, graduate schools, and professional schools. Even after graduation you must usually pass at least one standardized test to be licensed in a profession, and more and more fields are adopting this requirement. If you want to get a Civil Service job you will probably have to take a standardized test as did 1,616,178 people in fiscal year 1978 for the federal government alone.[4] If you want a promotion within the Civil Service system you will likely have to endure yet more standardized tests. And then you can watch the cycle start all over again as your children begin the process, often with amazing speed—in Washington, D.C., for instance, some nursery schools try to coach the children so they will do well on the kindergarten entrance tests.[5]

Tests are almost a universal passport or barrier today both in the schools and at the workplace. The tests are used in the name of efficiency: they claim to be good at picking out which students or workers will do the best. These claims, by and large, are more than the tests can live up to. What's more, the public tends to exaggerate the claims far beyond what even the test publishers assert. Because the tests are not well understood, some people believe they are completely accurate and are an end in themselves. And many people believe the tests do the job they set out to do. Standardized tests enjoy high public esteem. Ironically, while the tests have a good reputation with the public at large, they are the source of heated controversy and fierce criticism within the community of testing and statistical experts.

The basic claim for these standardized tests, in addition to their efficiency, is that they are fair, scientific, and objective in their assessments of the ability of the people who take them. And that, after all, is part of our creed: people should get ahead on their own merit, on the basis of what they can do, and not who they know or who their parents are. Most of us want society to operate that way: a fair test for all, no strings pulled, and may the best woman or man win. Standardized tests seem to avoid the possible prejudices and personality conflicts that can arise when individuals judge individuals directly. But are we deluding ourselves? Are standardized tests fair, scientific, objective? Are they the impartial judges of merit we seek?

Let's look at a little history. The most widely used and most influential standardized test for admission to college is the Scholastic Aptitude Test (SAT). The SAT goes back over fifty years to 1926 when it was first given to college applicants. The man who developed this test, Carl Brigham, had some very strong ideas about intelligence and the worth of various segments of the American public. Brigham wrote a book called *A Study of American Intelligence,* which was published in 1923, three years before the first SAT was given. In this book Brigham explained the conclusions he had reached from standardized tests given to army draftees during World War I. Brigham retracted his *statistical* analysis of these tests in 1930. But in his book, here is how Brigham characterized various American ethnic groups:

> The Nordics are . . . rulers, organizers, and aristocrats . . . individualistic, self-reliant, and jealous of their personal freedom . . . as a result they are usually Protestant. . . . The Alpine race is always and everywhere a race of peasants. . . . The Alpine is the perfect slave, the ideal serf . . . the unstable temperament and the lack of reasoning power so often found among the Irish. . . . Our figures, then, would rather tend to disprove the popular belief that the Jew is intelligent . . . he has the head form, stature, and colour of his Slavic neighbors. He is an Alpine Slav.[6]

Brigham did not neglect to make some "scientific" observations about American blacks as well:

> We must face a possibility of racial admixture here that is infinitely worse than that faced by any European country today, for we are incorporating the negro into our racial stock, while all of Europe is comparatively free from this taint. . . . The decline of American intelligence will be more rapid than the decline of the intelligence of European national groups, owing to the presence here of the negro.[7]

These are some of the beliefs Brigham professed before writing the first SAT.[8] Fair, scientific, objective?

Brigham was not considered an isolated bigot in his day, although some other testers and laymen did criticize his conclusions. In many ways, Brigham seemed to be following in the footsteps of Henry Goddard. In 1912, Goddard went to Ellis Island, which was the main port of entry in New York City for immigrants from around the world who sought refuge and freedom in the United States. Goddard saw his job as keeping out as many of these immigrants as possible. What Goddard did was to give IQ tests to great numbers of these would-be Americans when they landed at Ellis Island. When they did not do well on the tests, Goddard claimed that they were "feebleminded" people not fit to come to America. Goddard argued that the IQ tests proved that 83 percent of the Jews, 80 percent of the Hungarians, 79 percent of the Italians, and 87 percent of the Russians were "feebleminded," that is, of subnormal intelligence. By 1914, Goddard was pleased to note that the number of deportations for "feeblemindedness" was up by almost 600 percent, thanks to the instrument of the IQ tests.[9] What a triumph for science!

Goddard was not without his critics. Some people noted the wave of nativist sentiment that was sweeping America and said the IQ tests were rigged. The critics said that the tests were being used to provide a supposedly scientific justification for a political decision to cut back on the number of immigrants because they were now coming from the "wrong" countries. But Goddard was most serene in his position. He dismissed the criticisms about the test results as being only able to "arouse a smile and a feeling akin to that which the physician would have for one who might launch a tirade against the value of the clinical thermometer."[10] He was arguing that the critics were mad at the messenger for bringing the bad news that the immigrants were feebleminded. Rather than facing up to this sad fact, the critics resorted to attacks on the value of the tests, or so Goddard thought.

The sad thing is that many Americans believed what Goddard was telling them. How much of this came from a desire to believe that the strange new immigrants really were inferior, and how much from awe at the numbers and apparent scientific precision Goddard flaunted is open to debate. What is not open to debate is that there was a hole in Goddard's reasoning (perhaps, indeed, in his intelligence) big enough to fly a 747 through. The IQ tests at Ellis Island were given to the immigrants in English, which was a fairly important consideration since most of these immigrants from southern and eastern Europe did not speak the English language at the time they arrived in this country. An informed guess tells us that we probably would not do tremendously well on an IQ test given in Russian, Italian, Hungarian, or Hebrew if we did not speak the language. So it should not have been surprising that non-English speakers did not do well on tests in English. Instead, they were labeled as mentally defective, and the fear that they would pass their "mentally defective genes" on to their children was responsible for keeping a lot of them out of America. An interesting fact is that the children of those immigrants who did get in, children who inherited the English tongue, scored well on their IQ tests. An even more interesting fact is that those immigrants who were admitted to the U.S. even with low scores on the supposedly constant IQ test, when retested years later, ended up with much higher scores. There are two theories to account for this: they either became more intelligent with age, or they had learned English. Was the use of those IQ tests fair, scientific, objective?

Years later, after Goddard had brought disgrace to Ellis Island, and after Brigham had written the SAT, the National Education Association met at Atlantic City and lashed out at standardized tests. These criticisms indicated a greater sophistication on the part of American educators about the limits and possible abuses of standardized tests. Perhaps now the rush to overreliance on tests would be reversed. Dr. Harold G. Campbell, the deputy superintendent of schools for New York City, said, "Ten years ago we would have said that the intelligence tests gave us a yardstick for discovering the attitudes and aptitudes of our pupils. We have found, however, so many cases of lack of correlation between these tests and achievement that few of us are willing to take them as a sole guide."[11] Dr. Garry Meyers of Western Reserve University had harsher words: "As part of our fine machinery have come standard tests. . . . Stop-watch drills will by and by be barred from the classroom as belonging to barbarity. . . . Two hundred years from now they will appear as curios in the museum alongside the torturing devices of the inquisitions."[12] With members of the education establishment uniting in opposition to test abuses, surely America would turn in the other direction? But such was not the case. This conference took place in 1932, when standardized testing was a mere fraction of what it is today.

Something significant happened five years later in 1937 when the Stanford-Binet IQ test was restandardized. Basically what that means is that this particular IQ test was overhauled so that the proportion of various questions asked was changed and a new group was found whose scores on this test would be used as the benchmark for all those who took the test in following years (until the next restandardization). That in itself is not unusual.

But what was unusual was the candor with which the test re-writers set about their task. Up until this time, men had consistently scored higher on the Stanford-Binet test than women. This was troubling, for if this test really measured innate intelligence, then it meant that men were intrinsically smarter than women. The people in charge of the rewrite decided this could not be; men and women must be of the same average intelligence and if the IQ test did not reflect that belief, then the IQ test would be changed. So they tinkered around with the questions, removing those which males tended to score better on (such as sports-oriented questions) and adding questions that females tended to score better on. They continued this process until they had an IQ test which yielded basically equal results for males and females alike.[13]

So far, so good. Indeed, the people who worked on this re-standardization might be congratulated for catching on to the fact that women are not intellectually inferior to men a little before that realization spread to all corners of this land. But think about what they did. They determined ahead of time through their selection of questions how people would do on their IQ test. They said men and women are of equal intelligence and we will adjust the test until the results conform to this principle. In this case we can applaud the outcome. But if the choice of questions used predetermines the results for groups of people taking the test, just how fair, scientific, and objective can these tests be? Could not the test writers sit down and decide how well Chicanos or Asian-Americans or whites from Scarsdale or Appalachia or Texans or Alaskans or any other recognizable group will do? Could they not sit down and either eliminate or create score discrepancies among various groups, merely by changing the questions asked? The fact is they could. No one is suggesting that the testers consciously do this sort of thing at present as part of some conspiracy to fix the tests. But the selection of the questions to be asked is such a powerful factor in determining how you do on the test that if subconscious class or cultural inclinations of the testers play a part in question selection, then test results can be seriously misleading. If you can fiddle with test questions in such a way as to control the outcome for test-takers, at the very least this means to me that I'd want to write the questions for a standardized test I had to take, and if that weren't possible, I'd want the test to be written by people as much like me as possible.

Apart from the issue of how much the test results are pre-determined is the matter of why more is not done to reduce existing disparities in standardized test scores, especially in the realm of intelligence and aptitude tests. In the public mind an intelligence test is thought to measure natural intelligence, and an aptitude test to measure native aptitude. We will see later that this is not what test publishers mean when they defend these tests, but that is what people think—at least those people who understand what these words mean in the English language and not in the special jargon of the testers. So, why isn't something done? If the Stanford-Binet people could change their tests in 1937, over forty years ago, so that men and women would score the same, why not equalize the tests for other groups? If the test writers and publishers really believe that blacks are as intelligent as whites, that the poor are not necessarily dumber than the rich, that people who live in rural areas are not mentally inferior to those who reside in urban areas, why not change the tests to reflect these beliefs as well? We will get into the arguments given by the standardized testing industry on this point later, although the basic argument consists of denying that intelligence and aptitude tests reveal intelligence and aptitude. For now, bear in mind the words of Chief U.S. District Judge Robert Peckham: "If variations in test scores arise, the test may be revised to remove the unwanted bias. An earlier version of at least the Stanford-Binet IQ test was modified in this way because the test yielded different scores for boys and girls and the testing experts assumed such differences were unacceptable. No such modification on racial grounds, however, has ever been tried by the testing companies according to the testimony at this trial. Rather, the experts have from the beginning been willing to tolerate or even encourage tests that portray minorities, especially blacks, as intellectually inferior."[14]

Walter Lippmann, the writer and columnist, bitterly criticized what he saw as the failings of the standardized intelligence tests as early as 1922. Some of his comments were so astute that they are equally valid today. This is partially a tribute to his intelligence, and partially a sad commentary on the relative lack of improvement in testing sophistication in the past fifty years. One of Lippmann's central concerns was that intelligence tests were claiming to measure something they couldn't even define. This is a neat trick. As you know, intelligence includes many things, including the ability to perform academic tasks and to adapt to and survive in your environment—like knowing enough to come in out of the noonday sun (with the possible exception of mad dogs and Englishmen) and the rain (with the possible exception of ducks). A person can be really smart in one area, unbelievably stupid in another, and average in others. How do you take all the parts of a person and add them up—scientifically, of course—and come out with a composite number that tells you just how intelligent that person is? How do you weigh oral skills against book learning, street smarts against wilderness survival instincts, musical talent against painting ability? Does determination and force of will to make the most of whatever intelligence one possesses enter into the computation? These are hard questions, questions which have been argued for many years and probably will be unanswered years from now.

Lippmann put the problem this way: "We cannot measure intelligence when we have never defined it. . . . The claim that Mr. Terman or anyone else is measuring hereditary intelligence has no more scientific foundation than a hundred other fads, vitamins and glands and amateur psychoanalysis and correspondence courses in will power, and it will pass with them into that limbo where phrenology and palmistry and characterology and the other Babu sciences are to be found. In all of these there was some admixture of primitive truth which the conscientious scientist retains long after the wave of popular credulity has spent itself."[15]

Well, all right. Some of the early writers and proponents of standardized testing had unsavory views and there were some problems with the abuse of test results and the technology hadn't been fully developed yet. But that's all ancient history, isn't it? Unfortunately, it's not just ancient history.

Dr. James Loewen, who earned a Ph.D. from Harvard in

sociology before teaching at Tougaloo College, the University of Vermont, and Catholic University, testified before Congress in 1979. He said:

> "Standardized tests" are the greatest single barrier to equal opportunity for disadvantaged groups, at least in the sphere of education. Minorities who get into higher education generally do so despite tests, not because of them, which is particularly ironic in light of the ostensible reason for the development of the tests themselves, to avoid petty prejudice and capricious or arbitrary rejections.[16]

Oscar Buros, the publisher and editor of the *Mental Measurements Yearbook* for many years until his recent death, was a widely respected figure in the world of testing. His *Yearbook* was a reputable review of the content and quality of standardized tests given in America. In 1977 Buros gave a speech to an audience of testers:

> Many of you know that I consider that most standardized tests are poorly constructed, of questionable or unknown validity, pretentious in their claims, and likely to be misused more often than not.[17]

A few years earlier, Buros had written this dismaying assessment of the state of standardized testing:

> At present, no matter how poor a test may be, if it is nicely packaged and if it promises to do all sorts of things which no test can do, the test will find many gullible buyers. When we initiated critical test reviewing in the 1938 *Yearbook,* we had no idea how difficult it would be to discourage the use of poorly constructed tests of unknown validity.[18]

Bernard Feder holds a Ph.D. in education from New York University and has written a book, published in 1979, entitled *The Complete Guide to Taking Tests.* In his book, Feder comments about the use of standardized achievement tests in our schools today:

Thumbing through the reviews in Buros' *Mental Measurements Yearbook* can be pretty depressing when you realize how much garbage is bought by schools each year to make critical and often irreversible decisions about students' personal worth and their future.[19]

On top of all this, even the standardized tests that have generally been conceded to be the best have run into a string of what might loosely be called scoring errors. Scoring errors aren't supposed to happen when the scoring is done by computers which are above human mistake. Nonetheless, in the five years from 1975 to 1980 alone, a host of mistakes have been uncovered and publicized. Here are some of the most noteworthy instances.

• In May 1978, the American College Testing Program (ACT), which administers the Medical College Admissions Test (MCAT), wrote to medical schools to inform them that the MCAT scores they had been sent were incorrect. Due to an error in the scoring key sent to ACT by the MCAT development agency, the scores of roughly 90 percent of the test-takers were too low.[20]

• In November 1977, the Graduate Management Aptitude Test (GMAT), which is used for admission to business schools and is administered by the Educational Testing Service (ETS), went wrong. An error threw scores off by about 10 points on a scale ranging from 200 to 800 points.[21]

• ETS changed the content of the Law School Admission Test (LSAT) between the July and October 1977 administrations, apparently without notifying the nation's law schools. The result was that nearly twice as many students scored 750 or better in October than July, with triple the number of perfect 800 scores reported. Law schools with rolling admissions policies (that is, admitting applicants when the application is completed as opposed to waiting for a set date to look at all the applications at the same time) admitted students on the false assumption that LSAT scores from October 1977 meant the same thing as those from July 1977 and earlier. Students who took the LSAT in July 1977 or earlier were, in effect, penalized in terms of their chances for admission. The score variances weren't explained to law schools by ETS until February 1978.[22]

• During the 1975–76 applicant years, ETS admitted to having erroneously designated some law school applicants as "unacknowledged repeaters," i.e., persons who took the LSAT more than once while denying that fact on the information sheet filled out prior to taking the test. In effect, law schools that received this information were being told mistakenly that certain candidates were certified liars—information hardly likely to improve their chances of admission. A report about the incident published in the *New Republic* concluded that "individuals whose lives are crucially affected have no way of checking the accuracy of information ETS supplies to schools, universities, and state accreditation boards."[23] Critics also charged that even after the error was discovered ETS kept it relatively quiet and that no effort was made to correct past mistakes or inform those students who may have been harmed.

• In February 1979, a graduate of the Georgetown Law Center took the Maryland bar examination. Part of this examination consisted of the Multistate Bar Examination (MBE), a standardized test administered by ETS. In April 1979 the student was told that he had failed the bar exam and would have to take it again if he wanted to pass. People do fail the bar exam. What people usually do not do is then find out that they had actually passed the bar exam and that the computer had fouled up. That's what happened to this student. ETS offered the explanation that when some human beings went over this particular MBE test as part of a quality control check, they discovered a "crinkle" in the answer sheet. This had covered part of the answers the student had made, and the computer had scored that portion as all incorrect. When human beings rescored the exam, they found that the student had indeed made enough correct answers to pass.[24]

• As of February, 1980, lawyers in South Carolina were investigating the possibility of obtaining redress on behalf of an assertedly wronged teacher who took the National Teachers' Examination (NTE) in the recent past. The NTE was used in this teacher's school district as part of the job certification process. Although she already had a teaching job when her low score on the NTE was reported, that low score made her ineligible for the job. Later, after enduring the loss of this job for almost two years, she was informed that there had been a mistake. The NTE reported score was wrong and she had really scored higher. She was then rehired by the district, fortunately, and began exploring how to secure compensation for her losses.[25]

• In January 1980, it was learned that computer problems were causing disruptions in ETS's reporting of LSAT scores and LSDAS (Law School Data Assembly Service) forms to law schools. Processing of these forms was expected to run at least six weeks late for over 80,000 applicants applying to over 170 law schools. The executive director of the Law School Admissions Council (LSAC) was quoted as saying: "Law schools are broadly concerned. Many schools have had to change their patterns. Some people are angry, some are resigned."[26] Some of the angry people might include those 80,000 students. The charge by ETS for the LSAT is $15, plus another $38 to send LSDAS reports to five law schools. The LSAC was reported to be planning to take over the administration of the LSAT itself when its contract with ETS expires.[27]

This is not the sort of litany that would inspire great confidence in the current state of standardized testing in this country. What's more, this is just the tip of the iceberg. To begin with, we have no way of knowing how many undiscovered, unreported errors there have been for every one that has reached the attention of the public. This is because the test companies are the sole official inspectors of their products and operations. There are no government regulations or inspectors for these tests. There is no recourse for a test-taker who thinks a test may have been in error other than to ask the test company to please check again, or to go to court and try to convince a judge to require release of the test. The sponsoring bodies for the tests act less as independent oversight boards and more as satisfied customers who do not want to rock the boat. In the end, we have to trust the companies to be as diligent in rooting out errors, as scrupulous in reporting their shortcomings, as skeptical of any unproven assumptions as an outside investigator would be. We have to trust the test companies to rise above their vested interests in protecting the reputation and sales of their tests by publicly calling into question their own performance whenever errors crop up. It is no slur upon the basic integrity and decency of the people working for the standardized testing industry to suggest that this is asking a lot, especially considering the problems other people have had even in areas that are formally regulated by government agencies. The idea of a system of checks and balances is about as natural to an American as an appetite for ice cream, but as far as these tests are concerned the companies take our checks and balance their own interests before releasing information to the public.

But even if the testing companies devoted their unrelenting efforts to ferreting out these scoring errors and then telling us all there is to know about each and every mistake, we are barely scratching the surface of objections to the pervasive use and misuse of tests. For scoring errors such as we've seen to date are only the most visible, the most easily detected, and the least significant of all the things that can go wrong with standardized tests. All we've been talking about so far are instances where surface errors have lead to inaccurate reporting of scores or other information. But all this assumes that the tests are basically good, that they are worth the time and trouble of scoring correctly. The more serious concerns about the standardized tests focus on the value of the tests even when they are scored perfectly. If there are bad questions, or racial and cultural biases, or a serious potential for misuse and overreliance lurking within the very structure of the tests themselves, then seeing to it that the tests are accurately scored is the least of our worries.

CHAPTER TWO

The Impact
of Test Abuse

Test abuse occurs either when a test does not perform as well as it is billed, or when officials rely too heavily upon test results in carrying out their responsibilities. Test abuse takes place today at all levels of our educational, governmental, and business sectors. It is one thing to realize this in the abstract. Then it can be shrugged off as some vague statistical event. It is another thing entirely when you focus upon some of the individuals who are suffering because of this malady. What follows might be thought of as an album of snapshots of people who have been victimized by standardized tests. These are not faded photographs from the dim past—all of these snapshots come from the past five years.

State Senator Donald Halperin of New York testified before Congress in 1979 about one such person who did not do well at the hands of the standardized tests. Halperin narrates the tale of this person's constant struggle against the tests. This is the story of "a young man who worked in my law office as a clerk. When he took the SAT he got such low grades that he was told a monkey could have done as well. Yet he was valedictorian of his class in high school. One good college was willing to take a chance and he was accepted. He did fantastically well. He made Dean's list and was considered for a number of very fine fellowships.

"Then it came time to go to law school, so he took the LSAT

and once again ranked as high as a Rhesus monkey. This time he wasn't as lucky and no law school was willing to consider him, even with his grades. He then took the job at my law firm and took the test again. This time his average went up a few points; according to him, merely a matter of luck. After a new search he found a school willing to accept him. I recently called to find out how he is doing in law school. Not quite as well as college. Not a valedictorian, but he successfully completed his first semester and felt he was doing much better in his second semester."[1] This young man demonstrated that he was fully capable of doing the work at each stage of the educational ladder, but because he was not a whiz on the standardized tests that stood between him and advancement, he was continually reduced to pleading that someone pay attention to what he actually did and not to what the tests predicted he might do.

At least this young man has been able to point to his grades when seeking admission so far, and has had some luck, perhaps, on his second go-around with the LSAT. Others have not been so fortunate. I have a friend—his identity is irrelevant, so I'll call him Charles—who wants to be licensed to practice law in the District of Columbia. Charles has a long and proven history of scoring poorly on standardized tests yet doing incredibly well in top-notch schools. Charles had terrible SATs, yet because he had fantastic high school grades and recommendations, and because the admissions staff at one of the nation's best universities was willing to make an exception and overlook the test scores, he was admitted. He then tore up the place academically, receiving top grades. Charles then took the LSAT and to no one's surprise did terribly. Once more he mounted a successful drive for admission to a top-ranked law school by hollering for attention to his grades, recommendations, and history of trouble with standardized tests. Again he beat the odds and got in. He then pulled down superb grades in law school, ending up in the top 10 percent of his class.

But now Charles is out of rope. In order to become a lawyer in D.C. he has to pass the D.C. bar exam. One half of that exam is made up of the Multistate Bar Examination (MBE), a standardized test given by ETS. Charles continues to do poorly on standardized exams, so his MBE score has dragged him down to failing the D.C. bar exam on several attempts. Charles has studied and restudied the material for the MBE and then studied it more. He has taken review courses. All to no avail. I think his problem is twofold: he is too intelligent and knows the material so well that he sees subtle problems with answers that are scored as correct; and he is understandably very tense when he takes the MBE because of his past experiences and the pressure on him to pass. Charles will be one of the best lawyers in D.C. if he ever gets the chance. He is sharp, quick-witted in conversation, and well organized. But the rub is that he can't get around the MBE. No one at this level has helped out by looking at his past history of poor test scores and excellent performance, by noting the recommendations of his law school professors and classmates, by saying this system doesn't make sense. You could have a straight A average from Stanford or Yale Law School, you could have recommendations that would make any Supreme Court justice cry out in envy, but if you fail the MBE by one point, that's just too bad.

Charles loses out at this point, but so do the clients and law firms in D.C. that will be deprived of his services if he doesn't manage to pick up the trick of handling the MBE. What's more, Charles hasn't been allowed to peep at his MBE answer sheet for one minute to see if there's any pattern to his difficulties. The MBE is secret, and if you take the test in any of a number of states you're not given the opportunity to look at your MBE answers after the results are in. You don't get a chance to figure out what you're doing wrong so that you can better prepare for the next time you take the MBE. You don't have the opportunity to see if they made a mistake on your exam as they did with the student who took the Maryland bar exam. You are not given an opportunity to challenge the supposed relation between doing well on this six-hour standardized test and being a competent and honest lawyer. You *are* free, however, to begin questioning your own worth and intelligence as a professional. You may know in your head that there are a lot of problems with standardized tests, you may carry the assurance of years of success culminating in graduation from law school, but in your heart doubt begins to creep in. If you take the MBE results as a commentary on yourself (and it's almost impossible not to, no matter how well you understand the limits of these tests), you are in trouble. A belief that you can't handle the MBE may prove to be a self-fulfilling prophecy. Even if you do pass on a later try, the embarrassment, loss of confidence, and fear of discovery will linger.

Some people go through this agony in public. A few years ago the D.C. newspapers were full of the story of a particular black youngster who was by all accounts an exemplary person: he was valedictorian of his high school with all A's on his report card and high ratings for his personal traits. But he was rejected from college after college because of low SAT scores until the publicity came out and some colleges began to take a second look.[2] The story of another young man was told in a 1979 issue of *U.S. News & World Report*. This student was said to be seventh in his class at Columbia University, a member of Phi Beta Kappa, and a reject because of low LSAT marks from fourteen out of fourteen law schools to which he applied.[3] Terry Herndon, the president of the National Education Association, a union of some 1,800,000 educators, is outraged by the type of thinking that these cases typify. Herndon said: "We often see the newspaper story that features the valedictorian who was not admitted to a college because he didn't do well on the test. And the assumption is that this particular student was not accurately measured in the school experience and that the one day that he applied himself to this examination is a more valid measurement of his ability and aptitude for future development than was twelve years of prior school experience. I think that's an absurdity and it attributes a kind of accuracy and reliability to these tests that simply doesn't exist."[4]

Problems with the accuracy and reliability of standardized group-administered IQ tests have dominated the news during the past year. These tests had been banned previously in schools in New York City, California, and Washington, D.C. for use in tracking children because of concerns about their validity. Yet the ruling handed down by the Chief U.S. District Judge for Northern California on October 11, 1979, sent shock waves throughout the testing world. Judge Peckham enjoined the California State Board of Education, the Superintendent of Public Instruction, and the San Francisco Unified School District from "utilizing, permitting the use of, or approving the use of any standardized intelligence tests" for the purpose of placing black schoolchildren in classes for the mentally retarded.[5] This was one of the most prominent cases to challenge the fairness and scientific accuracy of some IQ tests. The repercussions have yet to be felt nationwide, but it is expected that more school districts will choose to cut back on the use of IQ tests on their own, while further legal attacks on questionable test practices cannot be far behind. The complexity of this case, known as *Larry P. v. Riles,* was so great that it took eight years from the time a complaint was filed until Judge Peckham's final order was issued. The trial transcript alone runs over 10,000 pages.

Larry P. is a textbook example of how standardized tests can mutate from potentially useful tools for diagnosis of learning difficulties into rigid instruments which tyrannize and sentence children to educational tracks which virtually guarantee failure. In California there is a program known as "E.M.R.," which stands for the "educably mentally retarded." The idea behind the program is a good one. Some children do not have the mental ability to keep up with their classmates in a regular course of instruction, but are able to benefit from classes geared to their level. So what California wanted to do was to find those children who needed the attention of E.M.R. classes and then place them in the appropriate section. In theory this would benefit both the children who received the specialized instruction of the E.M.R. classes and the children remaining in the regular program, since they would not have to compete for attention alongside the E.M.R. youngsters and since their curriculum would not have to accommodate slower learners.

What actually happened made a mockery of these desirable goals. Standardized IQ tests were used to do the sorting. The IQ tests used tended to score black children 10 to 15 points lower than white children, and as a consequence, black schoolchildren, who account for roughly 10 percent of all California schoolchildren, made up fully 25 percent of the enrollment in E.M.R. classes. Judge Peckham heard testimony from statisticians about just how remarkable this was. This is his finding: ". . . there is less than a one in a million chance that the overenrollment of black children and the underenrollment of nonblack children in the E.M.R. classes in 1976–77 would have resulted under a color-blind system of placement."[6] Judge Peckham even considered the possibility that California blacks might somehow have less intelligence for one reason or another and still found the IQ tests badly wanting in accuracy. He wrote: "If it is assumed that black children have a 50 percent greater incidence of this type of mental retardation, there is still less than a one in 100,000 chance that the enrollment could be so skewed toward black children."[7] Those are pretty high odds.

Moreover, this is not a benign mistake likely to work out for the best for the black child of average or better-than-average intelligence who is erroneously assigned to an E.M.R. section, for the simple reason that the E.M.R. classes were never intended to help students catch up with students in the regular classes. The best a child can do is keep up with the E.M.R. class, which is steadily falling behind the pace set by the regular classes. In fact, it's not unlikely that a student misplaced in an E.M.R. class would be both bored and angered by being certified as a "slow" student. He might rebel by misbehaving and refusing to do any work at all, or by taking any other of a number of self-destructive but readily understandable courses of action. One professor testified in the *Larry P.* case that less than 20 percent of those sent to E.M.R. classes ever return to the regular classrooms in California.[8] To Judge Peckham, then, the use of IQ tests in California "doomed large numbers of black children to E.M.R. status, racially imbalanced classes, an inferior and 'dead-end' education, and the stigma that inevitably comes from the use of the label 'retarded.' "[9]

Judge Peckham found that despite arguments to the contrary by California school officials, placement in these E.M.R. groups was determined primarily on the basis of scores received on the IQ test administered to schoolchildren.[10] What is more surprising is the way the California educational bureaucracy selected the IQ tests to be used in making these placements. People working in the standardized testing field have been aware of charges for at least fifty years that blacks tend to do worse on certain types of IQ tests than whites due to cultural and economic biases built into the tests themselves. You might think with this history that California officials would have exercised special care to select an IQ test that had been thoroughly checked out for problems of cultural bias and the like. Instead, the testimony shows that the tests were chosen because they were the most widely used at the time. According to Judge Peckham, when the decision was made to rely on the most commonly used tests, "they opted to perpetuate any discriminatory effects of those tests."[11] Ironically, the California School Board assumed both that the particular IQ tests chosen were picked by experts and that the experts looked at the issue of cultural bias in the process. Judge Peckham concluded that "neither assumption was correct."[12]

We don't know exactly how many children in California were unfairly denied their chance at a quality education because they were misplaced in E.M.R. classes. Since IQ tests appeared to be the prime factor according to Judge Peckham, we can be pretty sure that some children of every racial and ethnic background in the state were misplaced, because no test is 100 percent accurate. Cultural biases can harm whites who come from poorer families or neighborhoods with different cultural systems than the national norm for whites. We do know that in California black children suffered an unfairly high number of these misplacements. Even where school administrators and test publishers fought to stop overreliance on the IQ tests they apparently fought a losing battle until a federal judge put a stop to the practice. As Judge J. Skelly Wright ruled in another case involving the practice of tracking in D.C. schools: "Although test publishers and school administrators may exhort against taking test scores at face value, the magic of numbers is strong."[13]

The legacy of the use of standardized IQ tests can be seen in the faces of the young schoolchildren wrongly assigned to E.M.R. classes where learning took place at a pace much slower than they were capable of. You can see a look of puzzlement turning to frustration, anger, and most sadly, resignation and withdrawal. Judge Peckham draws a clear moral. He writes: "Educators have too often been able to rationalize inaction by blaming educational failure on an assumed intellectual inferiority of disproportionate numbers of black children. That assumption without validation is unacceptable, and it is made all the more invidious when 'legitimated' by ostensibly neutral, scientific IQ scores."[14]

Terrible as this is, you might be tempted at least to derive some satisfaction that we are no longer repeating our mistake from the Ellis Island days of testing people in an unfamiliar language and calling them defective when they fail the tests. Resist the temptation. In the fall of 1979, the *New York Times* told the story of a ten-year-old Hispanic girl named Elena who had been placed in a California E.M.R. class several years earlier. Elena was put in the E.M.R. section because a standardized IQ test spit back the number 45 when asked to quantify Elena's capabilities. The normal range on an IQ test is considered to lie between 85 and 115. For those who believe in the power of IQ tests, a 45 would suggest either great difficulties for a child or an almost total unfamiliarity with the English language. Somehow no one considered the second possibility until a guidance counselor, Olivia Martinez, found out that the young girl had only been in the U.S. for six months after leaving her home in Nicaragua. Martinez had Elena and the other Hispanic children in the class retested, but this time in Spanish. Elena came out in the normal range with a 94, and some 80 percent of the retested children showed they did not belong in the E.M.R. program. Elena had been a "six-hour retardant," that is, a normal kid who was wrongly treated as retarded at school.[15] Some sixty years after Ellis Island, citizens of this country are still subject to standardized IQ tests apt to label them as feebleminded if they're weak in English. The tests don't single them out as individuals who need to learn English; the tests just assign them a number indicating subnormal abilities.

Not only do the tests err (a human characteristic), but they also help to determine what is taught in the nation's schoolrooms. They require teachers not only to prepare students for the tests, but also to administer the tests, and then to explain the results before preparing for the next round. This steals time that could be used for normal teaching. Remember, even the best of the standardized tests cover only a small subset of the material taught in the school curriculum. A California schoolteacher complained to me that the teachers she knew were upset, because they were too busy prepping students for standardized tests to teach them many of the fundamentals. The painful experience of New York City in 1979 incorporated these elements in an especially vivid way.

Once every year all the elementary and junior high school students are given what is called a reading achievement test. The test purports to measure how well the students are reading, and gives them a "grade level equivalent" score. This score consists of two digits separated by a decimal point. Say your child in fourth grade takes the test and gets a 4.6 score. This means, according to the testers, that your child's reading skills are more or less the same as the norm for a national sample of students in the sixth month of fourth grade. If your child received a 4.5 it would mean the score was comparable to those of students in the fifth month of fourth grade, and so on. That's the theory anyway. In March 1979, some 460,000 students in New York City schools, grades 2 through 8, took the Metropolitan Achievement Test, published by the Psychological Corporation. These test results would have important consequences. They would be used by the school chancellor to rank the schools in terms of quality, to track students, to see how much federal money New York was entitled to for special programs, and to enter into decisions on whether children would be promoted to the next grade. The results were also sure to be published prominently in the *New York Times,* which would influence public opinion of specific schools as well as the school system overall.

It was big news, then, when School Chancellor Frank Macchiarola announced in mid-May 1979 that he had ordered school principals not to make any decisions on the basis of the citywide reading test. According to Macchiarola, something had gone wrong with the tests, as revealed by a strange scoring pattern. For example, while fifth graders in city schools had a median score of 5.6 (meaning that half the fifth graders got scores higher than 5.6 and half got lower), the median score for the city's seventh graders was 5.7. It was not intuitively obvious why the scores would indicate that an extra two years of schooling yielded exactly one month's reading progress. This was especially surprising since the fifth graders apparently were close to the national average. In any event, another school official was quoted as saying that two other grades had scored too high by approximately two years, while yet another grade had scored too low by about the same amount.[16] Macchiarola later ordered the 460,000 students who had taken the original test to take a different reading test on June 6 because of the flaws he saw in the original.[17] This sort of incident is costly in terms of administrative expense, teacher time, and time lost from other school subjects.

As a further indication of his displeasure, Macchiarola proclaimed that an investigation would be held to determine whether the source of the problem was "technical flaws in the test or its scoring." And he refused to pay the test company the $433,000 it charged for the tests, at least pending the results of his investigation.[18] This frontal assault on the quality of the test used to measure reading levels citywide was a dramatic development, for the same test is used by school districts across the country. If the problem was in the test itself, was this problem limited to New York, or could it show itself in other areas? Why weren't there complaints from other sections of the U.S.? Just how were these tests chosen anyway, and how would children be affected by a switch from one test to another? The testing company rescored the tests and came up with a second set of results that didn't look as odd as the first, but the controversy continues in New York. Prior to this incident the reading tests in the city had been criticized because of reports of rampant cheating.[19]

In addition, many voices were raised in opposition to the basic concepts behind the administration of these standardized reading tests. Some teachers object to the thousands of hours of time lost from teaching that is funneled into coaching for these tests every spring. Further, as the particular reading test changes, the focus of instruction in the schools changes to reflect what the new tests stress as important. This is only human nature. With the results of the reading tests watched so closely, with schools, principals, and teachers judged on the basis of the performance of their students, it is only natural to try to get a leg up by drilling classes on subjects known to be on the test. Of course this means that the teacher is not teaching what he or she decides is most important for the children to learn, but rather whatever material has been selected for inclusion on the test by a private company. This leads to a rudderless curriculum and a kind of faddishness in what is taught from year to year. New York teachers used to stress learning pairs of words that had opposite meanings, since that was tested by the Metropolitan tests. The new test chosen by the city doesn't include an emphasis on antonyms, so teachers aren't pushing them now.[20] The importance of learning antonyms varies from one year to the next not because of a reasoned change in curriculum adopted by the school board, but because a different reading test has been selected for use.

There are some other interesting side effects to an over-zealous devotion to standardized reading tests. First of all, those grade level equivalents are deceptively precise. They say a child is reading at the 3.7 level or the 4.2 level or the 4.3 level. What does that mean? And how can they measure within one month the child's "true" reading ability? Things are not what they seem to be. What actually happens is that when a youngster takes this test she is compared to all the other children in the nation in the same grade who take the test, using a percentile score. Let's say she scored in the 50th percentile. This means she got more an-swers correct than about half the children who took the test, and fewer than the other half. By most definitions this would be an "average" score. She would be said to be reading "at grade level." If she were in the sixth month of fifth grade when she took the test, her percentile score would be converted into a grade level equivalent score of 5.6.

But this process of taking a percentile score and converting it to a grade level equivalent can be terribly misleading. This is especially true for children who score at either extreme. When this happens, the test publishers extrapolate the scores in figuring out the grade level equivalents. There are complicated statistical procedures for doing this, but the common sense implications are clear.[21] For example, if you have an eighth grader who can barely read at all, who scores in the 4th percentile, that student would likely receive a grade level equivalent score of somewhere around 5.0. That seems to say the eighth grader is a poor reader who is reading at the fifth grade level. But in reality, fifth graders who are reading at their grade level can read vastly better than this eighth grader. It can work the other way as well. Say a second grader is the best reader in all of the second grades in the coun-try and gets a score in the 99th percentile. Depending upon the scales the testing company uses for extrapolating scores, the second grader may be said to be reading at the 8.4 level. That seems to tell the teacher and parents that the second grader is a tremendous reader who is going as well as students in the fourth month of eighth grade. But that's not necessarily true. If the second grader were to take the reading test given to the eighth graders, she could come out with a lower score such as 7.2. She would still be a tremendous reader for her age, but now a different level has been pegged. If this sounds confusing, it's because it is.

Grade level equivalent scores are inherently confusing and are no more scientifically accurate than percentile scores. In fact, grade level equivalents are worse than percentiles because they more easily give rise to misunderstanding and misuse. But testers defend grade level equivalents because they say that's what the schools and parents want. If they do, that would mean people prefer the appearance of exact measurement to less tidy but more realistic alternatives. I'm not so sure that's what the parents of schoolchildren want at all. Grade level equivalents make it easier to disguise hard decisions as easy ones which can be made by standardized tests.[22] Compare two cases. Say there is a question whether your daughter, Lisa, now in the fourth grade, is to be promoted to the fifth grade. Lisa took a standardized reading test in the fifth month of fourth grade and got a 3.7. This makes the choice look fairly simple—one shouldn't promote to the fifth grade a student who is still reading at the third grade level. Now look at it another way. Instead of getting a grade level equivalent score when she took the test, Lisa was told she ranked in the 34th percentile. Now if Lisa's teacher told you Lisa should be held back on the basis of the reading test scores you might be a little more inclined to question the decision and the test. After all, the 34th percentile is not that far from the normal range around the 50th percentile. Should students in the 40th percentile be promoted while Lisa is not? Has she improved since the test was given? Was she sick on the day of the test or was there some other problem that might have affected her score? Most importantly, how well is she actually doing in school and on her reading? Is she getting good grades and able to handle the work? These are questions you would want answers to in deciding what is best for Lisa. These are questions you will insist on when you aren't intimidated into an uneasy silence by an overly precise, apparently scientific grade level equivalent score.

Of course, when you've heard about what has happened in Maryland in just the past few years on these standardized reading tests, you might ask some additional and harsher questions. In September 1978, the principal of an elementary school in Ann Arundel County retired in the face of stories that students in his school had been given extra time to finish the tests in order to inflate the scores. This principal had been chosen as the Elementary School Principal of the Year for Maryland on three different occasions. The county school superintendent was quoted in the *Washington Post* as saying, "This business of making comparisons between schools is causing unhealthy situations to develop. This would be one of them."[23] The pressure to do well on these standardized reading tests is not limited to the students who take them. Teachers and, yes, principals apparently feel it as well. The Ann Arundel County incident does not stand by itself. One year earlier the principal of a Worcester County, Maryland, school resigned under fire. Because this school is in a poor area, it had received attention for its high test scores. Then the allegations began, and it was discovered that some pupils had been given the test for practice prior to the official administration.[24]

Moving over to Prince Georges County, Maryland, we notice similar problems in the administration of reading tests. In March 1978, the Iowa Test of Basic Skills (ITBS) had to be given a second time to 23,000 seventh and ninth graders in Prince Georges' schools. This time it turned out that some study guides for the ITBS put together by two teachers had some of the same questions that later turned up on the test. These study guides had made their way through many of the classes and school officials were worried that the results of the test would no longer be valid. A determination was made that the teachers who assembled the study guide had not intentionally done anything wrong.[25]

Still, damage had been done to the security of the test. The direct cost of the new testing was $8,950. The indirect costs were much higher. Students were subjected to another round of test preparation classes, and lost learning time during those classes and during the several days it took to administer the new test. The *Prince Georges' Sentinel* headline over the story about this sequence of events read, " 'Obsession with test scores' blamed for teachers' blunder." Obsession seems a fair word for the attitude many educators and parents have about these tests, and not just in Prince Georges County. Dr. Louise Waynant, the director of instructional services for the county, was quoted as charging, "A tremendous stress has been placed nationwide on evaluating a school system through standardized test scores."[26]

The concentration on test scores in this Maryland county is not atypical for the nation, although the need to retest is still a rare event. The pressures are clear to see. The year before this happened, Prince Georges' students had scored below the state-wide average almost across the board and there was heat to raise those scores. Officially, it was denied that coaching for this test took place at the price of neglect of other areas of learning. But one schoolteacher said she had started to coach the students three weeks before it was given, and that other teachers had started even earlier. She was quoted on her version of events: "We had meeting after meeting about practicing with the kids. That's all we heard about all year. [The superintendent] just doesn't want to be embarrassed again. . . . They put so much pressure on all of us to get those scores up. I said years ago if they want us to teach the test, why don't they just give us a copy of the test. It finally happened, and they're not happy."[27] The kids weren't really happy either. One junior high guidance counselor summed it up this way: "At this point, I think the kids are just tested out. Every time you turn around there's another test. They've just tested the hell out of them."[28] And they will continue to do so, not just in Prince Georges County, but in virtually every school district in the U.S. as long as the public is convinced that the reading tests are fair, scientific, objective, and not misleading.

We have talked about three separate instances of reading test problems in just three counties of the single state of Maryland in a period of two years. How much of this is going on in the rest of the country? How many situations of "bending the testing rules" are never uncovered? How many schools spend how much time coaching for tests of reading ability when they could be spending that time teaching reading? There are no national statistics on these questions. How many people are taken in by the magic of numbers to accept decisions about their children that make little sense on any other grounds? The National PTA, among other organizations, has been trying to circulate materials which debunk many of the myths surrounding the standardized reading tests, but progress is difficult. There is a general feeling that the schools are not doing their job well enough, so parents want outside measures of school performance. That's evidence of a healthy interest. However, that desire sometimes leaves the way open for out-and-out test worship.

There are, of course, good reasons for wanting to make sure that the students in our public schools receive a good education. But we must ask ourselves seriously if the rush to require yet one more standardized test is a means likely to lead to that end. Minimum competency tests have sprung up across the country. Yet there are times when those tests do things other than simply tell us whether a pupil has learned all the subjects we consider necessary for adequate functioning in today's society. On July 13, 1979, for example, U.S. District Judge George Carr ruled that use of a functional literacy test as a requirement for a high school diploma in Florida was illegal, at least for the next four years. This case, known as *Debra P.* v. *Turlington,* presented some interesting facts.[29] These facts suggested that many more black students were having trouble with the test than were white students. It was said that while blacks made up just 19 percent of Florida high school seniors, they comprised 64 percent of those students who were scheduled to be denied their diplomas for failing the test three times.[30] Something has been going on here. Either the public schools of Florida have been neglecting their duties with regard to black students, the test is biased in terms of content and format against black students, or some combination of those two factors has taken place.

Judge Carr did not rule that the test itself was discriminatory despite evidence introduced by the plaintiffs, but based his decision to suspend its use at least temporarily on another ground. He said that the black students due to graduate in the next four years had entered Florida schools when the schools were still racially segregated, and that this poor performance might be traced to past discrimination.[31] Moreover, the point was raised that there needed to be adequate time to phase in these tests. The idea was that since the functional literacy test was a new requirement, care had to be taken to ensure that students had actually been taught the required subject material during their years of schooling. It would be patently unfair to deny students diplomas for not knowing information that had never been mentioned in school. A more basic question, of course, is how are we to select the questions for such a test. What are the essentials? Who exactly will make that decision? And what are the costs and benefits of such an exercise? It is quite possible that if the Florida test is resumed in the mid-1980s, students will be so thoroughly prepared for that one test that the pass rates will skyrocket. But will that truly mean the students have learned more, or will it just be a by-product of dropping attention to all the subjects and areas not officially covered on the test? These questions are more extensively explored in Chapter 11. Judge Carr's decision has been appealed to the U.S. Court of Appeals, with the U.S. Department of Education refusing so far to intervene on either side. In the meantime the students in Florida at least will be spared the potential for test abuse inherent in awarding a diploma on the basis of one test rather than the completion of twelve years of satisfactory performance in school.

A prime instance of test abuse revolves around the whole controversial area of coaching. We have already seen that many school districts try to coach their students for standardized tests. But does coaching actually raise test scores? Most of the test publishers would have you believe that the answer is no. That is essential to the fairness of the tests, for if coaching does make a noticeable difference, then students who have been coached will have a distinct advantage over those who have not. This in turn would penalize students and schools who did not go in for coaching on the standardized tests. At the college and graduate school level, where the competition for admission is intense and standardized tests are a significant part of the process, the difference in scores between a coached and uncoached student could tip the scales in favor of the former.

So who thinks that coaching courses can raise test scores despite disclaimers from the testing industry? Well, many students do. Estimates of the annual income of coaching schools run to $60 million.[32] Over 50,000 students are thought to enroll in these courses each year, courses that can cost several hundred dollars per student per test prepared for.[33] Common sense would lead to a belief that test preparation through coaching could be helpful. If you had a choice between taking a standardized test that you had never even heard of before, and one on which you knew the subject matter and type of questions asked, would you consider that a tough choice? Test publishers often say that their tests measure something called "developed reasoning ability" which is the product of years of learning in schools. But why can't the kinds of "developed reasoning ability" measured on standardized tests be taught in a separate intensive course, especially one that meets over a period of several months as opposed to a few days?

Moreover, one should not underestimate the advantages of being familiar with test-taking techniques. Previous exposure to testing formats increases self-confidence in taking the actual test in many instances, and decreases the odds that one will suddenly panic when asked new and strange questions in a highly pressurized environment. There are other not-so-incidental benefits that may flow to you if you have the money to pay for one of these courses. You might have already seen some of the questions asked on the test. Senator Donald Halperin of New York, for one, had this experience. He took a cram course before taking the bar exam. While taking that exam he realized that he "had seen those questions and the reason I had seen them is not because anybody saw the test ahead of time, but because over the years the same questions are used, and the people who put together these courses have a little system worked out where they select certain people to remember certain questions and they come back and actually have a list of all the questions that are asked year after year and . . . so . . . I already had an advantage because I was able to afford the cost or thought it important enough to take the course."[34] Then there are questions that are changed from year to year but bear enough resemblance to their predecessors that it is definitely slightly advantageous to have seen them before the exam.

Who else thinks coaching can make a difference? Lewis Pike does. Pike was working for one of the biggest test companies of all, the Educational Testing Service (ETS) of Princeton, New Jersey, in 1972. At the time ETS was loudly and publicly denying that coaching had any appreciable effect on their tests. But in 1972 Pike wrote an internal memo for ETS that concluded coaching could change scores on the SAT (a test published by ETS and used by about 2,500 colleges and universities as part of their admissions process). Pike's findings were based on an experiment which showed scores improved as much as 13 percent on the SAT after coaching, although increases of no more than 5 percent would be expected from chance alone. Pike said, "Our studies showed a concentrated review of math and repeated practice with sample questions substantially raised student scores. Performance was particularly improved on the more complicated test items, which ETS uses more frequently now."[35] ETS shrugged off the Pike report, later commenting that Pike's coaching was more "intense" than that typically available in coaching schools.[36] One might ask exactly how ETS knows this and whether it is relevant to the question of whether coaching can work. One might also ask if that means those coaching schools which do provide the "intense" review are then doubly valuable in preparing for standardized tests. You will probably not be shocked to hear that ETS didn't go out of its way to publicize the results of the Pike report.

Despite these straws in the wind, the question on the minds of most experts in 1976 was whether the coaching schools were consumer rip-offs that ought to be put out of business for the public good. Such was the prestige of the standardized testing industry that their disclaimers of coachability carried more weight with the powers that be than all the conflicting and highly visible signals. In 1976 the Federal Trade Commission (FTC) set out to investigate this matter. The FTC didn't decide to investigate the testing industry for overstated claims about the accuracy and uncoachability of their tests. Not at all. The FTC was going to put the coaching schools in the dock and make them defend themselves against charges of false and misleading advertising in their search for customers.[37]

The FTC assigned this investigation to its Boston office. The staff attorney in charge was Arthur Levine. Levine has said that when he started his work he was convinced that the test publishers were correct in claiming their tests couldn't be coached. After all, Levine had taken and done well on those tests, so he had no ax to grind. Besides, the test publishers were considered to be virtually above reproach. But as he got deeper into the study and began comparing scores of coached students with the scores of uncoached students, Levine found himself forced to the conclusion that coaching did make a difference, and an important difference. Levine wrote his report along with the supporting documentation, and then a very strange thing happened. The D.C. office of the FTC refused to release the report or the data used in the study.[38] After months of silence from the FTC, Levine resigned and filed a Freedom of Information Act suit on behalf of the National Education Association demanding the release of this information to the public. Shortly thereafter the FTC was finally moved to action.[39]

What the FTC did was to release two reports and withhold the underlying data, which is still the subject of a lawsuit. One of the reports was the one Levine had written, and the second was a new report based upon a "reanalysis" of Levine's work. To make a long story short, the reanalysis found much less benefit to coaching schools than Levine had seen. But this second, more cautious report still found an average gain attributable to coaching of 25 points on both the SAT verbal portion and the SAT math portion. That adds up to an increase of 50 points on average. Some students would gain more, some less. All things being equal, you'd have to want to be the applicant who took a coaching course and presented SAT scores to the admissions committee 50 points higher than the person of equal ability who didn't have the money to pay for such a course.

This bears repeating. The staff of the national office of the FTC reanalyzed Levine's findings and still came up with this large an improvement in scores among students who took a particular commercial coaching course. Here is how they put it:

> This study contains an analysis of the impact on Scholastic Aptitude Test (SAT) scores of coaching at two commercial coaching schools. Data were obtained from the Educational Testing Service (ETS) and from the coaching schools, enabling a nonexperimental study to be conducted.
>
> Separate analyses were executed for the two schools for students who were coached before their first SAT exam

and for students who were coached between their first and second exams. It was found that coaching was effective at one of the two schools, contributing on the average approximately 25 points to students' scores on both the verbal and math SAT exams.[40]

The coaching school that registered these gains, in case you're curious, was the Stanley Kaplan chain.

What was the reaction of ETS to the release of these reports? After their long history of steadfastly maintaining their standardized tests were impervious to coaching, did they say "maybe we've been wrong, and we're certainly going to look into it"? Did they say that because of this information and their own Pike study and all the criticisms made over the years about their claim of coach-proof tests, that this was a serious matter deserving of public scrutiny? Did they undertake a massive program to bring this new information to the attention of college admissions personnel and prospective SAT-takers? Not quite. ETS issued this statement: "Although some students on some occasions have increased their scores after attending some coaching courses, we believe that the propagation of erroneous conclusions based on poorly designed research can have serious and adverse effects on most students."[41] It seems to me that placing too much credence in this ETS response could also have "serious and adverse effects on most students," or at least those for whom an extra 50 SAT points could make the difference between being accepted or rejected at the college of their choice.

If these bits and pieces of evidence about the coachability of standardized tests hold up, and there is every reason to think they will, then the fairness and objectivity of these tests has to be open to grave doubt. If you can improve your score by taking an expensive coaching course, then the test begins to measure how affluent you are, not how much scholastic aptitude or intelligence or developed reasoning ability you possess. We could save a lot of trouble and expense by assigning standardized test scores on the basis of how much money your parents make. If you come from a rich family, you get a high score. If you come from a poor family, you get a low score. There is some exaggeration here, but much less than any of us would want in such a statement. To start with, that report which found an average gain of 50 points on the SAT at one coaching school also presented some data to the effect that the affluent do take advantage of coaching. Students at the coaching course studied were more likely to have attended private schools than the uncoached students. Moreover, 41 percent of the coached students came from families with annual incomes of $30,000 or more, while only 17 percent of the students in the uncoached group came from families with incomes that high.[42]

If I seriously proposed that students should receive SAT scores based upon the amount of money their parents earned, you would no doubt be outraged. After all, just because you have affluent parents doesn't mean you are a better student or smarter than someone whose parents make less money. And the whole concept of being able to "buy" your way into a prestigious college fell out of favor many years ago. Indeed, the SAT and many other standardized tests were at least partly an effort to eliminate that old system of protecting those from the "right" families from their more talented kin from the wrong side of the tracks. We would not accept any system as fair, scientific, and objective if it meant automatically giving a student from a family making $20,000 a year a 625 on the SAT, and a student from a family making $9,000 a year a 225 on the SAT. Now look at some figures recently released by the College Entrance Examination Board (CEEB), the group which oversees the administration of the SAT by ETS.[43] These figures are for 1974. The column on the left represents an average score obtained on the SAT, and the column on the right is the average family income for students with those SAT scores.

ETS has offered some plausible explanations that might partially explain why income and SAT scores seem to go hand in hand, and I do not for a moment mean to imply that this relationship is intentional on the part of the testers. Nor should it be overlooked that these are only average, and some students from rich families don't do well on the SATs while some students from the poverty level do very well indeed. But given all that, there is something distressing about the way this standardized

SAT Score Range	Average Family Income
800–750	$24,124
749–700	$21,980
699–650	$21,292
649–600	$20,330
599–550	$19,481
549–500	$18,824
499–450	$18,122
449–400	$17,387
399–350	$16,182
349–300	$14,355
299–250	$11,428
249–200	$ 8,639

test which is thought to measure scholastic aptitude seems to mirror so exactly the economic status of those who are tested. James Fallows said it well in an article for the *Atlantic Monthly:* "One can of course argue that intelligence is hereditary, as in part it is, and that intelligence earns money, as to some extent it does. But these general tendencies do not explain the lockstep correlation between parental income and student scores. Unless one is willing to set aside the evidence of daily life and conclude that all smart people are rich, these results can only mean one thing: that standardized tests, created to offset one kind of privilege, have merely enshrined a different kind."[44]

So you can add some more portraits to the gallery of victims of test abuse. You might start with the poor. Then add those who are not really poor, but who can't afford the cost of coaching courses for the more crucial standardized tests, those that determine admission to the more elite colleges, graduate schools, and professions. You might have to find room to include those students who could have saved for and benefited from such courses, but decided against spending the time and money because of the assurances of various testing outfits. And there are still a few more who have been hurt by test abuse that you should find out about. For the most part these are stories about individuals, but then it is individuals who suffer when they are unfairly denied opportunities.

I was told by an acquaintance that her husband served on

the admissions committee of one of the best colleges in the country. The husband was still expressing regret that he had not been able to convince the committee to admit an extremely promising student because of a single low score this student had received on a subtest. There was a numerical formula for admission and that one low score blew the kid out of the water as far as the committee was concerned.

David McClelland, professor of psychology at Harvard University, told the tale of an encounter he had with the rigidity of some people in interpreting admission test scores. This passage comes from McClelland's celebrated essay, "Testing for Competence Rather Than for 'Intelligence,'" published in 1973. He writes: "I will never forget an instance of a black student applicant for graduate school at Harvard who scored in something like the 5th percentile in the Miller Analogies Test, but who obviously could write and think clearly and effectively as shown by the stories he had written as a reporter in the college paper. I could not convince my colleagues to admit him despite the fact that he had shown the criterion behavior the Analogies Test is supposed to predict. Yet if he were admitted, as a psychologist, he would be writing papers in the future, not doing analogies for his colleagues. It is amazing to me how often my colleagues say things like: 'I don't care how well he can write. Just look at those test scores.' Testers may shudder at this, and write public disclaimers, but what practically have they done to stop the spread of this blind faith in test scores?"[45]

Academics are not alone in displaying an absolute determination to cling to test scores as the truth in the face of an avalanche of indications to the contrary. Members of the news media have fallen into this trap at times. One representative of the College Board told a meeting of the National Consortium on Testing about an incident that took place in early 1976.[46] This was a time when Jimmy Carter and George Wallace were expected to battle each other tooth and nail for support in the Democratic primaries in Southern states. A reporter called the College Board and wanted to know what the average score of students taking the SAT in Georgia was compared to the average score in Alabama. This was going to be used to "show" whether Carter had done more for education while he was governor of Georgia than

Wallace had as governor of Alabama. The comparison might have a little surface appeal, but some thought shows it makes no sense whatsoever.

To begin with, neither governor had much direct control over education in their states since they were caught between local school boards who wanted to preserve their independence and the federal government with its massive subsidies and accompanying strings. Further, if you wanted to compare performance anyway, you'd want to look at the change in scores during the time the men were in office, not just current standings. That's because one governor might have come into office with his state's average way below the other state's and narrowed that gap considerably without quite catching up. Moreover, there are other ways of judging the quality of schools than SAT averages; ETS will tell you that the SATs were never intended to be used for school comparison and that they are inadequate for that job. Beyond these fallacies, you have to understand that the pattern with the SATs has been that as more people take them, the average score tends to go down. The theory behind this is that the "best" students were already taking the SATs and that when more students decided to go to college more students likely to get lower scores started signing up for the SAT. This would have the effect of lowering the average.

The answer to the reporter's question was that Alabama had the higher SAT average while at the same time it had a much lower percentage of its high school students taking the SAT at all. So you'd be hard-pressed to make any worthwhile comparisons between Georgia and Alabama public schools on this basis alone. To the extent that you could say anything, you'd probably conclude that Georgia was doing the better job insofar as it was managing to prepare many more of its students to attend college, or at least to think about it by taking the SAT. Yet a presidential candidate who turned out to be a president could have been tarred with a very sloppy brush because of an almost instinctive willingness to suspend disbelief in the face of standardized test scores. An entire state's school system and student body would also be denigrated, almost in passing.

Let's bring this chapter to a close by looking at two more victims of standardized testing: a police officer in eastern Massa-

chusetts and the quality of writing in the United States. The police officer has put in thirteen years of solid work and wants to
become a sergeant so that he can earn more money to provide
for his family. But in order to make sergeant, this patrolman has
to pass a Civil Service examination, and he has a handicap which
makes that task exceedingly difficult. He has dyslexia, which
means a tendency to see some letters and symbols in reverse order. The relationship of dyslexia to intelligence or his ability to
do the job is roughly equivalent to that of athlete's foot or a
need for glasses, which is to say there is no relationship. This
police officer doesn't want to duck the Civil Service test. He just
wants an opportunity to take it verbally or with a longer time to
finish or any way that would give him a fighting chance to surmount his dyslexia. As of January 1979 this determined officer
was getting a cold shoulder in these efforts. The *Boston Globe*
reported the kicker that since word of his dyslexia has reached
the public, some police officers have asked him to quit as secretary for the local union out of fear that he couldn't handle that
job.[47]

As to the quality of writing in this country, Thomas Wheeler
makes the argument that the use of the multiple-choice SAT to
measure writing skills in place of essay exams "bears a terrible
responsibility for the decline of writing in the United States."[48]
Wheeler has the idea that you should measure writing ability by
asking students to write, not by giving them examples of sentences and asking them to decide which of four or five alternative
structures is incorrect. As Wheeler sees it, "Writing requires not
only grammar but ideas and the ability to organize material.
These abilities show up only in actual writing."[49] When students
realize the SAT does not test them on actual writing, they tend
to slack off on the subject. Wheeler writes: "The testing services
that dominate our educational system may be able to justify tests
in mathematics, but they shouldn't be allowed to sap the strength
from our language with objective tests in writing. If we are given
another generation of tests, writing will become a rare art."[50]
Not an attractive prospect.

When excerpts from Wheeler's book, *The Great American
Writing Block,* appeared in the *New York Times Magazine,* an
assistant professor from the United States Military Academy at

West Point was moved to these remarks in a letter to the editor: "Every year we congratulate ourselves for recruiting a group of freshmen whose Scholastic Aptitude Test (S.A.T.) scores greatly exceed the national average, and by mid-September every year we are again disillusioned by their poor performance in class. The problem is, as Thomas Wheeler points out, that what is being taught at the secondary level is not how to write, but rather, how to take the S.A.T."[51] This is not exactly a new concern. Dr. Louis Zahner, then chairman of the English Department at Groton School, complained some twenty years ago: "Few teachers, administrators, or businessmen who employ the product of schools and colleges would deny that written composition is deteriorating. The wholesale substitution of objective tests for essay examinations in all subjects may well be a major cause of the deterioration; for testing influences teaching to a degree little short of control."[52] We are beginning to reap some of the consequences for surrendering responsibility on the tough decisions about students to the standardized testing industry.

These are just some examples of what can and does happen when standardized tests are abused. You've probably had similar experiences yourself or have family or friends who ran into these conditions. Yet it is not at all accidental that standardized tests have such a strong grip on us. These tests have been written, promoted, sold, and defended by an organized industry with a vested interest in the preservation of the importance of standardized testing. The fact that testing is an industry is not in itself good or bad, as is true with most industries. But it is important to understand that testing in America is an industry and not merely the incidental offshoot of some absentminded professors who have absolutely no considerations other than the perfection of our educational and vocational selections.

CHAPTER THREE

An Industry
Out of Control

How could anyone say there is such a thing as a standardized testing "industry," and that this industry is running out of control? Don't these tests just happen, without business concerns entering into it? The answer is no. Standardized tests are the product of an active, clever, and powerful industry. The classic definition of an industry is a collection of businesses all making the same, or very similar, goods and selling them for a profit (of one kind or another). Breakfast cereals, television sets, and automobiles are all the products of industries, and so are standardized tests. Yet one important difference is that while the production and sale of cereals, TVs, and cars are all regulated to some extent (or even overregulated at times), the production, sale, and use of standardized tests take place without government safeguards. The people who run this industry don't have to answer to people outside the industry—such as the people who have to take the tests and pay for them. You've heard of setting the fox to guard the hens? Well, the analogy often used for the testing industry is that it is the same as letting a student grade his or her own test and then announce the result.

There are oversight boards or sponsoring bodies who could exercise some degree of control over the work of the test companies with whom they contract. Unfortunately, because of overlapping directorates and a preformed faith in the tests, the test companies and the test sponsors tend to blur together. The relationship of sponsors to test publishers is often like that of college trustees to a college president. While the trustees have the formal power to fire the president and to make all decisions, this power is rarely exercised. After all, the trustees chose the president in the first place, so an admission of presidential incompetence would reflect badly on them as well. No one wants to rock the boat. Moreover, an industrious president can sharply tilt the odds in her favor since she is the one in charge of supplying the information to the trustees upon which they will act, indeed often setting the agenda. And even if the sponsors were holding test companies on a tight leash, just whom are the sponsors accountable to? Certainly not the test consumers, the people who take the tests. So the testing industry is out of control in the sense that it is given incredible freedom to operate in a manner of its own choosing in order to pursue its own ends.

How big is this industry? The numbers are impressive. There are estimates that every year between 400 and 500 million multiple-choice standardized tests are given in the U.S. alone.[1] That's almost enough to give two standardized tests a year to every man, woman, child, and infant in this country. It has been written that about one-third of the American population is the subject of one or more standardized tests each year.[2] Children in grades 1 through 12 are said to be the subjects of about 300 million tests per year, with roughly three out of four public school systems in the U.S. using a systematic scheme of standardized testing. Direct revenue for the industry is thought to run around $200 to $300 million a year.[3] This does not include additional income from coaching schools and the sale of test preparation books. If you think this is insignificant, the next time you are in a bookstore go to the section that contains test preparation aids and books and just stare at the mass of printed material available.

Let's put these numbers into some perspective that will give a good idea of the impact testing has on us. The National Education Association has recently released figures indicating that every year about 47,000,000 children in elementary and secondary schools take standardized tests. And still within the educational sphere, another 2,500,000 or so students take postsecondary standardized tests every year.[4] The *New York Times* printed a 1977 estimate that over 50,000,000 of America's youth would be exposed to up to three standardized tests each during their years of schooling.[5] Actually, this is a conservative figure since a youngster exposed to one or two IQ tests, a reading readiness test, several reading achievement tests, a minimum competency test, a PSAT, and an SAT or ACT—which is not an extraordinary sequence today—has already gone well beyond the "three standardized tests" estimate. Others believe that we in this country are subjected to more standardized psychological tests than all the rest of the people in the world taken together.[6] These figures are inexact because no one has been able to gather precise sales figures from all the testing companies. For the most part, these testers are not even required to report such sales figures, so we cannot know the scope of their operations precisely. This is another sense in which the industry can be said to be out of control—indeed, it might be more accurate to say portions of the industry manage to keep themselves hidden from sight, let alone control.

On top of all this, testing is expanding rapidly, both in numbers of tests given and in new subject and occupation areas. It is estimated that over 5 million standardized tests were given per year by 1930, over 100 million by 1960, and now we are in the 400 to 500 million range.[7] That's a phenomenal growth record. These numbers reflect the ability of the industry to keep reaching out, to keep spreading its shadow over more and more parts of American life. Testing programs and requirements exist in schooling, employment, and psychological evaluation programs. Minimum competency testing has become the latest boon for the industry, while research on new targets of opportunity goes on in fields such as infant intelligence, midcareer employment changes, and even nonacademic character traits for admissions programs. You are not immune to the virus of testing just because you are now out of school. As Bernard Feder writes: "Each year, the range of formal testing grows broader. In the armed forces, recruits are routinely tested for placement; in the professions, the right to practice what one has spent years learning depends on the results of a test that lasts for several hours or several days. Applicants for Civil Service and for an increasing number of jobs in business and industry, candidates for promotion in a wide variety of occupations, craftsmen seeking permission to practice their trades, and citizens who want to drive their automobiles all face qualifying paper-and-pencil tests—many of them only remotely related to the skills they purport to measure."[8] Again, in sheer numbers, in the spread of its use to all sectors of our economy and our schools, standardized testing is an industry running out of control.

Who are the members of the testing industry? There are thought to be some 400 companies in the field, but a few testers really dominate. The top 10 percent of testing companies, that is, forty to fifty test publishers, are responsible for roughly 90 percent of the tests used in the U.S.[9] One analysis published several years ago found that of 2,585 standardized tests in use at the time, 1,678 of them were written by the leading forty-five companies. The giants in this breakdown were the Educational Testing Service (ETS), the College Entrance Examination Board (CEEB), and Harcourt Brace Jovanovich (HBJ). ETS and CEEB between them accounted for 315 tests, or 14.3 percent of the tests in use. HBJ and its associated firms wrote 7.9 percent of the tests.[10] Some of the other large test publishers include such groups as the American College Testing Program (ACT); McGraw-Hill Publishers; Science Research Associates (SRA), a subsidiary of IBM; and Houghton Mifflin Publishers. To give you an idea of how firms and tests sometimes interact, consider what are called the "Iowa tests." The Iowa tests are used for assessment at the elementary and high school level. The same man who developed the initial Iowa Tests of Educational Development (ITED) also helped create the Iowa Tests of Basic Skills (ITBS). But now the ITED is handled by SRA, while Houghton Mifflin has the ITBS. One source estimates that these two tests alone are taken by about 10 million students a year.[11]

By far the most important firm in the industry is the Educational Testing Service (ETS) of Princeton, New Jersey. ETS is the flagship outfit of standardized testing. To paraphrase one of ETS's favorite forms for questions, please consider this.

ETS is to testing as _____ is to _____?

    (a) The New York Yankees/ baseball.

    (b) General Motors/ cars.

    (c) UCLA/ college basketball.

    (d) Howard Hughes/ secrecy.

    (e) All of the above.

Those of you who picked answer (e) selected the best of the alternatives presented, but that answer might understate ETS's preeminent position a mite. ETS is at the top of the testing heap whether you consider the top to mean earning the most money, having the highest reputation for the quality of their tests, being the trend-setter in research and new tests, or just being the most visible of the lot. By the way, despite its location in Princeton, ETS does not have any formal connections to Princeton University.

Let's look at some of the numbers that at least partially explain why ETS is perched at the top. During the 1977–78 school year, 1,488,300 students took the Scholastic Aptitude Test (SAT) and its related Achievement Tests.[12] These tests, written and administered by ETS, play a key role for many students in deciding which colleges they will apply to, and which colleges will admit them. Students don't take these tests as an optional exercise; they are required for admission. What's more, the SAT is especially in evidence in the admissions processes of prestigious colleges, such as those of the Ivy League and the Seven Sisters. In that same year, 166,000 students took the Graduate Management Aptitude Test (GMAT) to get into business schools. Some 314,000 students took the Graduate Record Examination (GRE) as part of their application to graduate schools. And 128,000 students took the Law School Admission Test (LSAT) in hopes of obtaining admission to law schools.[13] It should come as no surprise to you to hear that the GMAT, the GRE, and the LSAT are all written and administered by ETS, although they do not by any means begin to exhaust the list of ETS tests.

At last count, ETS was designing tests for over 350 different groups.[14] In addition to its scholastic tests, ETS writes occupational tests used to determine whether you can be licensed in real estate work, in automobile mechanics, in insecticide application, or move up in the world of the State Department.[15] ETS now makes approximately $94 million by administering some 8 million tests a year.[16] ETS has been able to almost double its income every six years since its post-World War II beginning. The full-time staff of ETS comes to over 2,000 people spread among the headquarters in New Jersey and eight branch offices including one in Puerto Rico.[17] One startling statistic is that very few ETS employees actually do the question writing for the multitude of ETS tests. One critic of ETS cited a figure of only sixty-seven ETS employees engaged in test writing, which comes to just over 3 percent of the total work force.[18]

These numbers by themselves, while impressive, do not do full justice to the influence ETS exerts on the nation. A recent *Newsweek* article contained this statement: "By common agreement, few people land high-prestige positions in the U.S. today without encountering—and doing well on—at least one ETS test. The company's IBM computers—the world's largest educational and psychological data bank—tabulate and store information twenty-four hours a day and hold exam scores for at least 15 million citizens."[19] Ralph Nader has criticized "the destruction of the self-confidence of millions of students who incorporate as a measure of their own esteem and self-worth evaluations set by the Educational Testing Service. ETS and the other major testing firms decide who has 'aptitude' and 'intelligence,' and significantly decide who has access to educational and professional opportunities. They are regulators of the human mind."[20] On a more personal level, you may recall your own nervous reactions to any envelope arriving at your door with a return address in Princeton, New Jersey. It is hard to imagine just how much adrenaline has poured into American bloodstreams at the prospect of taking, and getting the results of, an ETS test.

ETS describes itself in a rather modest fashion, sort of like a bashful, barefoot boy of testing. ETS says it is "a private, nonprofit organization devoted to measurement and research, primarily in the field of education. It was founded in 1947 by the American Council of Education, the Carnegie Foundation for the Advancement of Teaching, and the College Board."[21] This humble origin is akin to having a Rockefeller, a Getty, a Mellon, and a Kennedy for grandparents. ETS does seem to conduct its operations as if it were to the manor born. The headquarters is located on 400 beautiful country acres, complete with a plush home for the president, and a $3 million conference center. To preserve the multiple-choice image, visitors and overseers can choose between the ETS swimming pool and tennis courts when in need of relaxation.[22] Some people, though, are not relaxed by these comfortable surroundings. Chuck Stone, the senior editor of the *Philadelphia Daily News* and former director of minority affairs for ETS, might be numbered in this group. Stone unleashed a blistering attack on the ETS life-style while testifying before the New York State legislature in 1979.

Here is what Mr. Stone told the legislators: "The American people would be horrified if they knew how their hard-earned salaries are manipulated to pamper overpriced researchers who sit all day and contemplate their psychometric navels while the rest of the nation is out trying to make ends meet in these economically uncertain times. Ironically, the College Entrance Examination Board, which provides 40 percent of ETS's income, maintains comparatively spartan offices on a couple of floors in a mid-Manhattan building while ETS has built an educational country club with inflated test fees, excessive charges for its services, and built-in profit margins for its government contracts."[23] ETS has defended itself on several grounds, including comparisons of cost per square foot and a claim of economic foresight in obtaining its land at bargain prices.[24] There is something to be said for these explanations. But aside from the underlying reality, ETS by its conscious choice has set a tone and created the appearance of great luxury in its domain.

Part of the controversy stems from ETS's nonprofit status. All that nonprofit means is that you have met certain government rules, the chief of which is that no stockholders be allowed and no "profit" be generated. A nonprofit corporation, then, cannot pay out dividends and in theory has no reason to pile up the big dollars. Within certain guidelines, a nonprofit body must spend as much as it makes, which avoids the problem of profits (profits are basically whatever you have left over when you subtract expenses from earnings). Of course, a nonprofit company can rack up prestige points in comparison to a competing private company. After all, we know a private company is out to make money and might be tempted to cut corners in the process. But what does a nonprofit firm stand to gain by elevating revenues over costs? It could be a great deal. While nonprofit corporations don't have shareholders to give the surplus to, there are other ways of spending money which don't violate the government regulations. You could raise the salaries of all your employees and make sure they were working in superbly furnished and equipped offices, with generous benefits. If you had money left after that, you could plow it back into more research to bolster sales of your product, and to create new ones which would allow you to increase revenues and hire more employees and garner more prestige and so on. There is nothing wrong with doing these things lawfully. But notice that the behavior of a nonprofit organization may be attributable to many of the same motivations found in a private firm. In other words, "nonprofit" does not automatically mean disinterested or selfless. There is no reason to use "nonprofit" as an epithet; but neither does it mean "morally superior to profit-making companies."

The halo may have come off ETS's nonprofit crown simply because it grew so big. And ETS may have been able to grow so big by capitalizing on the goodwill that nonprofit groups have with the public at large. Paul Pottinger, executive director of the National Center for the Study of the Professions, was quoted on the former point. He said, "When ETS began to report $80 million in revenues, student perceptions about it began to change. They now realize that it is not just a benign friend of the university helping us get through. It is a big business that is affecting our lives."[25] Jerry Schechter, a psychology professor at the State University of New York at Stony Brook, has written on the latter point, "ETS has become the preeminent firm in the standardized testing industry, partly because it produces the most tests and partly because its nonprofit status implies it is more interested in science than it is in making money."[26] Some of ETS's competitors have complained publicly about the nonprofit status. For one thing, a nonprofit group doesn't have to pay taxes, a tremendous competitive advantage over a private concern meeting its tax burden. And Roger Lennon, associate to the chairman at HBJ, was cited in the *New York Times* to the effect that ETS can use the prestige of its nonprofit label as a "selling point."[27]

It does seem that if an outfit such as ETS intends to invoke the benefits of instant credibility associated with its nonprofit designation, and they do almost constantly, then it should live up to the higher standards applicable to nonprofit groups. ETS has not always lived up to these standards. This is not a new criticism, but it is a powerful one, and it is powerfully stated by Martin Mayer in his book, *The Schools*. Mayer writes: "If there is one proposition upon which educational philosophers of all schools are agreed, it is that tests and examinations are at best a necessary evil. But ETS is publicly committed to the proposition that testing is indispensable and always beneficent. . . . Such activity by a profit-making corporation would be excusable if unattractive; but the officers of a tax-exempt, charitably supported organization accept with their powerful quasi-public positions a moral obligation to keep their public statements well this side of hard-sell salesmanship."[28] This criticism by Mayer goes back to 1961, but the problem continues.

How well has ETS met this "moral obligation" lately? You might recall the ETS attack on the reports released by the FTC, the reports which dared to contradict ETS's oft-repeated assurances that coaching would not improve scores appreciably on its Scholastic Aptitude Test. You might consider a tendency on the part of some ETS spokesmen to engage in ad hominem attacks against individuals who dare to criticize ETS. In 1979, ETS published a paper that had been given to the American Psychological Association by a person who had just completed a year as the first "ETS Visiting Scholar in Measurement and Public Policy." This individual, I grant, is a noted psychologist and attorney more than entitled to her opinion. But listen to her response to the opinions of some testing critics. "On a more personal, individual level, tests tell us that the grandiose self-evaluations and inflated expectations for success and stardom increasingly common among some middle-class youths are just that: grandiose and inflated. In focusing on self-indulgent narcissistic youth of this sort at this point, I do not mean to suggest that they are the only ones who bitterly resent objective evaluations and respond by attacking their evaluators and the instruments they use.

Nader's young raiders are, after all, relatively fresh troops in this war."[29] That's certainly showing respect for the other party to a debate and rebutting the issues and concerns they have raised in a straightforward manner.

One need not be a devoted follower of Ralph Nader, as I am not, or even a "Nader's raider," as I have never been, to suspect there's a certain amount of overreaction in this ETS document. One could point out that there are a number of people who have questioned ETS and testing policies who have earned very high scores indeed on the ETS tests. One might also suggest that the above speaker herself has responded to outside evaluations by "attacking [the] evaluators." I hesitate to make such suggestions because of another allegation by the above speaker in the same talk. She charged that ". . . the attack on tests is, to a very considerable and very frightening degree, an attack on truth itself. . . ."[30] The last thing I want is to be accused of attacking truth itself or of criticizing someone who defends truth in a public address.

The most thorough outside study of ETS available to the public is the Ralph Nader report entitled, "The Reign of ETS." The report runs 554 pages and is the result of six years of work by researcher Allan Nairn and his associates. The report. is heavily critical of ETS, and reasonable women and men could differ with many of its conclusions and some of its methodology. Yet it is a serious work. A *New York Times* editorial said that despite some differences of opinion, there was "genuine value [to] the study. It is worthwhile if only because it publishes a good deal of research that test makers heretofore have kept to themselves. And the study can have additional value by helping to moderate the inflated importance that many people—admissions officers included—now attach to the tests."[31] The ETS response? Among a host of negative statements made by ETS spokesmen, one ETS official was quoted as saying the report was "deliberately fraudulent," and charged data had been distorted.[32] This is all somewhat ironic. ETS is fond of pointing out how much it tells test users about the limitations of its tests and how forcefully it admonishes against test misuse through overreliance. But ETS may think it has proprietary rights to those warnings, for when a report comes out that helps "to moderate the inflated importance that many . . . now attach to the tests," the report itself is roundly denounced in no uncertain terms.

ETS does many good things in the area of testing, and they certainly don't hold a monopoly on the less desirable actions either. Far from it. Overall, ETS is a class outfit, but it often turns out to be its own worst enemy with the public because of misleading or contradictory statements by its officials and staff. In addition, as with the tallest building or tree in a thunderstorm, ETS often draws the lightning because it towers above the others in its field. Critics out to make a point about test problems will often use ETS as the example because, as Banesh Hoffmann has written, "one makes the strongest case by criticizing the best test makers, not the worst."[33] ETS has some trouble with this concept. I have never heard them refusing the accolade of being the top-rated tester in the public mind, but some ETS officials seem defensive, even self-pitying, when the knocks that come with the top position are put on them. If ETS could bring itself to acknowledge valid criticisms less grudgingly, it might do a whole lot more to improve its image than it could ever gain by repeated attacks on the motivations and integrity of its critics.

Who are some of the other notable members of the standardized testing industry? Well, the College Entrance Examination Board (CEEB), often referred to as the College Board, is the largest sponsoring body at the postsecondary school level. The College Board is made up of over 2,500 individual colleges that have banded together for a number of purposes, including testing. The Board was founded in 1900 largely in an effort to devise a uniform way of testing applicants for college and thereby saving both students and schools a lot of trouble. Up until then most colleges had their own individual tests for admission, and it was becoming cumbersome for students to take all those different tests and for colleges to write and mark them. College Board tests were started to reduce this overlapping effort and to expand the pool of college applicants so that member institutions could grow.[34] Grow they did. Now the College Board, which is both parent to ETS and the sponsor of the SAT, contracts for the testing of more college applicants than all other groups put together.[35]

The main rival to the SAT test sponsored by CEEB and written and administered by ETS, is the American College Testing Program (ACT). ACT has its headquarters in Iowa City, Iowa. ACT is a relative newcomer on the scene since it didn't get its start as a nonprofit organization until 1959. Despite its youth, ACT has made great headway in its field. ACT is best known for two tests. The first, which ACT writes and administers, is the ACT Assessment, a test used by college admissions officers in selecting and placing students.[36] The other well-known test is the Medical College Admission Test (MCAT), a test ACT administers but does not write, which is required by most medical schools as part of their admissions decision process. In the 1976–77 school year, 923,241 students took the ACT Assessment, while another 60,000 or so medical school applicants took the MCAT.[37] The ACT is required or accepted in lieu of the SAT at more than 2,600 institutions of higher learning. Interestingly, the SAT seems to have its firmest grip on the Northeastern schools, while the ACT Assessment finds its strength proportionally greatest in the South, the Midwest, and the Far West.[38]

So much for some of the bigger nonprofit testing organizations. How about some of the private companies that publish tests? The Psychological Corporation (sometimes called the Psych Corp for short), a subsidiary of HBJ, is the biggest commercial test publisher. Next in line is the California Test Bureau, which is a subsidiary of McGraw-Hill. Also in the field is the group known as Science Research Associates (SRA), a subsidiary of IBM.[39] We will focus on HBJ/The Psychological Corporation as the largest private test publisher.

HBJ is a descendant of the original World Book Company, and has been publishing tests since 1918, while the Psych Corp got its start in 1921. HBJ as the parent body is responsible for more than 100 tests. Some of the better known tests in this flock include the Stanford Achievement Test, the Metropolitan Achievement Test, the Stanford-Binet IQ Test, and the Miller Analogies Test. A partial list of HBJ tests gives an idea of the diversity of its subject matter. HBJ directly, or through the Psych Corp, publishes tests for: obtaining a license in fields such as neurosurgical nursing, cosmetology, occupational therapy, marketing communications, and more; and for admission to some graduate schools and schools of pharmacy, optometry, veterinary medicine, nursing, and more. A spokesman for HBJ told Congress in 1979 that HBJ concentrates on tests for elementary and secondary schools, but added that the concentration was not exclusive, and recited an extensive litany of HBJ tests of which the tests mentioned above were just a fraction.[40]

Some of the commercial test publishers are sensitive to the spread of criticisms of testing in general, and the activities of some of the nonprofit firms (with an emphasis on ETS) in particular. This sensitivity has led some of the private firms to try and put some distance between themselves and the nonprofit groups lest they be engulfed by a rising tide of reform legislation. In 1979, Dr. Frank Snyder, the publisher of the California Test Bureau/McGraw-Hill, testified before Congress in his capacity as a representative of the Association of American Publishers (AAP). The AAP is a general organization of U.S. publishers, including many of the test publishers, but not HBJ or SRA. During his testimony, Dr. Snyder noted the existence of a "deep concern about the adequacy of examinations required for entrance to institutions of higher learning and the nonprofit organizations that produce them." Dr. Snyder went on to express the concern of the AAP that "inappropriate actions" would be taken against the commercial publishers. He made a plea that any legislation should regard commercial publishers as those who conduct "operations . . . of a much lesser magnitude, involve a different constituency, and whose trade practices are by nature markedly different."[41] Only time will tell if this is the beginning of a real schism within the testing orthodoxy, and what the consequences of such a split would be for the standardized testing industry as a whole.

Whatever the future of the industry, one of the most amazing things about it is the way in which it has been able to avoid direct accountability to the public. (The one possible exception to this statement, New York's Truth-in-Testing law, is discussed in detail in Chapter 14.) This ability to fend off outside groups such as students, teachers, and state and national government from any significant role in the manufacture and promotion of tests is remarkable. It is remarkable because of the vital importance of these tests to so many lives, and because of so many doubts that have been raised about the quality and efficacy of these tests. President Terry Herndon of the NEA argues: "Ninety million lives have been affected by data gathered by ETS. They're unaccountable to the political community, unaccountable to the educational community, unaccountable to the legal community."[42] There is little question on the power of the tests and test companies. One writer has proclaimed that "testing agencies . . . have long had the power to destroy a person's academic and career aspirations in a single morning."[43]

Yet there is considerable inquiry into the actual value of these tests; people are asking if the results of our testing policies are worth the cost and heartbreak involved. Bernard Feder, for one, reaches the conclusion that "many (if not most) highly regarded standardized tests used in this country are badly conceived, poorly designed, carelessly administered, and—most commonly —thoughtlessly interpreted and used for questionable purposes."[44] Despite the fury of this storm of criticism by reputable observers, the industry has kept itself warm and dry, snugly insulated from any outside regulation. This seemed strange twenty years ago, when Professors John Rothney, Paul Danielson, and Robert Heimann wrote: ". . . in a country in which butchers' and grocers' scales are regularly checked and policed, and clothiers' tags of '100 percent wool' must be validated if the sellers of such products are to avoid imprisonment . . . a test distributor may sell his products without any supervision or regulation."[45] This lack of control seems even stranger today after twenty years of dismaying revelations about the misuse of tests. The moral may be that we insist upon precision and policing whenever meats or vegetables are to be weighed, but when the human mind—that precious commodity—is weighed, we are content to sit back and let the testing industry serve as its own Bureau of Weights and Measurements. Butchers have been known to slip a finger on the scales, and grocers have sometimes slipped spoiled goods in with the fresh, but we just don't worry about those things when it comes to testing.

What are some of the possible consequences of leaving the entire testing industry alone to oversee its own products? We have already looked at a number of instances of test misuse. Not all, perhaps not even most, of this misuse can be traced to the door of the industry. Certainly the admissions people or employment officers who either inadequately understand the tests or who choose to close their eyes to test limitations for reasons of expediency bear responsibility for their actions. Yet the industry wants to have it both ways. While deploring examples of test abuse, they continue to stress heavily the fairness, the accuracy, the objectivity they claim for their tests. In short, at a minimum the insistence of the industry upon secrecy and self-regulation may be providing a hospitable environment in which the culture of testing misuse can thrive. In addition, the absence of outside evaluators can give rise to pressures for overpricing some tests to subsidize others in a publisher's stable, and to slow down the introduction of new technology to prolong the life span of outdated tests.[46]

This lack of control can lead some members of the industry to delude themselves into thinking that they are above "mere business" in their behavior. One official of the College Board told an audience in 1979, "I thought I was in education all these years, and now I find out I was in industry or business, [but we're] not trying to rip anyone off."[47] To begin with, the mere fact of being in business is not equivalent to trying to rip people off. That's a rather condescending attitude, and one that is just plain inaccurate. By the same token, altruistic intentions are noble but by themselves are no guarantee that good results will follow and that no more paving will be done on the road to hell. With very few exceptions the people I have met in the testing industry seem to have admirable goals, professional integrity, and a genuine interest in the proper use of tests. Why then do cases of poor tests and industry misbehavior occur? And why do members of the industry fight so hard against the notion that there is such a thing as a testing industry and that they belong to it?

It is hard to pinpoint a single source of these problems. Part of the answer must be that testing companies, for that matter the testing industry itself, do not operate as monolithic structures. There are research segments, and production departments, and sales and public relations divisions, and an administrative hierarchy to supervise the parts. But somewhere the sum of well-intentioned parts manages too often to go astray. One critic, Paul Pottinger, testified before Congress in 1979 about his analysis of the behavior of some testers. "Fear of accountability has already led to widespread hypocrisy and deceit by some testing companies. For example, to persuade us that they are public servants rather than salespeople, some of them claim that they do not market their products or compete with one another for business. They even call themselves testing agencies rather than companies to disguise their revenue-seeking motives. Yet, ETS reported one million dollars in excess revenue after expenditures in 1978—out of a total of $80 million in revenue. I see nothing wrong with their seeking revenue, but if they cannot be open and aboveboard about something so obvious as their desire to make money, how can we trust their statements about less obvious matters? Their statements breed mistrust and lead many of us not to believe them even when they are not lying to us."[48] Test companies will have a difficult time dispelling this mistrust under the best of circumstances. They will have no success in the effort if they continue to view testing as a private preserve.

The test companies are not ignorant of the problems that have been pointed out about their tests. Some actually admit the validity of at least some of the complaints. For example, the president of ETS, William Turnbull, wrote words to that effect in an unpublished internal ETS memo dated August 14, 1978. This 17-page memorandum, accompanied by five pages of charts, sets forth Turnbull's evaluation of the change in public attitudes towards standardized tests and suggests ways to influence those attitudes in ETS' favor. Turnbull seemed moved to action, not necessarily because there were test flaws, but because there were flaws and an aroused group of critics. ETS has not granted permission to reprint portions of this memorandum so I will have to paraphrase Turnbull's statements. However, you can find excerpts in the Spring, 1980 issue of *The Testing Digest* on pages 1, 6, and 7 and in *The Reign of ETS* by Allan Nairn and Associates (the Ralph Nader Report on the Educational Testing Service) beginning on page 379. Turnbull makes numerous points, and some might read this memorandum as building a framework for increased communication with ETS constituencies. Still, there are parts of this memorandum that are troubling. In the memorandum, for instance, Turnbull wrote at one point that a passive ETS response would be appropriate if the test criticism were without substance. However, since the controversy is receiving public attention and is likely to continue, Turnbull stated that an "activist strategy" was called for.[49] So is ETS going to mount a determined drive to root out the problems and work on reducing and eliminating them? To be sure Turnbull's memo indicates there will be some efforts in that direction: he states that ETS should work to ensure that a faith in the tests is valid, as well as to encourage a favorable public attitude.[50] But the heart of the memo seems addressed to improving the image the public has of tests.

How does Turnbull propose to do this? He seems inclined toward the "divide and conquer" stratagem. He wrote at one point that alliances should be sought with any favorably inclined segments existing within larger groups (such as minorities, students, education groups and social critics) thought to take a more skeptical stand toward tests in general.[51] As for the more intransigent types, Turnbull did not suggest breaking off contact. Far from it. He wrote that such groups should be continually deluged with ETS communications. The object of this exercise, as Turnbull wrote, was not so much to develop "cooperative projects," as to establish the strength of ETS' position.[52] The best strategy would seem to be responding to, and correcting for, the criticisms of substance that Turnbull acknowledged from the start. Look again at what Turnbull has written. First, that hostile groups should be kept on the receiving end of ETS communication. It seems like an intention to drown the opposition in a flood of press releases, with no real intent to engage in a meaningful exchange. Second, that cooperative projects with test critics are not worth the effort. That is probably so if ETS is absolutely bound and determined to maintain the status quo, but if that is the case ETS would be devoted to resisting test improvement itself. Third, ETS is going to be establishing the strength of its position. That sounds more like a holding action than a genuine commitment to mutual efforts toward the common end of better tests for ourselves and our children.

What are the conclusions Turnbull draws about all the turmoil over testing? In the concluding three paragraphs of his memo, Turnbull wrote that the entire staff of ETS, not just the public information division, needed to increase its work with the public. He suggested that the next three to four years would be a crucial period and that extraordinary efforts would be required. To back up this judgment, Turnbull proposed taking an extra $200,000, $150,000, and $100,000 from ETS' net proceeds for the years 1978–79 through 1981 and spending it on his program for altering the public's perception of ETS.[53] This would in practice have the likely incidental effect of increasing spending for ETS public relations and other divisions (reducing the ETS surplus after expenses, making ETS look even more "nonprofit").

Maybe a public relations campaign could reduce the public clamor and make the tests at least more apparently palatable. So that extra allocation might be money well spent by ETS. But to my way of thinking, that money would be even better spent on a thorough review and overhaul of ETS operations and a consideration of alternative procedures and tests. ETS may choose to blow its own horn, of course, but they might be better advised to design an improved instrument. ETS has a right to ensure that its views are heard, but if they are serious about their nonprofit status, they also have an obligation to listen to the views of others. ETS might generate more public goodwill (and maybe even better tests in the bargain) by seizing this time of unusual importance to mount a crash program of test research in full partnership with even its harshest critics. That would pose a risk of failure and continued criticism, but it would be unquestioned evidence of sincerity of intent. If any organization is capable of taking a risk of this nature, one that bills itself as "nonprofit . . . devoted to measurement and research, primarily in the field of education" should be in the vanguard.

The record of some of the testers to date indicates more of a tendency to indulge in defensive reactions to criticism than to engage in bold moves to satisfy it. Banesh Hoffmann ran up against this mindset nearly twenty years ago, and wrote of his experiences in a pioneering book called *The Tyranny of Testing*. Hoffmann reported a number of test questions that were poorly written due to ambiguity or misleading factors. When he chided the test publisher about some of these unsatisfactory questions, he tells of meeting with this response. "It [the publisher] does not say 'Oops, Sorry!' It brazens the matter out. Such conduct is disturbing in itself; no matter how well it may accord with acceptable standards of behavior in business, politics, propaganda, and the cold war, it is unbecoming in a test-making organization that would have the public regard it as objective and scientific."[54]

If we are to be able to sort the brazen replies from the legitimate ones, we need to know some things about the theory of tests and the special language used by testers. This language often has the effect of obscuring the facts from the public rather than clarifying them. As Hoffmann wrote in his book about some members of the standardized testing industry, when challenged on the facts, "they grow arrogant, claim to be scientific, and use their statistics as a smokescreen."[55] In the next two chapters we will work on building a fan of understanding that will help us blow away the smokescreen surrounding the tests. Once the smoke is dissipated, we will have a better view of what is illusion and what is real in the land of testing.

CHAPTER FOUR

False Claims
of Objectivity

"But 'glory' doesn't mean 'a nice knock-down argument,'"
Alice objected.

"When I use a word," Humpty Dumpty said, in a rather
scornful tone, "it means just what I choose it to mean—neither
more nor less."

"The question is," said Alice, "whether you can make words
mean so many different things."

"The question is," said Humpty Dumpty, "which is to be
master———that's all."

Lewis Carroll
Through the Looking-Glass

When publishers of standardized tests say that their tests are "objective," they are defining "objective" in a particular manner. When you think of an "objective" test, you are probably thinking of the common English meaning of the word. Unless you are acquainted with the jargon that surrounds standardized testing, you think of an "objective" test as a test that is totally fair, impartial, free of human bias—in other words, the opposite of a "subjective" test. If that's what you think, you are mistaken. In general, an "objective" test is nothing more than a subjective test that has been dressed up in statistical clothing designed to hide some of the sources of subjectivity.

Essay exams have often been cited as examples of subjective tests. This is a fair assessment if we understand subjective tests to be the kind where the judgment of the individuals who write and grade the exam influences how well the test-taker does. If you are taking an essay exam, your grade may vary according to who wrote the exam and who graded it, even though your understanding of the subject and performance on the exam stays the same. This makes sense if you think about it. The choice of questions, and the wording of those questions, is up to the exam writer. He may choose questions that are in your areas of strength or weakness. His choice of wording may give you an opportunity to display the depth of your understanding, or may lock you into a narrow subset of the course where rote memorization is vital. Whoever grades the essay exam can also affect the grade you receive. If the grader is inclined to be flexible, or in a good mood, or in accord with your views, or just finished reading a truly awful essay, you might do better than expected. Of course, the reverse could be true as well. If your essay were read by three different examiners, they might disagree among themselves about your performance: one might give you an "A," another a "C," and the third an "F." Thus, an essay exam is truly subjective: the grade you earn may vary according to the identity of the exam writer and grader.

The claim for standardized tests, on the other hand, is that they are "objective," meaning that no matter who marks your test you will receive the identical score. It's true that your score on a test will stay the same no matter who grades it, once we allow for the occasional slipups when a computer misreads the answer sheet (because it's folded or has stray pencil marks, etc.). This "objectivity" is readily explained. When a multiple-choice standardized test is written, one of the choices is designated as correct for each question, and the rest are declared wrong. Then, when the test is scored, whether by hand or by computer, no personal judgment is allowed to enter the process. You either filled in the space for the designated answer, or you didn't. If you did, you got the answer right, and a point is added to your score. If you didn't, you got the answer wrong and, depending upon the type of standardized test, you either get no credit or have some number subtracted from your score. The test scorer is not allowed to give partial credit for other answers that may seem credible, or to vary from the given instructions in any way.

Isn't that, then, an objective test in anyone's sense of the word? If the test results don't change depending upon who scores the test, it would seem there is no opportunity for subjective human judgment—or bias—to affect the outcome. But that is not entirely true. The first part of that statement is true: standardized test scores don't change from one grader to the next. But that does not mean there is no opportunity for subjective human judgment to affect the outcome. This is like the old game with several shells with a pea under one of them. If you think of subjectivity as the pea, everyone's looking for it under the shell labeled "grading," and it's not there. Some people then leap to the conclusion that subjectivity doesn't exist on the standardized tests. But if you're a little more careful, you look under the shells labeled "test format" and "question writing," and you find peas under both.

In a standardized test the subjective elements come into play before the test is given. The choice of test format—whether the test is to be multiple choice, how much time is to be allowed, what subjects are to be covered, how many questions will be asked—is a subjective choice. There is no single scientifically-required test format, but a multitude of options. Human judgment is used to select from these options. And these subjective choices have important consequences: some people of the same ability will do better, and some will do worse, according to the length of the test, the areas emphasized, and the time allowed per question. The choice of specific questions to be asked on the test along with the specific alternative answers that will be provided to the test-taker is largely subjective. There is no intrinsic, unassailable justification for using particular combinations on given questions. What's more, the choice of the specific questions and alternatives on a test has a tremendous impact on the scores the test-takers get.

When you get down to it, essay exams and standardized tests are both subjective according to the common meaning of the word. In an essay exam, the bulk of the subjectivity is at the end of the process when the grader is evaluating the quality of the answers. On a standardized test, the bulk of the subjectivity is found in the selection of test format and questions. This may be a less visible portion of the test, but it is every bit as important as the grading portion. In short, the main practical difference between an essay exam and a standardized test is that the latter can be graded rapidly and in great quantity by a computer scanner. Since all the subjectivity on a standardized test has been concentrated in earlier stages, all the computer scanner has to do is conduct a mechanical search for filled-in answer slots and count them up. The use of a computer only means that the subjectivity has been squeezed into a different part of the test, not that the test is somehow more scientific by virtue of its connection with computers. If testers wanted to be more precise about their "objective" tests they would rename them "computer-graded" tests.

But the testers persist in calling their standardized tests "objective," despite the danger that many will be misled into thinking that their so-called "objective" tests are truly objective. That is a serious error which can lead to test misuse, since test users and test-takers are more likely to place unwarranted faith in "objective" tests than "computer-graded" tests. Many people don't know this specialized definition, and the standardized testing industry doesn't seem to be going out of its way to make the definition known. It may be that this represents a failure of the public to inform itself about the meaning of "objective" tests and that the testers are justified to use their specialized language even though it is likely to lead to confusion in the public mind. This use, of course, is not at odds with their own interest in maintaining as high a level of respect for the value of tests as possible. But at a minimum, testers have an obligation to avoid placing their particular jargon in any context that makes it even harder for the layman to interpret than it already is.

"Then you should say what you mean," the March Hare went on.

"I do," Alice hastily replied; "at least—at least I mean what I say—that's the same thing, you know."

"Not the same thing a bit!" said the Hatter. "Why, you might just as well say that 'I see what I eat' is the same thing as 'I eat what I see'!"

Lewis Carroll
Alice's Adventures in Wonderland

Listen to the spokesmen for two of the most reputable firms in the testing industry. I can only assume they are completely aware of the meaning of "objective" tests, for if they are not, it would be a sad commentary that one could rise so high in a testing firm without knowing some of the basics about tests. Yet both these men, one testifying before the New York State legislature and the other before the U.S. Congress, used the term "objective" in a fashion that could readily confuse their audiences. In a strict sense they did not misuse the term; but they did use it in such a way that an erroneous implication, favorable to their firms, could be easily drawn. The spokesman for ETS said: "The answer to real educational and job opportunity lies not in setting aside careful objective assessment of developed abilities."[1] And a spokesman for ACT testified: "We remain convinced that so long as persons are responsible for making decisions about the future of others in the context of instruction, guidance, or selection, they deserve to have significant objective help."[2] Go back and replace "objective" in both those statements with "computer-graded" and see how different the statements sound.[3] Consciously or not, some testers are playing on public ignorance. The testers sometimes use their carefully defined term in a setting that could convey a false notion to anyone who hasn't learned the language of testing in self-defense.

These fundamental misunderstandings may be accidental, but they are nonetheless deplorable. People don't always have the time or the opportunity to translate the pronouncements of some test firms into their own language. Sloppy usage by testers can either mislead other parties to the testing controversy or lead them to their own incomplete statements. This effect is not limited to legislators or the parents of schoolchildren. Some educational professionals may face this result if they are not excessively wary of everything they read and hear. For example, Albert Shanker, the president of the American Federation of Teachers (AFT), is a controversial figure at times, but is also an unquestionably intelligent and hard-working individual. Yet here is part of the written testimony that Shanker submitted to Congress in 1979: "The basic purpose behind the development of objective aptitude and achievement tests was to provide us with an objective standard of quality, that could be used in conjunction with various subjective measures like student grades and personal interviews, in making decisions about admissions to various postsecondary undergraduate and graduate programs. An objective test like the SAT, for example, can just as well be used to 'discover' the bright student who has done poorly by subjective grade standards as to raise questions about the possibly inflated subjective reports on a grade-A student."[4] Go back and insert "computer-graded" for "objective" and see how much of the meaning of this statement is lost.

Shanker is dealing with some important matters in his statement. He may well be right in his assessment of the purpose behind the creation of standardized tests, and he is right about the subjective nature of school grades and the fact that the SAT can sometimes be a blessing for those who earn low grades. But he also seems to be saying that standardized tests are objective and free of the taint of subjectivity found in grades, and that is not totally accurate. We have already seen that subjective human elements enter into the process of creating and writing standardized "objective" tests. Moreover, if subjectivity is the "Original Sin" of school grades, then standardized "objective" tests are unavoidably sinful as well, because all that these tests try to do is to predict the grades you will receive in the future. If grades are subjective, and they are, then tests which purport to predict grades must be subjective as well, insofar as the tests use those grades as a yardstick. To return to Shanker, it is clear that he raised valuable points in his testimony. But the technical definition of "objective" is hard to keep sorted from the everyday use of the word. If a person of Shanker's background and ability runs into this problem, then surely many more people who have less training and talent in the realm of education must have run aground on the hard rock of testing jargon.

Jacques Barzun has made the argument that the search for a perfectly objective test is likely to be futile in any event. He has argued that the subjectivity so apparent in an essay exam, and somewhat hidden though no less real in an "objective" test, is not really a flaw but instead is an indisputable fact of life. Barzun wrote: "The further argument that essay examinations cannot be graded uniformly, even by the same reader, only shows again the character of mind itself: it is not an object to be weighed or sampled by volume like a peck of potatoes or a cord of wood. Variations in performance and estimate will always exist. Hence an objective test of mind is a contradiction in terms, though a fair test, a searching examination, a just estimate, are not."[5] A vital first step in securing fair tests is clarifying the testing jargon so that tests can be placed in the proper perspective.

Another term that lends itself to misunderstanding is the "intelligence" test (sometimes called an IQ test). We have already discussed IQ tests briefly, so it probably has occurred to you that the term "intelligence test" is a misnomer. The test does not measure "intelligence" as you or I would think of it, but rather measures some specialized skills. Judge Peckham had this to say about IQ tests: "While many think of the IQ as an objective measure of innate, fixed intelligence, the testimony of the experts overwhelmingly demonstrated that this conception of IQ is erroneous. Defendants' expert witnesses, even those closely affiliated with the companies that devise and distribute the standardized intelligence tests, agreed, with one exception, that we cannot truly define, much less measure, intelligence."[6] Despite this agreement that "intelligence" tests are not intelligence tests, companies still market IQ tests without changing their name.

Once again, a feel for language and definitions is essential for anyone who wants to keep firm footing while treading in the land of tests. You will recall the stratagem employed by some testers of saying that intelligence is that which intelligence tests measure. As Banesh Hoffmann wrote, the use of this peculiar definition "put them in a strong position. They could no longer be accused of measuring something other than intelligence as thus defined, yet they could still reap the benefits of the connotations of the word 'intelligence' in its original, nontechnical sense.

They persisted, for example, in the custom of referring to students with extremely high IQ's as geniuses, though they knew very well that genius is not significantly related to extremely high intelligence in the ordinary sense of the word nor to extremely high intelligence in the testers' sense of the word. To allow a word like 'genius'—to say nothing of 'intelligence'—to be polluted and bastardized in this way is hardly becoming conduct on the part of testers."[7] It seems that some of the same people who are bringing you tests of great precision and rigor are unable to combat some looseness in language, or unwilling to mount the effort.

Why should we care? The answer is that the use of these terms is like an unfunny double entendre because the joke is on us. These terms foster an atmosphere of misunderstanding which can lead to overreliance on tests, such as the mislabeling of children as mentally retarded in the cases we examined earlier. Sometimes our school officials may end up spending thousands of tax dollars for tests that are either unneeded or actually counterproductive. The testing professionals may say that this is all very unfortunate, but they are using words they have clearly defined among themselves and are not responsible if their language is misapplied by the outside world. But that argument does not hold, especially when the testers themselves start to confuse the regular meaning of the words with their specialized definition.

Mary Jo Bane and Christopher Jencks have written about how the testers are prone to walk unaware into the very snares that they themselves have set. They say it is like Humpty Dumpty claiming, with a trace of scorn, that he can use words to mean whatever he damn well pleases. "The trouble is that psychologists are *not* the masters of language, and they cannot assign arbitrary meanings to words without causing all kinds of confusion. In the real world, people cannot use a term like intelligence without assuming that it means many different things at once—all very important. . . . Having said that 'intelligence is what IQ tests measure,' psychologists always end up assuming that what IQ tests measure *must* be important, because 'intelligence' is important."[8] The easiest way around this pitfall would be to rename the tests so they more accurately reflect what the tests do. We might call such a step "truth-in-titling." Banesh Hoffmann, for one, has suggested that IQ tests be renamed "iquination" tests.[9] "Iquination" is as good a term as any to cover what the IQ tests are about, and would be less likely to mislead students, parents, and teachers as to what the tests measure. Hoffmann argues that saying a kid has "low iquination" is not as potentially distorting and harmful as saying a child has "low intelligence." What does "iquination" mean anyway? I don't know myself, but that's okay because we can always just say that iquination is what iquination tests measure.

"Coaching" is another word that may have a different meaning for some testers than it does for the average person. If asked what coaching for a standardized test consists of, you might reply that it is a period of intensive study for the particular types of questions appearing on a test. Or, in other words, that coaching is that combination of instruction and studying that goes on at the better test-coaching courses. If you wanted to determine if that sort of coaching is effective, you could set up an experiment where some students are coached for a test while others are not. Then you would compare the scores and draw your conclusions, being careful to account if possible for other factors besides attendance at the coaching schools that might have influenced the outcome. But if you define "coaching" in a different way, it could affect your conclusion as to whether coaching is effective.

For example, the College Board has defined "coaching" since 1965 not as what goes on at the good coaching courses, but as something rather different. The College Board decided they would define "coaching" as intensive and short-term drilling on test subjects.[10] Using this definition the Board has been able to deny that coaching is effective even in the face of the FTC report that found an average SAT improvement of 50 points. By the Board's own definition they are probably right. Sitting around for a couple of weeks trying to memorize vocabulary cards and the like is probably not going to make a significant difference in how you do on the SAT. But that's very different from what a good coaching course will do, namely take months rather than weeks to stress the types of reasoning skills measured by the tests. A good coaching course will explain test-taking techniques and insist that the students analyze their mistakes on practice tests. By its choice of definitions, the College Board has almost defined the problem posed by successful coaching courses out of existence. The Board can say with a straight face that its studies show no significant effect for coaching. But the public which gets this message is likely to misinterpret it unless they look very cautiously for the fine print where the Board explains its special use of the term "coaching."

It is true that there is no single universally accepted definition for "coaching," so it is fair for testers to experiment with different meanings of the word in exploring the effectiveness of test preparation. But it is stretching it quite a bit to adopt a very narrow definition of the term, one which is unlikely to have much effect on test scores, and then to stick to that definition exclusively for a period of years. If a car manufacturer were to define "miles per gallon" as the number of miles a car could go when in neutral on a steady downhill slope, then howls of outrage and the banshees of the government regulatory bureaucracy would be unleashed in an instant. But there is much more freedom to define terms to suit your own convenience in the area of testing. After the FTC study had been released, the chairman of the College Board repeated in testimony to Congress that "we believe coaching has no significant effect."[11] At about the same time, an ETS vice-president was quoted as saying that "intensive short-term study is not likely to raise scores significantly."[12] Note how carefully crafted these statements are and how an uncritical reader could construe them to mean that coaching schools won't help you. Both statements use the specialized definition of coaching, and both hedge their bets by throwing in the qualifier about "significance." The casual reader is not going to know whether CEEB and ETS mean to say that coaching gains are not statistically significant or are too small for anyone to get excited over or aren't great enough by themselves to make the difference between admission and rejection. It might be pretty tough to tell just how small a difference is "insignificant" in all cases, especially for an applicant who is right on the borderline between getting in and being locked out.

A few months after those statements by CEEB and ETS, something incredible happened. The New York State Department of Education announced that it was voiding the scores of 12,000 people who had taken a national test for registered nurses in the summer of 1979 in New York.[13] The reason for this was that claims had been made that copies of the test had been sold to some test-takers before the test was given. Some interesting things had taken place on this "nursing boards" test to certify registered nurses. The passing score was a 350 on the standard scale to 800. On this administration, more people passed than usual and some people who had previously failed registered score increases of up to 400 points. The percentage of foreign-trained nurses passing the test went up from the usual 10 to 15 percent to 30 percent. So, at least on the surface, there was some reason to wonder if the test had been tampered with.

Approximately one month after the announcement that the test results would not be honored in New York State, the state education commissioner decided that the results would be used after all.[14] The commissioner defended his decision on the basis that it would be unfair to penalize all 12,000 test-takers, who had paid $60 in test fees each, on the strength of unproven allegations. The commissioner explained the score increases: according to him, interviews with some of the alleged cheaters found they had all taken test review courses at least once. In effect, the commissioner was saying that test coaching could be expected to produce improvements of this magnitude, improvements of up to 400 points on the test.[15] Moreover, the commissioner's decision came hard on the heels of a court order to honor the scores since the court saw no evidence of cheating. So now, at least for the nursing tests in question, gains of up to 400 points have been credited to the use of coaching schools. That surely is a significant improvement if truly the result of coaching.

You will recall that the College Board is on record as opposing the notion that test coaching will lead to significant score improvements, at least on the SAT. Yet not all colleges and universities behave as if they believe this assertion. Adelphi University, for example, regularly runs ads in the *New York Times* promoting its own coaching program for the LSAT. The Adelphi University coaching course is conducted in cooperation with the "National Center for Educational Testing, Inc."[16] Now, unless Adelphi is publicly participating in a fraud on the public—which I sincerely doubt—then it must believe that coaching for the LSAT is effective. It is hard to imagine how the LSAT could be coachable if the SAT were impervious to coaching, since the tests share many characteristics. Some might even say that the difference between the LSAT and the SAT is about the same as the difference between a wasp and a hornet. According to Arthur Levine, the author of its Boston-FTC report, a number of College Board members offer coaching for graduate level tests. What's even more unexpected, also according to Levine, is that St. John's University offers coaching courses for the SAT itself.[17] This presents an obvious paradox. How could St. John's adhere to the CEEB position that the SATs can't be coached and then turn around and charge for a SAT-coaching course? How should St. John's use SAT scores in its own admissions process—are they considered uncoachable or coachable then? Should students who took the coaching course get a bonus for their foresight or should the admissions committee discount their SAT scores as being high because they took the course? St. John's may well be doing the right thing in offering a coaching course. It's the implied contradiction that is disturbing.

Problems in dealing with the coaching issue have popped up in other areas as well. In early 1979, ETS got a $15,000 settlement from a suit against a New York SAT-coaching school. This school, not one of the nationally known ones, had, according to ETS, used some questions in its program that were identical to those appearing on the SAT at roughly the same time. ETS cancelled the scores of some 150 students of this course. Those students then had the option of retaking the SAT at no additional charge.[18] There is no way of knowing for certain how many similar incidents occur throughout the standardized testing industry.

The test publishers don't always get along with the test coaching schools since their interests are not parallel. Even the reputable coaching schools which follow the letter of the law make test publishers nervous, for they stand as a challenge to claims of uncoachability by their very existence. And a representative of ACT told Congress in September 1979 that the test preparation courses which don't qualify as instructional in nature have "procedures [which] frequently conflict with the sponsors' test security measures."[19]

What was the ACT spokesman talking about? Perhaps he

had in mind the sort of thing Senator Halperin claims happened to him. Senator Halperin said in May 1979, "I was a beneficiary of the existing system. I was one of those whose family was able to afford a course which helped to raise my grades from the PSAT to the SAT by 200 points in English and by over 100 points in math. A well-known and highly organized tutoring course that I was able to participate in had people taking the test year after year, extracting questions which, as the test people say, are used year after year. A whole list of questions were [sic] accumulated and our course entailed going over those questions and knowing how to answer them. So when I saw many of them for the 'first time,' I was no stranger to them."[20] Dr. Paul Jacobs of Thomas Edison College testified that the long and the short of it is that "under the present system, those students who can afford to pay for private coaching and who can afford to take an exam many times have partial access to previously used questions; less privileged students do not."[21] That certainly cuts against the grain of the notion that all test-takers start out with an equal chance to show their skills on a given standardized test. As James Fallows wrote: "If courses can be designed for the specific purpose of increasing scores on the tests, does that not suggest that the tests reveal, rather than 'aptitude' or 'achievement,' only mastery of an unusual and specialized system of thought?"[22]

One crucial aspect of this system of thought is the ability to deal with the multiple-choice format common on standardized tests. You know this format—it's the kind where you're given a question and told to pick one of four or five alternative answers as the best. This particular format has been steadily criticized for years as being inadequate for measuring intellectual competence. The problems are legion. To begin with, a multiple-choice test does not allow a test-taker to explain her reasons for picking a given answer. This means two things. First, a multiple-choice test can't tell if the student has arrived at a designated "wrong" answer through a brilliant chain of reasoning or because of defective wording in the question itself. Second, a multiple-choice test will give full credit for a correct answer even if the student had no idea what was going on and just made a lucky guess.

Both of these flaws could be alleviated if students were required to give some reason for their choices, but then the test would no longer be "objective" or "computer-graded." The reason for this is that human judgment would have to come into play in deciding which reasons were acceptable and which were not. This, then, is a trade-off. If you want the benefit of an "objective" test which can use computers to process hundreds of thousands of tests very quickly, you have to sacrifice the ability to look directly at the quality of reasoning employed by the test-takers. Banesh Hoffmann, along with many others, doesn't think the tradeoff is worth the cost. Hoffmann wrote that "the crucial question is with us still: what sense is there in giving tests in which the candidate just picks answers, and is not allowed to give reasons for his choices?"[23] Nor should we worry only about students who use the right reasons to arrive at an answer deemed wrong by the test publisher. A person might use wrong logic to reach a wrong answer on the test and still deserve a great deal of credit. Hoffmann explains: "The problem as stated in the examination might be a fairly straightforward one, but the student might misread it as a much harder problem. The harder problem might actually be beyond the capabilities of even the best students at his level to solve. But if he nevertheless made a brilliant attempt, and if this attempt failed because of subtle reasons that he could not be expected to perceive, then the wise examiner who knew his subject well would realize that he was dealing with a student of unusual ability."[24]

Banesh Hoffmann is especially concerned that our dependence on standardized tests could be depriving the world of another Einstein or Edison, since their kind of ability could be ignored on these tests. Hoffmann has some expertise in the matter: he was a close colleague of Albert Einstein, and is a recent biographer of the man who came up with the theory of relativity. Einstein might be called a "late-bloomer," since he had trouble conforming to the rigid dictates of his school days. Can you imagine giving Einstein a multiple-choice test and forbidding him from explaining his selections? Who would have the presumption to mark Einstein's answers incorrect in math or science without even inquiring what Einstein had in mind when he made the selections? To return to Hoffmann's example of a student misreading the question and then displaying superior talent in a vain quest to solve the harder question, someone might object that the student should be penalized. The student made a mistake: he misread the question. Therefore, shouldn't we feel comfortable in denying credit for a wrong answer? In a word, no. First of all, a multiple-choice test does not deny credit to a student who misreads the question and blunders by mistake into the "right" answer. More importantly, unless you are talking about a reading test, denying credit to our student would be deceptive. He would be hurt on his math or his science score for his problems in reading and not for any lack of math or science skill. Moreover, the misreading may be a product of nervousness or time pressure during the test or of ambiguity in the question itself.

Judah Schwartz is a professor at MIT and is one of the pioneers in developing alternatives to the standardized tests we have seen. He has written about another problem with multiple-choice tests' indifference to your reasoning process. Some forms of standardized tests, IQ tests among them, use a fair amount of analogy questions. You've seen this form of analogy before—sock: foot :: glove: hand (a sock is to your foot as a glove is to your hand). The problem is that when you ask an analogy question in a multiple-choice format, you open yourself up to heated arguments about which of the alternatives is the right answer, and why. Professor Schwartz thinks there is a clear reason for this dilemma: "An analogy question never has a unique answer. The quality of any answer offered can only be judged in the light of the respondent's stated rationale for his or her answer."[25] But you're not allowed to state a rationale for your answer on an "objective" test, so the scoring of these analogy questions is subject to an arbitrary judgment when the "correct" answer is designated by the test publisher.

Let's look at the multiple-choice format from the point of view of the person who has to take the test. Whenever she comes to a question which has two or more alternative answers that seem to be reasonable choices, she must resort to a kind of magic or mental telepathy in making her selection. Since the test publishers don't allow her to explain her reasoning, she has to guess which of the answers is not necessarily "correct," but the answer most likely to appeal to the people who wrote the test. In fact, because the tests are "pretested" to see which alternative answer people who score high on other parts of the test favor, her job is actually more complicated than it appears on first blush. Here is how Hoffmann described the task, this time for a male candidate: "He must pick the answer he believes most of the best candidates will pick; and mind you, he must pick not the answer he thinks they will honestly believe to be the best, but the answer he thinks they themselves will be guessing that the other best candidates will guess that they themselves will guess."[26] If such seriousness weren't attached to the results of these tests, the whole process would seem either funny or enjoyable, in the sense of solving a crossword puzzle, breaking a code, or using a Ouija board.

Nor does this exhaust the list of problems with multiple-choice tests. A typical feature of multiple-choice test is that many questions—sometimes several hundred—are asked in a tightly compressed amount of time. You don't have the luxury of stopping to think about the question and carefully weighing the worth of the alternatives. Instead, you are on a madcap tear through a forest of questions, rapidly reading and answering so that you can finish before time expires. This time limit in turn forces test publishers to use questions that are rarely deep and challenging, for no one would have time to answer that many clever questions. Moreover, if you want to do well on this sort of test, you'd better be wearing the same kind of multiple-choice thinking caps that the test publishers wear. If you have a "different" way of thinking about things, you will be at a disadvantage on this test, unless you go out and purchase a multiple-choice thinking cap through individual preparation or a coaching course.

Hoffmann's analysis of the implications of multiple-choice tests amounts to a clear condemnation. He writes of an individual facing a multiple-choice test: "If he is strong-minded, nonconformist, unusual, original, or creative—as so many of the truly important people are—he must stifle his impulses and conform as best he can to the norms that the multiple-choice testers set up in their unimaginative, scientific way. . . . These tests favor the nimble-witted, quick-reading candidates who form fast superficial judgments."[27] Are these really qualities we prize so highly? What will the consequences be to society when individuals skilled at making fast and superficial judgments have been slotted for the best schools and the most influential positions? We all know the story about the tortoise and the hare, but under the race conditions of a multiple-choice test the tortoise might as well pack it in at the start.

Multiple-choice questions are held in low repute by many testing experts. One incident serves to illustrate this point. On November 5, 1979, Professor Judah Schwartz rose to ask a question of the people who had gathered for the Fall Conference of the National Consortium on Testing (NCT). The membership list of the NCT reads like a "Who's Who" of the testing world, including test proponents and test critics alike. Some of the organizations that belong to the NCT include: ETS, ACT, the College Board, the American Educational Research Association (AERA), the National Council on Measurement in Education (NCME), and the Education Commission of the States (ECS). Professor Schwartz asked this question of the entire gathering at the NCT meeting: aside from the lower cost and ease of administration, was there anyone in the audience willing to defend the multiple-choice format on intellectual grounds? Professor Schwartz got exactly one taker from the entire crowd, and that gentleman was willing to defend the multiple-choice format only if he could argue with the publisher after the test about the merits of various answers.[28] People at the meeting may have remained silent for different reasons, ranging from the variety of defects in the multiple-choice format to an unwillingness to enter a discussion on the issue at that particular time. But the fact remains that in this distinguished company, the multiple-choice test could not muster one solitary supporter to wholeheartedly defend its merits as an intellectual proposition.

Aside from the multiple-choice format, critics have noted that the standardized "objective" tests suffer from a preoccupation with reading skill and a susceptibility to ambiguous or slanted questions. In order to do well on a standardized test, above all you must be a good and speedy reader. There is much to be said for reading as an important characteristic of success, but surely this can be overdone. When scores that purport to reveal a candidate's knowledge of history or biology or the rudiments of police work are heavily influenced by reading ability, then we are being misled. The ability to communicate effectively through the spoken word is being overlooked, as is the knack for understanding exactly what it is that people are saying to you. These are not unimportant skills in the real world. And there are other things in life beside language skills, whether they be written or oral. There is an entire range of traits we would consider absolute requirements for success in life that don't even register as a blip on the standardized test screen. Some of these "hidden" virtues include drive, integrity, common sense, creativity, and idealism. Phillip Morrison, a professor at MIT, has written, "It would be absurd to deny the primacy of language for human thought, but in a time when we recognize the complex nature of the two-sided brain, let alone the cultivated mind, it is at best premature and at worst dishonest to enthrone language and its nuances as the seat of human intelligence."[29] Yet the reliance on reading-based testing works to that end.

We will turn to a more detailed exploration of some of the failings that have been encountered in the test questions themselves when we discuss sources of test bias in Chapter 11. For now it is sufficient to recognize that a poorly worded question can discriminate against certain kinds of test-takers, be they candidates from different cultural backgrounds or persons who are brighter than the test writers so that they see things in the questions that the publishers haven't considered. As a brief illustration of how vulnerable anyone is to standardized tests which are geared to people of different backgrounds and experiences, consider the case of Koko the gorilla. Francine Patterson, a developmental psychologist, reported in the October 1978 *National Geographic* about her work with Koko.[30] Patterson wrote that she had tested Koko on the Stanford-Binet IQ test (through sign language, not by making the gorilla sit down at a desk with a number 2 pencil). Koko's scores were 95 and 85, both within the "average" range for humans. Some might interpret this to mean that Koko is as smart as the average person. A more logical conclusion is to regard the test with some skepticism if it is so narrowly focused that a gorilla can obtain an average human score.

Be that as it may, the more interesting aspect of Patterson's article involves her contention that Koko deserved an even higher score on the IQ test. On one question, Koko was asked to pick two of the following five items as good to eat: a block, an apple, a shoe, a flower, and ice cream. Koko went for the apple and the flower, which reflects gorilla tastes, but had to be scored as "wrong." On another question, Koko was asked which of the following four items was a good place to run to for shelter from the rain: a hat, a spoon, a tree, a house. As Patterson explains: "Koko naturally chose the tree. Rules for the scoring required that I record these responses as errors." This experience has led Patterson to the conclusion that IQ tests exhibit "a cultural bias toward humans that shows up when tests are administered to a gorilla." This is true and it's also amusing—in this instance. But when fellow humans are victimized by more subtle forms of cultural bias, there is nothing humorous about the consequences. A question and designated answer may appear to a test writer to be a universal truth, yet in reality be nothing more than an assumption shared by the testers and their associates.

It's time for us to look at some of the theory behind the construction of standardized tests and their scoring. In Chapter 5 we will examine the terminology and technique of standardized testing. Don't worry about the particular numbers that are used; the concepts themselves are the important thing and you will find they are pretty basic.

CHAPTER FIVE

The Illusion of Precision

Standardized tests convey an illusion of much greater precision than they are actually capable of achieving. The three-digit scores and the statistical summaries and the aura of science about these tests all give the impression that tests are exact and practically infallible instruments. A representative of the National PTA told Congress in 1979 of their concerns that "the present degree of the art of assessment is far less precise than we have been led to believe."[1] The public's awe for numbers, and for anyone who can fling them about with an air of assurance, is at the root of this belief in the precision of test scores. The mere use of numbers or elaborate statistical procedures in and of themselves does not make an argument any more correct than it was when standing on its own merits.

Our aim in this chapter is to avoid the mistake of excessive deference to testing statistics. This may strike you as an ambitious task, for the mystique of test complexity is strong. But the fundamental ideas behind the construction and use of tests are not beyond our understanding. Robert Ebel, a respected testing expert, addressed this issue in 1963. Ebel wrote: "Secrecy concerning educational tests and test scores has been justified on several grounds. One is that the information is simply too complex for untrained minds to grasp. Now it is true that some pretty elaborate theories can be built around our testing processes. It is also

true that we can perform some very fancy statistical manipulations with the scores they yield. But the essential information revealed by the scores on most educational tests is not particularly
complex. If we understand it ourselves, we can communicate it
clearly to most laymen without serious difficulty. To be quite
candid, we are not at all that much brighter than they are, much
as we may sometimes need the reassurance of thinking so."[2] Let's
take Ebel's words to heart and look past the illusion of tests to
their underlying substance.

Say you have taken a standardized, multiple-choice, objective, norm-referenced test a few months ago, and have just now
received your score. You have received a 479 on the TTAT (an
acronym for the fictitious Test-Taking Ability Test). Your information sheet from the publisher tells you that the reliability of the
TTAT is .92, and that the correlation of the TTAT to grades
earned by students at the College for Collage Designers is .57,
with an r^2 of .32. Well, that certainly seems to take care of that.
Your 479 isn't such a great score, and the TTAT is used as part
of the admissions process at the Collage College where it seems
to predict student grades pretty well. It looks as though your collage aptitude has been pegged precisely and you're just not cut
out to be collage material. Maybe you should give up your aspirations for Collage College and the field of collage design and
focus your energy on other areas where you will do better. After
all, the TTAT has all those impressive numbers, so the problem
must be with you.

But it ain't necessarily so. If you know something about
standardized tests, if you can see beyond all those numbers, you
might ask some questions. The problem may indeed be in the
test, in its inability to accurately measure your talents and ability
in this field for one of any number of reasons. When it says you
are a 479 and not a 478 or a 480, it may be much less precise
than it appears. What about the standard deviation of the test?
How many sources of possible bias have crept into the test? What
are the unproven assumptions behind the TTAT? How does the
TTAT measure up on the criteria of content validity and predictive validity and criterion validity? What group was the TTAT
standardized on? Who set the TTAT normal curve at what and
why? Once you know enough to ask these kinds of questions and

grasp the answers, you will never again be in awe of test precision, and you will have a better idea of what a test score does—and does not—mean.

It's time for us to build our own standardized test from scratch. This will enable us to get a feel for how the process is conducted, and for what makes the tests tick. Let's say that we have been hired by the sponsor of the TTAT to construct a new version of that test in a manner more or less consistent with the practices commonly employed in the standardized testing industry. Our new TTAT will be standardized, multiple-choice, objective, and norm-referenced just like most of the tests we have discussed so far. The first thing we have to do is decide just what it is we want our test to predict. We could try to write a test that predicts how well someone will do as a collage designer after they have graduated from college. That's a worthy goal, but it would be hard to do since we'd have to find a way to rank the work of all the people in this field. The effort would be expensive, time-consuming, and bound to result in disagreement among the experts we ask to rank the collage workers. So we'll settle for something that already exists, something we won't have to vouch for as our own standard. How about the grades students earn at the college? That's a good peg for us to hang our test scores on. The college already gives grades, and grades are widely accepted as some indication of academic performance.

We now have a *predictor variable* and a *response variable*. The predictor variable will be the score on our TTAT. The response variable will be the grades a student earns at the college. We will try to make our TTAT test scores predict student grades as closely as possible. If the professors at the college give grades arbitrarily so that the better students get the lower grades and vice versa, our test scores will still be pegged to grades and therefore will incorporate to some extent the professors' arbitrariness. We will not look at grades to see if they are "right" in some sense. If the professors are biased or indifferent or incompetent, we will still abide by their judgments about student performance. Grades, of course, are at least a step removed from real world competency, but the people who use our test will just have to live with that. If it turns out that the better students get the better grades, but that good grades in college aren't closely related to good work in the outside world, our test scores will not be affected. We will focus on student grades and leave these larger questions to others.

The question then is what grades we will use for our response variable. We could look at a student's grade point average (GPA) for the entire four years at the college, but there are some arguments against that. For one thing, our tests would always be lagging four years behind in adjusting for student grades. We won't know how well our first batch of test-takers does at college until four years from now when graduation looms. Besides, many things can happen over a period of four years. We would expect that the college would start to influence student performance in that time. If the college is a good one, even the poorer students should acquire new skills. And, quite frankly, if we use grades for the entire four-year period, our tests won't look as impressive, because in most cases they can't predict as well for a long period as they can for a short one.

So let's say we decide to tie our tests to the grades a student earns in his first year at the college. In some ways that may be the most critical year, and grades earned in the other three years will undoubtedly bear some relationship to those first-year grades. We will put a disclaimer in our promotional materials that our tests only predict for first-year grades and rely on the admissions personnel to make any necessary adjustments. Now we have another decision to make. How will we attempt to establish the validity of our test format for the TTAT? We have already determined that the TTAT will be standardized, multiple-choice, objective, and norm-referenced. Let's make sure we understand these terms before tackling test validity. When we say *standardized,* we mean that we will compare all future test-takers with an initial group of test-takers. We will use sophisticated techniques so that the scores of students who take the TTAT five years from now are close to the scores they would have received if they'd taken this year's tests. In other words, by standardizing the test on a particular group of test-takers today, we will be able to equate their scores with scores of subsequent test-takers so that a 479 today will mean the same as a 479 five years from now.

It is vital that the group we use to standardize the TTAT test be representative of the entire group of future TTAT test-takers. If there is a glaring discrepancy, our hopes of arriving at consistently meaningful scores may be dashed. For example, if we standardized the test on a group of 1,000 students, all of whom received sculpture awards in high school, and if we then posed a lot of sculpture questions on the TTAT, we would be asking for trouble. What could happen is that if many subsequent TTAT test-takers have painting and drawing backgrounds, they won't score as well on a test heavily weighted toward questions on sculpture as the sculpture whizzes in our standardization group did. Because sculpting talent is just one type of artistic ability, our test scores for painters could be misleading. This is because the standardizing group with their sculpture background will score well, while their successors without this background will score poorly, when in fact the overall artistic ability of both groups may be equal.

We have already talked about what *multiple-choice* means. This is simply a kind of pencil-and-paper test format where we write ahead of time both the questions and the alternative answers that the test-taker has to choose among. We decide before the test is given which answers will be marked correct, and which incorrect. If our questions or alternative answers are misleading or ambiguous, the worth of our TTAT test will be reduced because the better students may choose answers we have decided will be marked as wrong. If we ask the wrong questions on our test, we may be rewarding students with skills unrelated to getting good first-year grades at the college. By the same token, we might miss questions which would give test-takers with the potential to earn high first-year college grades a chance to show off their stuff. We have to worry about the possibility that candidates with low collage ability may score well on the TTAT because they have mastered the tricks of taking a multiple-choice test and vice versa.

In any event, because we have selected the multiple-choice format, we have an *objective* test. As we've discussed earlier, an objective test is basically a test that can be graded by a computer. We will make the test-takers record their answers by filling in bubbles on a special score sheet. We can then take these sheets and run them through a computer scanner which will see where the dark marks of a number 2 pencil have been made. The computer can add up the responses to arrive at a raw score of the number of right answers. The computer can then adjust this raw score for any other factors we want to include, and then print out the candidate's TTAT score.

Our test will also be *norm-referenced*. This has nothing to do with anyone named Norm, but merely means that we will grade the test on a curve. In this sense we are using the word "norm" to be short for normal or average or typical. In other words, we will rank all the people who take the TTAT not against their knowledge of a certain set of information, but against each other. We will determine ahead of time how many of the TTAT-takers will be allowed to get high scores and how many will be forced to accept low scores. There are some refinements on this by virtue of our equating process with the group we've used to standardize the TTAT, but essentially we are interested in relative skill, not absolute skill. Think of this in terms of an art class of thirty students. If the teacher grades on the curve, or gives norm-referenced grades, then most students will get C's, while some get B's and D's, and a few get A's and F's. If this is a strict curve, then even if all thirty were art geniuses— every single one a Picasso, a Van Gogh, a Rembrandt, a Michelangelo—that's too bad: some of them will receive D's and F's. Or if all thirty were absolutely abysmal artists they'd luck out: some would receive A's and B's just because they were a little less awful than the others. Contrast this with *criterion-referenced* measurement whereby students are marked on how well they handle the material in some absolute sense. Then our class of art geniuses would get thirty A's for their excellence, while the class of abysmal artists would get thirty F's for their mediocrity.

There is much to be said for criterion-referenced tests since they measure a student in terms of fixed standards. But the college we are writing the test for wants a test that will help them weed out some applicants, so we will use the norm-referenced system. This way we will not end up with all high or low scores, which might tell us about the ability of the candidates but wouldn't be much use in narrowing the field. Moreover, we would face a lot of arguments about what exactly the questions should be on a criterion-referenced test since different people may have different ideas about what is important in the field of art.

We can avoid that muddle by comparing each candidate to the other people who take the TTAT. What we have to do now is decide on a test scale and a curve for our test. A lot of other tests use a 200 to 800 scale, so we will too.

As to the test curve, we will use a *normal curve* since it is also widely used in the testing industry. A normal curve has a distinguishing shape and certain mathematical properties. Here is what a so-called normal curve looks like.

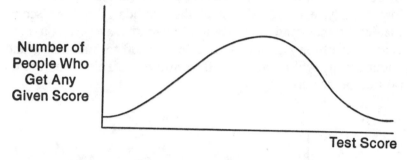

Number of People Who Get Any Given Score

Test Score

This is sometimes called a bell-shaped curve. There is no scientific reason why we have to pick this particular shape for our curve, but it is convenient for us because it will spread out the test-takers' scores.

We use the concept of a *standard deviation* in connection with our curve. A standard deviation is a statistical measure of how confident we can be about whether an event, or a score, is occurring by chance alone as opposed to a true reading. How does this work in practice? Let's go back to our normal curve. (The name normal curve does not mean that a curve of a different shape is somehow "abnormal." The term simply denotes a specific type of curve.) We will set our mean score at 500 (halfway between 200 and 800), and we will set one standard deviation as equal to 100 points on the test. We can choose the shape of the curve, the mean score, and the standard deviation ahead of time because we will decide which questions make up the test and how many points each correct answer earns. When we give our pretest later, we'll see how choosing the test questions affects the curve of test scores. Given the chosen curve, mean score, and standard deviation, we now know how the test scores will come out. The curve determines that about 68 percent of the test-takers will have scores within one standard deviation of the average either way. That is, if we give the TTAT to 1,000 people, about 680 of them will get scores higher than 400 and less than 600. These people fall in the shaded portion of the curve below. Another 14 percent of the TTAT-takers will have scores from one to two standard deviations from the average. So, about 140 scores will be in the 300 to 400 range, while another 140 will be between 600 and 700. This is the white area of the curve below. Finally, about 2 percent of the candidates will get scores that are three standard deviations from the average, on both ends. Some twenty people will be in the 200 to 300 range, and about twenty will be in the 700 to 800 area. This is the dotted portion of the curve below.

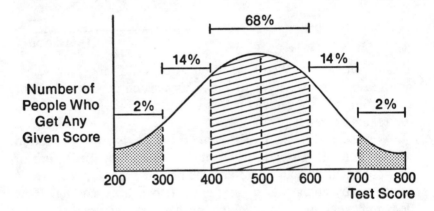

This outcome of score distributions has been predetermined by us. There is nothing overwhelmingly natural or normal about it. If we had chosen a different shape for our curve, we would have come up with different distributions. Talent and achievement can come in many different forms. We are assuming this "normal distribution" because it makes life easier for us as test writers. If we are wrong in this assumption, it will skew our test scores in a false direction. How could this happen? Well, say people turn out to be either very talented in collage work or very untalented, with few in between. Then we should have a curve for the TTAT that reflects those conditions. Such a curve would look something like this.

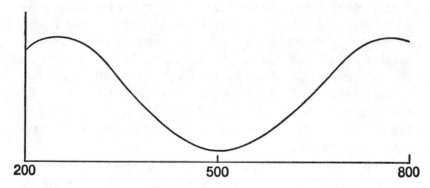

200   500   800

Or perhaps most people have some talent in this field, with very few who go to either extreme. A curve for that would look something like this.

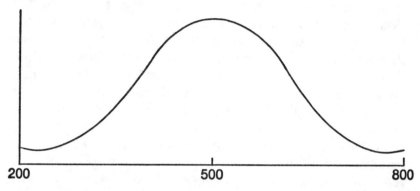

200   500   800

We don't know for certain what curve is right as we design our TTAT. We are betting on the normal curve. If we lose the bet, then our scores will be misleading.

Now we come to three key measures for any standardized test: reliability, standard deviation of an individual score, and validity. Let's take them in order. *Reliability* is simply a measure of the consistency of our test. Reliability tells us the probability that a student who takes the TTAT on Monday and gets a 479 will get a highly similar score if she retakes the TTAT the next day. It is important that our TTAT earn high reliability marks because an erratic test is generally a bad test. If the TTAT had low reliability, no one could count on it since a student's 479 score might have been a 227 or a 684 if she had taken the test a day earlier or later. In that case, the TTAT would be little more than a lottery. One thing we can do to boost our reliability index is to reduce the time given to students to complete the TTAT. Research has shown that a shorter test tends to have higher reliability overall.[4] Of course, by shortening the test we run the risk that some talented but painstaking workers will be discriminated against. And there is no guarantee that a test with a high reliability index will be a good test. The TTAT could very consistently give people the wrong scores, yet as long as it's consistent in doing this the reliability measure will be high.

The standard deviation of an individual score is a number that gives us an idea of how sensitive our test is to chance occurrences. No matter how good a test is, we would expect some variation in an individual's scores. This happens because you might have a cold the day you take the TTAT, or be distracted by a knuckle-cracker near you, or not have had a good night's sleep. The standard deviation of an individual score is the numerical measure of this variation. Recall that the overall distribution of scores for all students taking the test has a standard deviation, as well, which indicates how many scores will fall in a given range. This time we are concerned with the potential scores an individual might have received if she had taken the test on a different day, had more or less sleep, or sat next to an empty chair. Let's say that the standard deviation of an individual score for the TTAT is 30 points. This means that if you got a 479, your real score for that test is probably somewhere between 449 and 509. There is a one-third chance that your real score is actually outside this range. When we decide to give candidates three-digit scores we are leaving the door open to test abuse by admissions personnel who are not sophisticated in the use of test scores. How can this be?

Let's say you have two friends, Mary and John, who took the TTAT with you. Mary has a 429 and John has a 529 to show for their efforts. The temptation for you, for admissions people, for parents, is to say that John's 529 shows more ability than your 479, which shows more ability than Mary's 429. But not so fast. Shades of gray enter in when you examine these scores according to the ranges involved. John's range with a 529 extends from 499 to 559. It's possible, then, that his true score could be a 504—which could also be your true score. John may have had a good day when the test was given and you may have had a bad day, but your real ability could be exactly the same. While John's 529 looks more impressive than your 479 on the TTAT, a careful statistician would refrain from leaping to the conclusion that John is "better" than you. The same reasoning is applicable to the difference between your 479 and Mary's 429. The spread is not statistically significant. That is, a person who understands what the TTAT does would be unable to say with any assurance that your abilities as assessed by the test are any different from Mary's. However, we can be pretty sure that John's test-measured ability in this area really is greater than Mary's, since the 100-point gap is statistically significant.

Now we must look at test *validity*. Validity measures are numbers which attempt to tell us something about how well the test does what it sets out to do. There are three main kinds of validity measures: construct validity, criterion validity, and predictive validity. *Construct validity* asks whether the test seems to make sense on the surface. If this is a math test, are the questions math questions or literature questions? If they are math questions, then the test is likely to have construct validity; if they are literature questions, the opposite is true. *Criterion validity* asks if the test scores match other possible indicators of student ability. For example, if the students who take the TTAT and get high scores are the same students who are currently getting good grades in their high schools, then the TTAT is likely to possess criterion validity. The type of validity you are most likely to have heard of is the third type, predictive validity. *Predictive validity* is a measure of how well the TTAT scores correlate with, or predict, the grades these students will earn at the college. If the match is close, then the TTAT will be deemed to have predictive validity.

Predictive validity is sometimes measured by what is called a correlation coefficient. The symbol for a correlation coefficient is the lower-case letter r. You will see the absolute value of the correlation coefficient expressed as a decimal that is never smaller than 0, nor larger than 1. What does it mean? A correlation coefficient is an index of how much of our predictor variable (the test score) correlates with our response variable (grades at college). If there were absolutely no relationship between the two variables, then our r would equal 0. If there was a perfect match between the two, r would equal 1. In life we find that r will usually lie in between the two end points. For example, the correlation between a person's height and a person's weight is approximately .5.[5] Say you have to guess the weight of people you know absolutely nothing about. Sometimes you will guess correctly by sheer luck; often you will be way off, because you have no information to go on. Then say you are told how tall each person is before you have to guess that person's weight. Now you will probably do somewhat better on your guesses if you figure that the taller a person is, the more he will weigh. This is still a far from perfect system because there are some short people who weigh a lot, and some tall people who are light. But your guesses on average will be better if you know a person's height. Our correlation coefficient of .5 is simply an indication of how much weight corresponds to height.

There is a famous saying in statistics, and it is very important: Correlation does not equal causation. In other words, just because two events can be shown to occur together, it does not mean that one event caused the other. Does being tall "cause" you to be heavy, or being short "cause" you to be light? Of course not. We all know a number of people who do not fit this pattern. We may be able to guess on the basis of a pattern, but we cannot scientifically come to the conclusion that there is a causal relationship on the basis of the pattern alone. Here's another example. I have been to three "big" baseball games: two games were part of a World Series, and one was a playoff for the division championship. The teams I rooted for lost all three of those games. There is a perfect correlation here between the games I attended and the games my team lost, an r = 1.0. If you know absolutely nothing about baseball history, but only which team I was rooting for, you would guess correctly the losers in all three games. The correlation, the match, between my support and losing the big game could not be higher. But you would not for one second leap to the conclusion that I had somehow "caused" my team to lose all three times. Common sense has to enter in when you think about any claims of causation. An r of 1.0, as high as it is, can have nothing to do with one event causing the other.

When we want to evaluate how well our TTAT test does in predicting grades, we will need another number which is called r^2. We get this number by multiplying our correlation coefficient, r, by itself (r times r). This number r^2 is a measure of how much our guesses about the response variable are improved by knowing the predictor variable. The r number will always be higher than the r^2 value (unless $r = 0$ or $r = 1$). This is because r attempts to measure the strength of a relationship, while r^2 tells us how much our forecasting will improve over sheer luck by knowing the predictor variable. Remember when we were guessing weight without any information? We got some of those guesses right by plain luck. R^2 tells us how much better we do knowing people's heights. So, if the r for height to weight is .5, the r^2 is .5 $\times$ .5 = .25. We will make better guesses about weight given height, but while the relationship of weight to height is about .5, our improvement in prediction is only .25. Correlation coefficients look much more impressive than is warranted by the improvement in our forecasting power. When we publish our TTAT test, if we want to impress our clients we will stress the r value of our test and downplay the r^2 figure. There's another reason for this, namely that r values fall more slowly than do r^2 values at some intervals important for us.

Look at it this way. If our TTAT comes out with an r value of .5, the test will be doing as well or better than many of the standardized tests already on the market. That's not a very impressive r value to someone who knows about statistics, but it probably looks good to the unaware. After all, we can't expect many tests to have perfect r values equal to 1. Let's say we agree that an r of .8 would be superb for a standardized test (which, in fact, it would be). The average person might say that the .5 r value of our TTAT falls short of that .8 benchmark, but not too far off. Well, .5 does look to be at least somewhere near .8. That's as far as the average person might take the analysis. But if you know that the r^2 is a more significant measure, look at what happens. The r^2 for a test with an r of .5 is .25, while the r^2 for a test with an r of .8 is .64. Compare an r^2 of .25 to an r^2 of .64, and suddenly the tests don't look to be anywhere near each other in predictive power. There's more. Since an admissions committee will often look at an applicant's high school grades, and since those grades often correlate better with college grades than do test scores, the TTAT's r^2 of .25 may still be overstating the case. If the admissions people asked how much better the TTAT helps them predict college grades when they already know an applicant's high school grades, the odds are the answer would be much lower than the 25 percent the r^2 seems to indicate.

We are now ready to finish the construction of our new form of the TTAT test. We have selected the test format (a standardized, multiple-choice, objective, norm-referenced test). We have decided that the TTAT test score will be the predictor variable, and that first-year grades at the college will be the response variable we are trying to predict. We have selected a group to standardize the test on, and have decreed a scoring scale from 200 to 800 based on the normal curve. We expect a standard deviation for individual scores of 30 points on the TTAT. We are now intent on making our validity and reliability indices look as good as possible. For the sake of high reliability readings, and on the theory that the speed with which a candidate picks answers has some relation to his knowledge of the material, we will ask many questions in a short time. Let's say we decide on 100 questions in a three-hour test.

The challenge now is to write the test questions. We will gather a committee of question writers, some of them experts from the field of collage work. We will pay the members of the committee to write questions according to our format. We will have them write out 1,000 questions. We then assemble a second panel which is chaired by one of our employees, and includes other experts and members of various minority groups whom we have chosen to participate. We pay this panel to look at the questions and give us their opinion on whether they seem to be reasonably related to the area of collage work. We also ask the panel to throw out questions they think show bias. The panel reports back that they have eliminated 200 questions for unrelatedness or bias, and that they think the rest are adequate. On the basis of the approval of the panel which we selected and paid, we now feel that our TTAT test has construct validity. For the purpose of brevity, we will not worry about criterion validity on this hypothetical test.

We now pick 100 questions from the remaining 800, and

put those questions into a test question booklet. We also prepare an answer sheet that can be scored by a computer. We give our TTAT test to the group of 1,000 students for the standardization. We carefully record their scores for later comparisons. Now we perform what is called the "pretest." We look at individual questions and see how many people got them right, and which people got them right. To start with, we only want to keep questions which were answered correctly by a certain percentage of the candidates—let's say for our purposes by 55 to 65 percent of the students. If too many test-takers get a question correct, then we are not obtaining our normal curve—too many students would end up with high scores. If too few are getting a question correct, the opposite would occur—too many students would end up with low scores. So we discard questions that don't meet our distribution requirements.

There is a second part to this "pretest" process. We want to make sure that any given question will more often be answered correctly by the candidates who score higher on the overall test. For instance, let's say John has a high score of 700 while Jill has a low score of 300. We look to see if there are questions that Jill got right which John got wrong, and whenever we find questions like that we throw them away. If we left in questions that the Jills did well on while the Johns missed them, we'd ruin our curve. The low scorers would start getting higher scores, while the high scorers would see their results drop. Then we'd end up with almost all average scores around 500, instead of the spread we are determined to achieve. It may be that everyone should be scoring close to 500 because their abilities are pretty evenly matched, but that's not what we want. It may even be that the low scorers on the pretest should be getting higher scores than the high scorers, but we don't want to have to adjust for that. So we consciously and deliberately select questions so that the kind of people who scored low on the pretest will score low on subsequent tests. We do the same for the middle and high scorers. We are imposing our will on the outcome, so that the test scores will fall in the pattern we picked in the beginning.

We have a great power partially to predetermine from the outset what scores will show up on the TTAT, and who will do well and who will do poorly. Think of it another way. To some extent, this power is equivalent to the power political pollsters would have if they could dictate who would be allowed to vote in order to make their preelection results look good. Pollsters ask people before an election how they intend to vote. These interviews are somewhat like our pretests; both are used to make predictions. But sometimes pollsters look bad because their predictions don't hold up when citizens actually go to the polls and vote. That's because some people change their minds after an interview, some people may not vote who were expected to (and vice versa), and there is some statistical error in the process. But if the pollsters could stand outside the voting booth and decide who would be allowed to vote in accordance with their preelection sample, there would be far fewer surprises on election day. We test writers have the kind of power society has wisely withheld from the pollsters. We can reject questions that look good to our panel if they produce results we don't like, that is, if the questions don't discriminate among the takers in the prescribed fashion. Our assumptions about maintaining the consistency of scores through the use of the pretest had better be correct. If we're off, then kids who deserve to receive higher scores are being held down while others who don't deserve their high scores are being cushioned.

In any event, we've now built our TTAT test. We will compare TTAT scores with college grades in a year, and start accumulating data about the predictive validity of the test. We will try to raise the r and r^2 values by using more questions that the students who went on to get high grades in year one of college answered correctly on the test. We will continue to delete questions whose performance does not meet our expectations. We will promote the use of our test, and we will continue to recruit and pay experts in the field to serve on our committees and panels. If these people happen to be the same ones who will decide later in their careers which—if any—tests to use for selection at their institutions, all the better. Certainly these are men and women of integrity who cannot be "bought." But if they have early, favorable, and repeated experiences with our company, it is only natural that those memories are unlikely to hurt us if we seek a hearing later. The steps we have gone through in putting our TTAT together are a greatly simplified and abbreviated version of what is common in the testing industry. We have left out some details, and not all companies—or all tests—follow all the practices we have used. But if we haven't retraced the path of development for any test exactly step for step, we have hiked a long way into the heart of testing territory.

During the course of this hike we've been able to catch glimpses of some of the beasts that lurk in wait of unwary test users and test-takers. There are additional pitfalls and hidden dangers in the testing terrain that we've not yet spotted, but they will be encountered in the chapters to come. From this brief foray we should recognize that we allow numbers and statistics to replace good hard thinking at our peril. If you were about to go on a wilderness survival expedition, you'd want to know something about your guide. If your guide could recite numbers about how safe and reliable he is until he turns blue in the face, you'd be impressed. If he then confided in you after much prodding that the secret of his success is his firmly held assumption that the sun rises in the west, you'd find another guide quick, numbers or no. It is the same way with testing. A test could sport the best numbers since the last time Nadia Comaneci put on a gymnastics exhibition. But if that test is based on faulty assumptions, you'd better not put too much reliance on its reported results. When it comes to the precision of test results, pay attention to the warnings of the test publishers and then some. Some people hope that tests will give them exact readings. More likely, a test could tell you precisely whether you're in the Atlantic Ocean or the Pacific Ocean, but if you want a better location you're going to have to use additional instruments.

Althea Simmons, the director for the Washington Bureau of the National Association for the Advancement of Colored People (NAACP), warned Congress in 1979 about the need for better public understanding of the limits to test precision. Simmons said: "The public must be informed not only that the test scores are fallible and that their reliability is imperfect, but must be told the extent of that fallibility and imperfection. The public must be informed that test scores are *only* a sample of a student's performance and are never more than an estimate of truth."[6] This plea for information derives much of its force from the abuses of test scores that take place every day. As New York

State Senator Kenneth LaValle put it, "Despite this advice [by test publishers against using scores as the sole criterion], I have learned that admissions officers are using test scores to establish arbitrary cut-off points for admissions decisions. While the reasons for this are many, it is significant in that it portrays the attitude of the general public. The major test companies have become so complex that their product is often granted unwarranted value, regardless of its statistical validity."[7]

The next section covers the use of standardized tests in our society starting with schoolchildren and working up to adults in midcareer. Chapter 6 is about the heavy use of these tests as a way of sorting and branding our children at an unconscionably young age.

PART TWO

How Does Testing Dominate Us?

CHAPTER SIX

Branding Children

Taking standardized tests is not an ordeal reserved exclusively for mature adults competing for admission to some selective college or graduate program or for a job. Rather, our children are subjected to standardized tests almost from their first day in the public schools. Some children are exposed even earlier, sometimes even before entering nursery school or kindergarten. The process of winnowing out the select few and branding the rest as failures in a "meritocratic" contest can't even wait until the children reach adolescence. IQ tests, reading readiness tests, reading tests, tracking and achievement tests, all form a gauntlet that most children have to endure in the course of their schooling. How pervasive are these tests? In the mid-1970s, it was estimated that over 40 million elementary and secondary school youngsters took standardized tests at a direct cost of more than $250 million.[1] Just two types of IQ tests, the Stanford-Binet and the Wechsler editions, were administered to over 2 million children each year.[2] The Stanford Achievement Tests were in use in over 4,000 of the 17,000 school districts in this country.[3] One expert estimated that by the time a child completes the grades from kindergarten through high school, he will have been forced to take between six and twelve complete achievement test batteries —not counting the IQ and reading and minimum competency tests.[4]

The testing industry has participated in the growth of testing programs for schoolchildren. ETS, for example, reported revenues of $6,300,000 in 1979 from tests for elementary and secondary schoolchildren, up from the $1,100,000 reported in 1959.[5] School systems have become hooked on standardized tests, and some school employees are now dependent upon the continued use of these tests to protect their positions. For instance, Montgomery County in Maryland was testing a minimum of 60,000 students per year in the third, fifth, seventh, and ninth grades as of 1976. Montgomery County is not alone in maintaining a staff devoted solely to test administration, with a total direct test cost of $55,000.[6] It is hard to count the "indirect" costs—the value of the time lost to classwork, the harm from the emotional and mental disruption in a course of study, the expense in teacher time of giving the tests and evaluating the results, the loss of self-confidence and peer respect suffered by improperly labeled "slow" children—but they must be substantial.

Things have reached an absurd stage indeed when three- and four-year-old children at nursery schools are being coached on how to take standardized tests used in the admissions process to some kindergartens. But that's what is now going on, at least in the Washington, D.C. area. As the *New Republic* reported in 1979, "A major concern at many private nursery schools in the Washington area is preparing their children for the kindergarten admissions process."[7] Standardized tests even play a part in that process at the most selective nursery schools.[8] What exactly is a standardized test going to tell us at that age besides whether the child comes from the "right" family with the "right" income in the "right" neighborhood (who is possibly a product of the "right" nursery prep school)? Can it be long before someone comes up with the idea of giving standardized tests to infants in order to "fairly" and "scientifically" track them into fast and slow prenursery school programs? Where will it all end? If parents are nervous about the performance of their children on these tests, if they take the view that these tests will reveal the child's intellectual "worth" at such a tender age, can you imagine what fears and pressures the children themselves must feel? How many of them can shrug off this judgment from on high as just an estimate subject to error of some of their skills at a particular moment?

Can we really expect these children to display the sophistication and skepticism about test results so lacking in many adults who use standardized tests?

Schools use tests to sort children into reading sections and then to track them by grade and ability; to affect decisions on whether a child will be promoted, graduated, held back, or placed in a group for the mentally retarded; and as a rationale for their decisions by declaring that tests, not school personnel, are the ultimate and infallible arbiter of these matters. Of course, this can get a little tricky, especially when the standardized tests used do not overlap entirely with the materials taught in the particular school or class that the child has attended. One problem with the use of national standardized tests to measure "achievement" in the nation's schoolrooms is that there is no national curriculum. School systems differ on what is taught and the sequence in which subject areas are taught. Further, the mobility of Americans in moving from area to area, and school system to school system, means children in any given class have been taught a variety of skills with different degrees of emphasis. The National PTA has made the powerful argument that "a child should not be penalized because a local school system has chosen a different sequence than the test maker."[9]

School districts are becoming increasingly aware that excessive reliance on standardized tests can be doubly dangerous. Although the tests may facilitate the sorting of students in a relatively cheap fashion, missorted students would surely dispute the false economy involved. What's more, schools themselves may be evaluated in turn by the public on the basis of these test scores. School districts which rely on standardized tests to make the hard decisions for them are fostering a belief in test efficiency on the part of parents and students. When taxpayers then attempt to use these same tests as measures of school performance in the accountability movement, the schools are in a bind. They can't really plead the inaccuracy of the tests because if the tests are bad the public will ask why they have been used for so long. In any given instance it is possible that low school test scores are reflecting incompetence. But those scores could also be distorted reflections of other facts about the system. It is akin to staring into a fun house mirror—the image you see could be reality or it could be a monstrous reshaping of the true picture. There is no simple way to know, short of a close and careful examination of the test or the mirror.

The problem is that the use of test scores to judge how well a school is doing can be just as flawed as the use of those scores to banish children to the educational netherworld. It may be that the test is measuring skills different from the ones stressed in the school up to that point. The test could emphasize antonyms when the school has just finished its unit on synonyms. This doesn't mean the local school curriculum is inferior to the curriculum assumed by the national test publisher, just that the two are different. It may be just as sound, or even preferable, to teach synonyms before antonyms. Moreover, the use of scores to rank schools doesn't take starting points into account. Children might learn more at P.S. 1 in the time they're in school than comparable children at P.S. 2, but if they started way behind the kids at P.S. 2 they might not have caught up. On a straight ranking scale, P.S. 1 would be blamed for factors totally outside its control. To make matters worse, resources could be diverted from P.S. 1 to P.S. 2 on the basis of scores which superficially show P.S. 2 to be the "better" school.

Much of the public takes published test score reports at face value. For example, imagine the following headline in your local newspaper: "Local Schools in Shambles; A Full Half of Students Tested Fall Below the National Mean." That sounds pretty terrible, doesn't it? That headline could send school board members into hiding, or induce voters to grant them a permanent vacation from any further responsibility for the schools. But when you know about standardized tests, when you know that tests are graded on a curve, when you know that the word "mean" just means "average," that headline is no big deal. If half of the students in the district are below the national average, then the other half are above the national average, which basically means the schools scored at the national average overall. That may be no cause for gloating, but it is not cause for panic either. Furthermore, because test publishers will change their curves from time to time, the local schools might actually be doing a much better job than they were ten years ago without receiving any credit for the improvement. How could this happen?

It could happen because a national average is just an average, and we're talking about norm-referenced standardized tests. Let's say the test we've been talking about that gave rise to the headline has 100 questions. It may be that ten years ago the students in the local schools got an average of 70 of those questions right, which was also the national average at the time. But now, because of more attention to the contents of this particular test throughout the nation, the national average is up to 80. The students in our area also go up to 80. But as far as the curve is concerned, our students haven't made any progress because they are still "just average." Imagine a marathon runner doomed to run forever because every time she gets close to the finish line the officials move it back two miles. This is what can happen when the standardized tests rely on the curve. It brings back the words of the Queen in *Through the Looking-Glass:* "Now, here, you see, it takes all the running you can do, to keep in the same place. If you want to get somewhere else, you must run at least twice as fast as that!" There is an apocryphal story that the governor of one of our states made a campaign pledge that if elected he'd see to it that every schoolchild would score above the future statewide average.[10] That would be a neat trick, but it can't be done. That imaginary governor might labor mightily and improve schools so much in his state that every single student would know three times as much as before and get a raw score three times as high as before. But half of the students in the state will always score higher than the other half of the students on a curved standardized test. That's what a curve is about, and for parts of the public, test scores are like a wicked curve that's hard to follow.

When reading test scores or achievement test scores are published for schools and school districts without adequate explanation, more is at stake than the possibility of erroneous conclusions. Schools and teachers may feel compelled to teach to the tests in self-defence. This may only compound the difficulty since it means more time spent preparing for the tests, more influence for test subjects over school curriculum, and finally more importance placed on test results by students, parents, and the general public. Some leaders have spoken out against the gullibility inherent in accepting test results as precise, arguing that "in fact, it would make as much sense to take the blood pressure of each student, apply the usual statistical procedures, and publish the results district by district, to measure the health of the student body."[11] There is little question that some teachers are worried about the way test scores influence their reputations, as well as the impact on the children. One educator told the New York State legislature: "Many teachers are afraid that if test scores are continually emphasized, teaching and curriculum may become completely hitched to test-taking and test passing. Institutions fear that their worth will be judged on the basis of their students' scores on these tests."[12] If the tests measured teacher competence and student skills accurately, this form of test dominance wouldn't be a bad thing. There are bad schools and mediocre teachers and indifferent students, and if we could find a fair way to assess them and motivate them we'd be fortunate. Unfortunately, relying on a single set of test scores doesn't work. A bad teacher can be hidden behind a good class, and a teacher making headway with a class of slow learners can be unfairly attacked. To top it off, using test scores this way would put control of the pedagogy of local schools into the hands of a few national, nonelected test publishers.

This is not just a hypothetical problem we must consider in the future. A preoccupation with standardized test scores in our public schools exists at this moment. The underlying cause is understandable. As Frances Quinto of the National Education Association (NEA) told a gathering of the National Consortium on Testing (NCT), if teachers are going to be evaluated on the basis of their students' test scores, it is only logical to teach to the tests.[13] The more tests are relied on as an evaluation tool, the more the teachers will concentrate on preparing children for those tests. Then what have we accomplished? If subjects and skills that are too important and too complex to be measured on these tests are excluded from our children's education, we will have lost far more than we have gained. The unhappy prospect of turning out a generation of students who can breeze through multiple-choice tests and little else stares us in the face. We want schools to teach our kids how to read, write, use arithmetic, and then to use those skills in combination with an appreciation for the arts and the duties of citizenship. Constant practice in filling in tiny boxes with pencil marks does not necessarily lead us in that direction.

Be that as it may, Arthur Laughland, a school principal in New-ton, Massachusetts, has written that "teaching to the test has be-come a way of life for many of our high school teachers."[14]

The adverse effects of testing mania in the schools have been pointed out by the National PTA. In testimony to Congress, a PTA representative warned that overreliance on standardized tests can "develop patterns of expectation by teachers and school systems that often are totally unrelated to a child's true capabili-ties; and because the power to test is the power to influence cur-riculum, there is a tendency to reinforce curriculum patterns that respond only to the ultimate goal of 'looking good' on the na-tional tests."[15] This is hardly a new concern to professional edu-cators, but the public has not been fully informed about the scope of the problem. Back in 1961, Jane Sehmann, the director of admissions at Smith College, was quoted as saying, "As a re-sult of parental and other pressure, schools are substituting vo-cabulary drills and word study for meaningful work in reading and writing."[16] Obviously, parents would rather their children re-ceive high scores on the standardized tests they take in school than low scores. But parents have assumed that achieving high scores on those tests is the same thing as mastering the skills re-quired for meaningful work in reading and writing. Parents backed vocabulary drills because they thought raising test scores meant improving learning. After all, weren't these tests impartial appraisals of their children's performance across the board? But if parents are presented with the choice of drilling for tests for the sake of high scores alone, or using that time to teach the funda-mentals of reading and writing and so forth, it's not so clear they'd still opt for the test prepping.

By their very nature, standardized tests tend to narrow the broad abilities we seek for our children into a few specific sub-skills that can be measured in a multiple-choice format. Standard-ized tests as a rule are passive in nature. They do not ask the stu-dent to respond to a question with an individual answer using that student's talents and imagination. Rather, the student is just asked to choose one of the alternatives already written by the publisher. The ability to gather information and then distill it in cogent sentences is not the same as picking out an erroneous sen-tence fragment on a multiple-choice test. The PTA spells out this difference: "Multiple choice or short answer types of questions limit the ability to measure a full range of skills. For example, the ability to write well, to organize and transfer thoughts to paper, requires testing of a written sample, yet for many years we have tested writing skills by multiple choice questions. Why? Because it was easier to score. We reduce writing to the rote principles of grammar, spelling, and punctuation, and then wondered why children's writing skills deteriorated."[17] Can you imagine giving Shakespeare a multiple-choice test to see if he could write instead of looking at something he had written? Or telling a Mark Twain with his marvelous gift of writing dialogue in the vernacular that his test scores in formal English mark him as an inferior writer?

Some other undesirable side effects are connected with the worship of tests in our schools. Subjects such as art, music, shop, and physical education, among others, which are not readily measured by multiple-choice tests, are devalued for students. If these subjects don't show up on the tests, then schools and students alike can fall prey to the notion that they are not important in the overall scheme of things. Courses such as history and civics can get caught in the crunch, too, because it's hard for a test publisher to figure what a student in these courses is supposed to know by, say, eleventh grade. So what the publishers do to get around this quandary is to give what is essentially a reading test and call it a history test. It works like this: the publisher will supply all the factual information about historical events in reading passages, and then require the student to select answers based largely on reading those passages as opposed to any outside knowledge of history he may bring to the test. This way the publisher can say the "history" test is appropriate for all school districts in the U.S. since students aren't overtly penalized if their school hasn't covered certain materials—the information is on the test itself. But now a student gets test scores for history which may be almost identical with his reading scores. We end up testing the skill of reading as much or more than the subject of history and a student's understanding of historical forces.

It doesn't stop there either. Publishers of textbooks are tempted to gear the level of their books to the level and types of standardized tests widely used in that field. This is a selling point to school boards: "If you buy our textbooks, your students will automatically be preparing for the areas the tests will cover." Independent judgment by text publishers, local school boards, and individual teachers can become severely threatened in this cycle. You may applaud the result if you believe in a national curriculum, but this is surely bringing it in through the back door with a minimum of public awareness. Further, results of standardized tests are increasingly used by the national policymakers who control funding as a way of determining which policies will be continued and which discarded. Often these decisions can be made on the basis of a small sample of test items which are open to a number of valid objections as to their reliability and validity. It is clear that policymakers have latched on to the use of standardized tests as a way of forcing local schools to comply with their educational directives. What is not so clear is whether this is ultimately in the public interest. What is painfully evident is that this process of nationalization is taking place not as a result of deliberate policy considerations by elected representatives, but rather as an unintended consequence of reliance on tests to evaluate federally funded programs.

Why should we care about this tendency to let tests determine the curriculum? Simply because it can cheat our children out of the more important educational experiences in favor of the lower level, but more easily tested, skills. Ann Cook of the Community Resources Institute, has spoken on this topic. She says that standardized tests overlook the abilities we really care about in education, such as "knowing something in depth; taking intellectual responsibility and defending a position; reading a whole, entire, book; critically analyzing material; and developing written and oral arguments."[18] Standardized tests veer away from these abilities not because they are unimportant, but because they do not lend themselves to the quick and inadequate measurement provided by multiple-choice questions. The tragedy is that as we insist schools train children to do better on the tests, we may be depriving those children of the opportunity to acquire these more complicated abilities. A mad scramble to post higher scores is not a panacea for the admitted shortcomings of public education. Tests must be restored to some balance in the educational hierarchy lest we give our children the message that it is more important to acquire the superficial skills prized by the tests than the deeper accomplishments so needed by society. When this is done in the name of "objectivity" we are just fooling ourselves. As two educators have written: "We have placed our faith in these 'objective' tests because we did not trust the 'subjective' parents and teachers who know our children best. We forgot that the nameless 'theys' out there can also be subjective, biased, or plain stupid too. Only their subjectivity masks itself in 'science' and is even harder to combat."[19]

One of the most abhorrent words to enter the English language in conjunction with standardized tests is "overachiever." This is a term that has been used to damn children to a Kafkaesque region where reason and logic do not dwell. A child who does admirably in school—good grades, good behavior, and intellectual and social growth—is called an "overachiever" if her test scores are less outstanding than her grades. The idea is that she is working above her capacity in school and should accept a lesser status and stop trying so hard. The word "overachiever" literally does not make sense. How can you achieve more than you are capable of achieving? If you've actually obtained the good grades the test said were beyond your reach, then by definition those grades were within your grasp. The word "overachiever" is a marvel of misdirection. It gets you to thinking that somehow this child did what she can't do, instead of realizing that the true problem is in the test. As Banesh Hoffmann has written, the child in question is really an "underscorer" on the tests.[20] The test that said she couldn't do it was wrong—she did it. But we've been conditioned to think of this accomplishment by the youngster as an act of youthful insolence in refusing to conform to her test score. This situation is a flashing warning signal that the tests are imperfect, and not that the child is defiant.

What is inexcusable is that children who are labeled as "overachievers" are sometimes subject to pressures to conform. The child is told that she can't keep it up; that somehow she is abnormal and her success in school is not "real" in some mystical sense. This attitude goes against all we know about the limitations of tests, yet it exists. The opposite effect can be found in the term "underachiever," a person supposedly not living up to his "test-discovered" potential in school. As Hoffmann wrote, "The vice of these words, 'underachiever' and 'overachiever,' is that they all too often treat the tests as the standards: if the tests say the student is able, then able he is, no matter what his teachers think; and if the tests say he is not, nothing he does will make him otherwise."[21] How can we totally abandon our understanding of the complexity and unpredictability of children merely because one type of evaluation—a standardized test—renders a verdict at odds with all the other forms of evaluation practiced by teachers and parents? The very thought that an "overachiever" should give up rather than strive for excellence should make Americans' blood boil. In most spheres of life we preach a credo that an individual should do all she is capable of and not be held back by artificial restraints. But in the area of tests we have displayed a willingness to turn our backs on demonstrated competence in order to preserve the myth of test precision.

There are many reasons behind our susceptibility to ignoring performance when it contradicts the predictions of tests. There is a foundation of general accuracy in the more reputable tests which can readily be extended to an impression of total accuracy. Moreover, tests can make life easier for teachers and administrators in a number of instances. But the test industry has played its part in promoting an unhealthy suspension of disbelief in reviewing test scores. This faith in tests has been nurtured by some test publishers over decades through their literature and promotional activities. It should not be shocking to discover that after years of the testing industry's sowing indiscriminate praise of tests, the public should now be reaping the bitter fruits of test misuse. It is arguable that these tests are a response to public demand, but that "demand" has been carefully cultivated and stimulated by the standardized testing industry.

ETS is by no means a sole culprit, or even necessarily among the most culpable. But it has not been immune from past promotional practices that left much to be desired. Twenty years ago Martin Mayer wrote in his book, *The Schools:* ". . . every observer of the schools has noted that it is the administrators, not the teachers or children, who are enthusiastic about these tests. Indeed, the Educational Testing Service, a nonprofit group which runs the most 'scientific' test-selling operation in the country, has found it necessary in its literature to proclaim that 'If a teacher is unsympathetic to a testing program . . . she is abdicating her rightful position.' "[22] Of course a teacher who abandons his or her judgment in deference to a test score takes abdication to its limits. In a different passage, Mayer observes: "Certainly, ETS ought not to be sending out to schools literature which prates earnestly about 'underachievement' (caused by 'poor study habits, lack of motivation, or lack of challenge') and 'overachievement' (caused by 'undue tensions or pressures to do well'), when its own chief psychometrician, Henry Dyer, writes in the *Teachers College Record* that 'underachievement' and 'overachievement' are fallacies which his profession had hoped to eliminate in the 1930s."[23] We are living with the legacy of years of overstated if well-intentioned claims for the tests. The excesses of the past are felt in the present, most especially by the children who are less capable than adults of defending themselves when they encounter test abuse.

Test abuse comes in many guises. One of its most frightening forms is the use of test scores as an excuse to "blame the victims" of low scores and brand them "unteachable." Instead of taking a poor test score as an indication of the need for some kind of help, schools sometimes dump the poor scorer into the lowest priority group. After a while, that poor score may become a self-fulfilling prophecy, as the student attempts to "live' down" to those expectations of failure. The child and teacher may both give in to the "inevitability" of the child's continued poor performance, thus making that prediction a reality. If people thought of test scores as dimly lit snapshots instead of eternal monuments in stone, then poor test-takers would receive special attention to their needs rather than a sentence to the outer reaches of the school world. Snapshots can be blurred, and we know that new photos can show people who have changed in confidence and ability over time. Children must not be treated as outcasts unfit for redemption on the word of tests. If a test reveals educational ailments in a child, then the treatment should be directed to relieving those ailments, not to watching the worsening of those ailments with a smug air of having "told you so." Doctors give tests to diagnose the illnesses of their patients. Except in a crisis situation in which time is severely limited, doctors do not give tests to sort the relatively healthy from the sick in order to concentrate their attentions on the fit while dooming the ill through a lack of medical care. Even when standardized test scores are accurate in singling out a problem, they are not visions of what must be for a child, but only of what may be if the symptoms are not treated. This is a concept Ebeneezer Scrooge would understand (at least on Christmas Day). It is a concept we need to act upon.

Walter Lippmann anticipated this phenomenon of using test scores to rationalize the branding of children—and sometimes school districts and various ethnic and racial groups—as inferior, as hopeless cases. A triage system is necessary in medical crises, but it is a darn poor philosophy for our educational system. As Lippmann wrote, "The danger of the intelligence tests is that in a wholesale system of education, the less sophisticated or the more prejudiced will stop when they have classified and forget their duty is to educate."[24] We might all be better off, but the children especially, if we spent a little less time guessing about their potential to learn, and a lot more time improving their performance in learning. We don't send kids to school so that they can be labeled "bright" or "slow" and then sent back to us in essentially the same condition they started. We send them to learn. It is no excuse to say, "These kids will be hard to teach according to the scores." That's precisely the reason we send them to school in the first place. Lippmann put it this way: "The child's success with schoolwork cannot be a measure of the child's success in life. On the contrary, his success in life must be a significant measure of the school's success in developing the capacities of the child. If a child fails in school and then fails in life, the school cannot sit back and say: you see how accurately I predicted this. Unless we are to admit that education is essentially impotent, we have to throw back the child's failure at the school, and describe it as a failure not by the child but by the school."[25] To the extent that test scores are used to predict failure rather than work to avoid it, we also have to throw back these failures at test abuse.

This fascination with test prophecy to the detriment of hard work with the low scorers is doubly ironic. It is ironic first of all because one of the virtues of standardized tests in the schools is supposed to be the elimination of the "halo effect." The halo effect refers to a human tendency to consider subconsciously not just the content of schoolwork performed by a student, but also the background of that student. A teacher may grade Jane's essay too highly because Jane has written good essays in the past. And Jim, who has not written well in the past, may receive a grade that is too low on his most recent paper because the teacher is thinking of Jim's poor writing history when he reads the paper. Jane wears a halo in the teacher's mind—her work can look better than it really is because she has a good reputation. Poor Jim seems to be wearing horns when it is time for his paper to be read. Test scores were supposed to be immune from this possibility since a computer doesn't "know" whose test it is scanning. But now the mystique of tests produces its own halo effect. Teachers may alter their evaluations of a student's work based on his test history. A teacher may think, "This looks like garbage, but the tests say this kid is smart, so maybe there is something here I didn't see the first time." We all share an inclination to find what we are looking for, and given the right frame of mind, a "garbage" paper can look like genius. What's more, teachers may inadvertently find themselves spending more time and attention on the "gifted" students. This attention naturally helps the children to bloom. Tests can skew the way teachers' time is used. For example, a controversial experiment was conducted in California in 1964 which indicates that teachers may divide their attention in accord with test results and that this attention itself can influence future test results.[26]

Here's what happened. The experimenters gave all the children in a particular elementary school a standardized test. Then the experimenters told the teachers in that school that the tests revealed certain children were potentially better learners than the rest. The catch was that the experimenters just picked the kids they said belonged to this special group at random. Actual performance on the test was irrelevant. But the teachers weren't told this. One year later the experimenters came back to the school and tested all those children once again. The results? The children who had arbitrarily been designated as the best potential learners indeed turned out to be the same children who gained the most in their test scores. This experiment has been criticized by some as employing faulty technical procedures, so we should not place complete confidence in it until all the verdicts are in.[27] But it does stand as a remarkable event. How could these results have been produced? The logical assumption is that at least some of the teachers spent extra time on the chosen few, and that these kids responded to the attention and the teacher's conviction that they would do well. If this is the case, test results may be measures not of the child's innate capacities, but of external factors—such as teacher approval and attention—existing in our schools. Kids labeled smart may tend to live up to that label through their own efforts and the devotion of their teachers. Of course, the fear is that the reverse effect takes place as well. In either event, the halo effect lives on through the medium of the tests.

The second irony is that we as a people should sit still for a doctrine of predetermination in our schools. Test scores have a number of important consequences for our children with little opportunity for their individuality to shine through. We insist on individual rights in most areas, but we do not shrink from mass-labeling our children in their formative years. David Harman, of the Harvard University Graduate School of Education, wrote: "Test scores have significant implications for people over and above their use as determiners of reading ability. They are widely used as criteria for placing students in different classes, for accepting or rejecting students for different schools, and for guiding and counseling students into different avenues of academic and vocational pursuit. It is indeed one of the distinct ironies of the American experience that a cultural heritage predicated on the notion of rugged individualism should spawn a system of education that places so much credence in standardized and normed achievement testing."[28] Why do we do this? There are some valid reasons, including the way tests can help teachers and students when used properly. But surely the cost factor cannot be overlooked. Lawrence Plotkin, a psychologist at the City College of New York, explained: "It takes a real clinical expert to diagnose some of these problems. But why hire a lot of psychologists when you can do it for nineteen cents a test? And it takes the onus off the school officials because they didn't make the decision."[29] In point of fact, the school officials did make the decision on how their young charges would be treated when they selected the particular test or tests to which they surrendered their remaining responsibilities.

A vicious cycle is at work. If a child starts school behind on the skills that are measured by the tests, then the child may be relegated to the lower track or the slow classes. From there the child has less and less of a chance to catch up with the students receiving the more intensive training. What's most galling is that school authorities can then point to the child's later performance as proof that the tests were right all along. In some cases the tests are right. But they are also wrong in other cases, and this backward reasoning in justifying dependence on them is unacceptable. As Bernard Feder wrote: "If an extremely high correlation exists between IQ and school grades, this means, in effect, that schools grade students not on the results of *instruction,* but on abilities and aptitudes that those students had before they even walked into the classroom."[30] Why not just give the children who do well on standardized tests from the start a free pass to college if they will be able to coast through school on the strength of this skill? Conversely, we could just write off the chances of the low scorers who will only sink deeper in the educational quagmire with time. They will be placed in situations where they are unlikely to be pressed to expand their intellectual abilities to the fullest. As Vito Perrone, dean of the University of North Dakota and the president of the National Consortium on Testing, has written: "Children placed in such settings are often viewed as failures; expectations tend not to be high for them. And children in such settings quickly learn to view themselves as failures, producing little."[31] Judge Skelly Wright threw out the tracking system in D.C. schools for similar reasons, saying: "Even in concept the tracking system is undemocratic and discriminatory. Its creator admits it is designed to prepare some children for white-collar, and other children for blue-collar jobs. Considering the tests used to determine which children should receive the blue-collar special, and which the white, the danger of children completing their education wearing the wrong collar is too great for this democracy to tolerate."[32]

The danger of putting the wrong collars around the necks of our children is indeed great. We have already talked about the problem of tests which simply ratify the advantage some children have when they start school and then serve to perpetuate that advantage. We know this is unfair since children change rapidly and if left to their own devices will alter their relative academic positions many times during the school years. We also suspect that tests may be measuring skills which are a function of being born to affluent families, and skills which represent only a small portion of a child's abilities. But beyond all this, test results can be out and out misinterpreted. A poor score on a standardized math test could actually mean that the child is a whiz in math who can't fill in bubbles neatly. Edwin Taylor of the Education Development Center has written about this type of case.[33] According to Taylor, a concerned parent in a Boston suburb forced a showdown over the results of a standardized test given to his daughter. The test supposedly revealed his daughter to be so poor in English that she had to be placed in a "special learning" class. The parent had to threaten to sue the school board in order to see a copy of this test along with his daughter's answers.

What happened when the father and daughter were at last able to sit down and go over the test? Taylor wrote that it became evident the daughter's "difficulty is not with the test but with the separated answer form. For example, with a red pencil she easily corrects errors of punctuation and capitalization in a sample paragraph but makes mistakes in coding the corrections and transferring them to the answer sheet. For her, the original test was not at all a test of English but a test of clerical skill."[34] A test of clerical skill could have banned her from continuing with her regular class. How many other children run afoul of tests, not because they can't do the work desired, but because the test really measures something other than what it is said to cover? How many other parents have the nerve and the resources to challenge an entire school board to see if the test results are inaccurate in some way? Do we just turn and walk away from the danger that students, teachers, and parents are more likely to accept misleading test results than to challenge them?

MIT Physics Professor Emeritus Jerrold Zacharias lays down this law: "Adequate scrutiny of an item demands knowing not only what a child's response is, but also why he or she made that particular response."[35] This is the reason standardized tests can be so easily misinterpreted, with potentially devastating consequences for all concerned. We can see which boxes the child has marked, but we don't know why those choices were made by the child. There is an entire body of writing which details a number of poor quality questions that have been asked of children and others on these standardized tests. Most of these questions are considered poor because of their ambiguity to a test-taker, or for some form of bias. Here are some samples of standardized test questions that have been asked of children. These questions, along with the commentary on them, were compiled in a very informative book called *The Myth of Measurability*, edited by Paul Houts.

"Something you see in your sleep is a . . .
 ( ) dream ( ) fairy ( ) wish ( ) dread?
 Dr. Freud might answer wish or dread, and a kid who's lost a tooth and put it under the pillow might answer fairy. And, anyway, see is a poor choice of verbs. Did you see a dream last night?

"When a dove begins to associate with crows, its feathers remain _____, but its heart grows black.
 ( ) black ( ) white ( ) dirty ( ) spread
 ( ) good
 Not only is the statement itself erroneous, but think of the emotional impact of an item like this on a black child. (And, incidentally, not all doves are white.)

"How the _____ roses flush up in the cheeks!
 ( ) white ( ) pretty ( ) small ( ) yellow
 ( ) red
 The 'correct' answer is red—but only if the cheek in question is white. Note also the quaint phrasing.

"dollar   peso   mark   lira _____
 ( ) change ( ) franc ( ) foreign
 ( ) purchase ( ) bank
 This question might pose no difficulties for the well-traveled child, but it requires at least a smattering of global economics for the others."[36]

Can we really accept the assertion that children who answer these kinds of questions "correctly" possess some special, intrinsic intelligence while kids who pick the "wrong" choices with no right of explanation are inferior? These questions do measure what a child has been exposed to and how well he can guess what is on the test writer's mind. But it becomes very risky to make any broader claims about what these questions reveal of children's talents. Banesh Hoffmann writes of how creative children can run rings around the test writers in their responses. One first-grader, for instance, was asked on a school test to circle the figure that represented what he was like in the morning. One figure had a wide-awake face, the other a sleepy expression. The child drew a half-circle around each figure, because when he got up in the morning he was half awake and half asleep.[37] This disregard for instructions (he was told to circle one figure, not portions of each) will get any child into trouble on a standardized test, but shows a greater instinct for giving a true answer. Hoffmann and Ann Cook also made light of a favorite type of question used on standardized reading tests when they spoke at a recent NCT meeting.[38] Some reading tests will ask a student to pick out the "main idea" expressed in a reading passage, but Cook said this is a misleading question; what the tester is actually looking for is what has been talked about most. A student who tries to make a qualitative judgment about what is the most important thing mentioned will be marked wrong, while the student who only sees what has been repeated most will get the answer right. Hoffmann suggested that this sort of approach could lead to the following absurdity. A passage could read: "An atomic bomb devastated New York City yesterday. It was a rainy day. The rain poured down. It continued to rain all day." The child who picks the answer, "a rainy day in New York," could get the main idea right, which is not necessarily an indication of superior brainpower.

Edwin Taylor has taken a crack at some of the questions which have appeared on standardized science tests for elementary schoolchildren. Taylor's conclusions? "1) standardized science achievement tests are almost uniformly poor in quality. They are incorrect, misleading, skewed in emphasis, and irrelevant; and 2) any quick-answer, paper-and-pencil science test that has consequences for the child or the school is likely to be irrelevant and perhaps harmful to those activities most likely to interest children in science."[39] Some of the science questions Taylor has uncovered are given below, along with his commentary on them.

"Why would a trip to Pluto require more fuel than a trip to the moon?
( ) Pluto is much smaller than the moon
( ) Pluto is farther from Earth than the moon
( ) Pluto moves faster than the moon
( ) Pluto is closer to the sun than the moon
    The key idea, difference in gravitational potential in the field of the sun, is not mentioned. The fact that 'Pluto is farther from the Earth than the moon' is by itself irrelevant: in a frictionless environment, going far takes no more fuel than going near.

"If the earth did not turn on its axis, there would be no
( ) phases of the moon
( ) summer and winter
( ) months and years
( ) day and night
    and no test makers."[40]

Analyzing test questions is important to us because it reveals more fully how test scores can go astray. When questions are ambiguous, or imprecise in their facts, or ostensibly directed to history when they really measure reading, then we can only guess what was in the minds of the students as they chose their answers. Right and wrong answers become indistinguishable. At that point the entire concept of relying upon standardized tests must be called into question. The shield of secrecy which surrounds many of the standardized tests makes this difficult without free access by outsiders to the inner workings of the tests. As Virginia Sparling, the president of the National PTA, told Congress, "The appropriate question might well be, 'Are we buying instruments that tell us what we need to know?' If not, then we are already wasting $250 million. We cannot evaluate the changes that may be necessary unless we can review what the true costs of the present system cover."[41] Not least among these true costs is the trauma inflicted on the children who have to take the tests. Mayer has written, "The child, who knows that much of his future may be determined by his test scores, cannot approach tests in that calm frame of mind which the testers seem to regard as natural, 'once he knows that the test is there to serve him.' "[42] Amity Buxton, of the Oakland, California, Teacher Shelter, told of children in kindergarten who were crying and wetting their pants when forced to take a standardized test used to determine eligibility for federal funds.[43] Is it necessary to scare children this way?

The scaring and the scarring of children by tests have not gone unobserved. Listen to these witnesses discuss the costs to children of test abuse. Jerrold Zacharias wrote, "It is my belief that our efforts to measure so-called intelligence have had an imprisoning and destructive effect on the lives of children."[44] School Principal Arthur Laughland wrote, "Testing can mark innocent children with stigmata for the rest of their lives, tarnish schools' reputations, and ruin teaching careers. . . . [Testing] is not fun for the child who freezes; it is not fun for the child who struggles for small successes to be labeled a 'failure' time after time; and it is not fun for the child whose one bad day yields results that must be lived with until the next testing time."[45] Thomas Cottle of the Children's Defense Fund, wrote: "We ought to worry, too, about the child who goes home after learning that his test scores have earned him a place in the lowest academic track of his inadequate grammar school, and with tears in his eyes tells his parents: 'They told me in school that I'm stupid. I didn't know what they were talking about. They told me there was no talking back to them because they had it in their tests—everything they wanted to know about me. I said I should be in the other group because those kids were learning more and besides, they were getting all the best teachers in their classes. I didn't want them to put me in the class they put me in. But they said it wasn't what they wanted to do, it was what they had to do 'cause they don't decide what classes to put the student in, the tests decide that for them. People don't decide. . . .' "[46]

The cost of overreliance on standardized tests to this child, and to uncounted others, is hard to comprehend entirely. If you took a standardized test to get into a job position or college or graduate school, you must remember sweating out the results. If bad scores came your way, you probably recall the impact. You know your own talents and what you can do, but it is difficult to remember these if the test says you're not up to snuff. If you've always done well on the tests, you probably expect to do well again, but there is that nagging uncertainty that maybe this time the tables will turn. And then the previous high scores are of little comfort. Anyone who has lived by the tests can be denied by the tests. Yet whatever the outcome, adults know life goes on and that there are more important things in life than getting high test scores. Children do not have this buffer of age and experience. They are most vulnerable to being branded by tests, and least able to fight back against test abuse. But they are not the only ones who experience this plight. We turn now to their older sisters and brothers who are vying for admission to college.

CHAPTER SEVEN

Closing
College Doors

Late in their junior year of high school, or early in their senior year, millions of American students take part in a strange youth ritual. This ritual does not involve drinking or drugs or sex or roller skating or rock and roll. The two variations of the ritual are called "taking the SAT" and "taking the ACT." This ritual could be compared to the rites of initiation a pledge to a fraternity or sorority has to go through. Both require that the youngster exhibit specialized skills or behavior in order to maximize his or her chances of acceptance by the selecting group. Participants in this ritual are called "college applicants," and by and large they are frightened about the experience. They have reason for this apprehension, for their performance during this rite will have significant repercussions. The scores students get on the Scholastic Aptitude Test (SAT, also known as the College Boards) and/or the American College Testing Assessment (ACT) may be decisive in determining which colleges will welcome them, and which will shun them.

The SAT and ACT have a hold on the imaginations of college applicants in this country. Most of the better known colleges and universities require an applicant to take the SAT, or the ACT, before they will be considered for admission. Why do these standardized tests make students so nervous? Judith Weitzman, the assistant director of admissions at the Massachusetts Bay Community College, has written: "Mere mention of the

123

SAT sets teeth chattering, for it is a grueling three-hour race against the clock to select the winners of the Ivy League sweepstakes. High score: You win four years at the college of your choice. Low score means slim pickings."[1] This kind of pressure can turn normally brilliant minds into cottage cheese. Nor is this a fad of today's youth alone. Marian Schlesinger wrote of her participation in this contest back in the 1930s, in a passage from *Snatched from Oblivion:* "The terror of our lives was the College Boards, looming at the end of our senior year. I can still see the shape of those fateful little white sheets of paper and feel the panic spreading as I scanned the algebra problems or the French translations, all comprehension and memory seeming to fly out the window into the balmy June air."[2] Some students will excel on these tests and some will not. Members of both groups will get ill, lose sleep, and worry constantly over their prospective encounter with the SAT or ACT. The kids who worry too much about the tests are prone to choke on the day of the test because of the additional pressure they put on themselves. A bad day, produced by anxiety or illness, can lower an applicant's score on the test and lessen her prospects for that "right" college she wants to enter.

Just what does it mean to take the SAT or ACT? In general, it means getting up early on a Saturday, going to your local high school or test center, and working your way through a test that is supposed to predict to some extent what grades you will get in college. The SAT reports two main scores, one for your "verbal aptitude" and the other for your "math aptitude" (the former is known as the SAT-V, and the latter as the SAT-M). There is also a third score, called the Test of Standard Written English (TSWE), which purports to measure your writing ability by asking you a number of multiple-choice questions. This TSWE score seems to have much less importance in the eyes of admissions personnel than the SAT-V and SAT-M. The SAT is sponsored by the College Board, and it is written and administered by ETS. The ACT reports four main scores: Social Studies Reading, Natural Sciences Reading, English Usage, and Math Usage. These scores seem to be more widely used by colleges for placement purposes after admission than are the SAT results. The college you apply to specifies whether you must take the SAT or the ACT (and some schools give students the option of which test to take). The rest of this chapter we will focus on the SAT since it is taken by more students yearly than the ACT. Many of the comments about the SAT will be applicable to the ACT since they are both standardized, multiple-choice, objective tests used in college admissions. Yet the ACT is not identical to the SAT in structure or use, so do not automatically assume all criticisms of the SAT also cover the ACT.

The SAT can trace its direct lineage all the way back to June 23, 1926 when the first SAT was first given to 8,040 students.[3] ETS officials estimated that in the half-century since the first SAT was given, over 25 million people have shared the experience of taking the SAT.[4] From its relatively humble start the SAT has expanded to the point where it is now taken by well over one million applicants every year.[5] And the SAT has held its spot as "king of the hill." A recent article in *Newsweek* stated: "ETS's Scholastic Aptitude Test—the famous College Boards—is the country's best-known admissions standard."[6] That hold on the public imagination has been carved out over an even longer time than the SATs have been around. At the turn of this century, the College Board started an essay examination that was used to compare college applicants. That essay exam was prestigious and continued even after the College Board had created the multiple-choice form of the SAT in 1926. The essay exam was finally phased-out by the multiple-choice SAT offshoot in 1942.[7]

With time the SAT became firmly entrenched, especially at colleges in the eastern part of the country. Its main competitor, the ACT, has yet to surpass the SAT in either numbers or overall recognition. Yet the past two decades have witnessed many controversies whirling around the SAT. Part of this can be attributed to the imperfect nature of the SAT itself. Like any test, the SAT has a standard deviation for individual scores (roughly 30 points on the 200 to 800 scale), which means a given score may not accurately pinpoint a student's real ability to take the SAT. In addition, like most tests, the SAT is susceptible to what is called a "testing effect." This means that someone who has taken the SAT once is likely to learn from that experience and—all things being equal—will probably score higher on a second encounter with the SAT. About one-third of SAT-takers are thought to take the SAT at least twice. Of the students who take the SAT again, most will gain about 20 points on average while the rest will drop a few points.[8] And there is the whole matter of coaching. We have already discussed the potential for significant score gains through taking a reputable coaching course and working hard on test preparation. Finally, many students take what is called the Preliminary Scholastic Aptitude Test (PSAT) about one year before they first take the SAT. In effect, the PSAT is a trial run for prospective SAT-takers, although it is also used to select certain scholarship recipients. The PSAT is scored on a scale of 20 to 80, and many students will improve from their PSAT score (multiplied by ten to adjust for the different scale) to the SAT.

You begin to see the scope of the problem in determining what any given SAT score means for any given applicant. If Joe has a SAT score of 640, it could mean that his true ability on the skills tested by the SAT is currently at the 640 level. But that score could also mean a number of other things. Which way would the standard deviation cut? Has Joe taken the SAT before, and gained from the testing effect? Has Joe taken, and benefited from, a coaching course for the SAT? Has he taken the PSAT and received a 64? If his PSAT, or a prior SAT, score differs markedly from the 64/640 level, which of the scores are we to trust? There are no simple answers to these questions, which means that we must allow a wide berth for SAT scores when using them for admissions decisions. How wide? That's also hard to say definitely. We might get an idea of the range that 640 score could represent by combining the factors. With a standard deviation for individual scores of 30 points, we know the odds favor, but do not guarantee, that Joe's real score is between 610 and 670. If we consider a testing effect of 20 points, then we have to broaden the range further. We don't know if Joe's score is 20 points higher than it would have been if he hadn't taken the SAT before. We also don't know if Joe's score is 20 points lower than he could have received by retaking it. So now our range goes from 590 to 690. Finally, Joe might have done, perhaps, 50 points better or worse on the SAT depending upon whether he took a coaching course. So now our apparently firm SAT score of 640 may really be only an indication that Joe's SAT abilities should earn him a score somewhere between a 540 and a 740. That possible swing of 200 points is quite a ballpark for an estimate of college ability.

To be sure, this 200 point swing almost certainly overstates the uncertainty inherent in any SAT score. Yet ETS admits to a range of about 60 points (that is, the SAT score plus or minus 30 points), which may be̅ enough to tip admissions decisions by itself. It is certainly enough to make all the difference in the world at any school which uses cut-off scores for admission. A college might set a minimum of, say, 900 on your combined SAT-V and SAT-M scores for admission. You could have a combined score of 860 and just be out of luck, even though that puts you within the range of statistical uncertainty (equal to 60 points here: you add the 30 points that your reported score might have missed on the SAT-V plus another 30 points for the SAT-M). It's bizarre that colleges would use cut-off scores based only on SAT scores. For one thing, if they're going to use cut-offs, high school grades would be a better device since high school GPA has been shown to predict college grades consistently better than SAT scores. And ETS and the College Board have made a point of discouraging the use of a cut-off system based on test scores because of the margin of error on a standardized test. Yet, as Bernard Feder wrote, "A lot of colleges use 'cutting scores' on the SAT and the ACT. That means that if you get below a certain score, many admissions officers won't even look at your high school grades."[9]

Why would any institution of higher learning engage in such an arbitrary practice? Well, a lot of the explanation can be traced to the sheer number of applicants to some colleges. The admissions offices may not be staffed adequately to permit careful inspection of all the applications that come in. So, to save money and time, an artificial minimum test score is set. This provides a handy mechanism for reducing the flock of applicants to a more manageable size. Yet efficiency does not justify a technique which is statistically unwarranted. As Vito Perrone (head of the NCT) explains, "I am aware that many schools have large numbers of applicants and because of limited admissions staff tend to desire simple quantification over descriptive portfolios. I understand this but don't accept it as responsible practice."[10] What's more, despite their official policy of discouraging the practice of cut-off scores, the College Board, at least, has made some very sympathetic noises about this technique. Compare these two statements. One: "The College Board discourages the use of score cut-offs or the use of scores in isolation from a variety of other considerations in evaluating candidates for admission."[11] Two: "Well, they are drawn by some schools. I don't happen to agree with cut-off scores, but if they're set low enough there's probably good reason for doing that. . . . This is a matter of allocating resources. Colleges do have a conscience, and there's no need to recruit and admit a student who at the cheapest college will still be spending a fair amount of money, if they're not going to succeed in the program."[12] These two statements don't entirely square with each other.

However, both statements were made in 1979 by the same man, Fred Hargadon, the chairman of the College Board. Statement one was made in testimony to the U.S. Congress, while statement two occurred in the course of a discussion on the MacNeil/Lehrer Report on television. Hargadon is also the dean of admissions at Stanford University. I do not suggest for an instant that Dean Hargadon was intentionally contradictory in his statements. To me, statement one was a restatement of official CEEB policy, and statement two an expression of Dean Hargadon's personal views which certainly come from a base of experience. But surely this is an instance of the Board sending out conflicting messages to schools and the public. Or, perhaps the message is that the Board wishes the use of cut-offs would cease, but in the meantime they will tacitly tolerate the practice. This impression is reinforced in a booklet put out by CEEB entitled, "College Guide to the [SAT] Summary Reports." One section of this College Board publication shows how a change at a hypothetical college of the "SAT-average minimum" would affect the need of students for financial aid.[13] It seems strange to be condemning a practice on one hand while demonstrating ways it can be manipulated on the other. It would not seem strange if the staff of a college employing cut-offs concluded that the College Board really isn't all that upset about it.

To return to Dean Hargadon's second statement, it seems to contain a mighty big assumption. The assumption is that someone who gets below the cut-off score is "not going to succeed in the program." That's a broad assertion which doesn't seem to be backed up by what we know about statistical variation of test scores and so forth. A student might be excluded from a college because his score was under the cut-off point, yet that score might have been inaccurate. If you use an absolute minimum score, you run the serious risk of unfairly penalizing applicants who come within a few points of that score. It's true that the odds for success at a given college may go down with lower SAT scores, but even here we have a continuum. You cannot say that an applicant with a total score of 884 can make it at our school but every single person with a total score of 883 or below is incapable of succeeding. The SAT is not that precise, cannot be that precise, and the use of absolute cut-offs only fosters the cruel hoax of scientific precision in differences as low as one point out of 1,600.

If you want to be fair to an applicant you must look beyond her SAT scores alone. Why is this? Because for one thing, we have been conservative in our use of the standard deviation figure until now. Recall that the standard deviation on the SAT-V, for instance, is about 30 points in each direction. With an SAT score of 500, there is a two-thirds probability that the "true" score is between 470 and 530. But there is also a one-third chance the true score is outside of this range, with a one-sixth chance it should be lower and a one-sixth chance it should be higher. This is not a possibility to be sneezed at. It means that of the 1,488,300 students who took the SAT in the 1977–78 school year,[14] 486,-100 students received SAT scores that were more than 30 points away from their true score.[15] There will be some statistical variation on these numbers from year to year, but even allowing for this, that's still an awful lot of SAT scores that have wandered far away from home. Of those 496,100 scores, half will be too high and half too low. So 248,050 students probably got a break of better than 30 points, while another 248,050 got a raw deal by getting scores more than 30 points too low. Even at schools that don't use formal cut-offs, coming in more than 30 points behind your closest competitor for admission could spell the end of the race. In fact, 2 percent score 60 points too low. This is a serious difference. If your true SAT score should be a 560, but you had a bad day and ended up with a reported SAT score of 500, your "SAT value" to an admissions committee is hurt dramatically. Instead of ranking up in the 72nd percentile of all SAT-takers (with a 560), you're down to just an average 50th percentile score (500). The impact of this change will vary depending on the college and the rest of your credentials, but it's safe to say it's not doing you any good.

Do colleges really care about these SAT scores? The answer is yes. There would be little point in requiring college applicants to spend millions of dollars each year, not to mention nervous energy and time, all for a meaningless exercise. To be fair, unless you are applying to a college that uses a cut-off score approach, or to one of the most selective colleges, your SAT score probably won't be enough to keep you out by itself. Yet these colleges still add up to a noticeable bloc. The College Board tries to downplay the importance of the SAT scores. A survey sponsored by the Board and released in late 1979 found that only 1.8 percent of colleges admitted to relying on test scores as the single most important factor in admissions decisions. That was the finding that CEEB played up. But that survey also found that 30 percent of colleges had minimum SAT requirements (i.e., cut-offs).[16] If you are one of the applicants summarily turned away from a college because your combined SAT score was below an established minimum, then your SAT score most certainly was the single most important factor in the decision. Indeed, your SAT score was the only factor in the decision. Moreover, the survey further reported that almost 60 percent of the more competitive colleges admitted SAT scores were "very important" to them in selecting students. An additional 33 percent said they used the SAT as "one of several factors."[17] No matter how you play with those figures, they don't exactly add up to a conclusion that the SATs are just inconsequential ventures.

Vito Perrone addressed this point in his testimony to Congress. He wrote: "Now most selective admissions institutions insist that they use both test scores *and* high school grades in whatever formula they use. . . . But what is clear is that a student scoring very high on the SAT is more apt to be selected than individuals with lower scores, high school grades notwithstanding. Wing and Wallach, using *only* the SAT scores, were able to predict actual admissions decisions for several selective institutions at a 76 percent level."[18] Perrone is referring to a famous bit of investigation by Cliff Wing and Michael Wallach of Duke University. One of the things they did was to examine the contention by some selective colleges that test scores really shouldn't cause any worry because they're just a part of the whole package considered by an admissions committee. By gathering data on both the accepted and rejected candidates at several colleges, Wing and Wallach discovered they could account for the decision made by the college solely by looking at a candidate's SAT scores a staggering 76 percent of the time. This was hardly a reassuring finding for people concerned about an overemphasis on SAT scores. Wing and Wallach published their findings in 1971 in a book entitled, *College Admissions and the Psychology of Talent.*[19]

If an academic study is not enough to convince you of the importance placed on the SAT at many of the colleges where applicants outnumber openings, consider the evidence of the marketplace. Go to the reference section of your bookstore or library, and dig out some of the guides to American colleges such as the Barron's series. Thumb through these books, and you will see sections that contain admissions information for prospective applicants. For most colleges you can be sure that the median SAT or ACT scores of the entering classes will be prominently displayed. Average high school grades for entering classes will be emphasized only rarely. There may be admissions grids showing your odds of admission to a particular institution given certain SAT scores (or ACT scores or sometimes high school GPA). There's a pretty unmistakable message in all this for the college prospect. There is always the possibility that these commercial publications err in singling out SAT scores for special attention, and there is usually some fine print at the front of the guide telling applicants the test scores are just one of many factors. But few candidates who have been exposed to these materials can maintain a blissful indifference to their results on the SAT. News reports about how high school grade inflation has deepened college dependence on the SATs only reinforce this impression of importance.[20]

Why is the SAT assumed to have such significance when all it does is attempt to predict first-year college grades? When the success of the SAT on this rather limited task is unimpressive (their value for SAT scores and college grades usually fluctuates around the .5 level)?[21] When the fact is that the SAT scores by themselves usually predict college grades less well than high school GPA does?[22] When the SAT has been shown to be susceptible to certain kinds of coaching? When the SAT correlates so highly with parental income, as we saw in Chapter 2? When both ETS and the College Board at least formally warn against overreliance on the SAT? With all these limitations, how can admissions offices continue to cling to SAT scores as somehow immutable signposts in an era of changing directions? I don't know. There do seem to be some indications that the SAT is not as omnipotent as it once was. But it's not clear whether this can be attributed to a more balanced view of the SAT in the admissions offices of the country, or is just the result of a slackening in demand for college admission at some institutions as the baby boom recedes.

Yet even as demand lessens at some colleges, it remains strong at the most influential colleges. And these are the very institutions most likely to factor the SAT into their admissions process in a significant fashion. Even if the debate over the SATs is only a fight over who is admitted to the more elite colleges, there are still important consequences attached to the way we make those decisions. If positions of leadership, or even just job opportunities, flow first to graduates of the elite colleges —and one can make a strong argument that this is indeed the case—then who is selected matters to society, not just to the applicants. Perrone testified that "as college attendance has become more commonplace, especially in a sputtering economy that no longer absorbs graduates in the manner that was true in the 50s, 60s and early 70s, the *particular* college one attends is enlarging in consequence."[23] Our colleges are turning out more holders of bachelor's degrees than there are openings in the workforce for college graduates. As a result, many college graduates are forced to take jobs that formerly didn't require a college degree, and the holders of those jobs—people with a high school education or less —are being squeezed out. Talk to some friends who have graduated from college in the past five years with a nonspecialized liberal arts degree (i.e., not an engineer or economist) about their experiences in looking for a job. Ask them if they think it makes a difference which college they graduated from, not in regard to whether they are as qualified, but in terms of getting an interview in the first place, let alone a job.

Perrone saw this effect as being similar to the kinds of tracking systems used in elementary and secondary schools. He told Congress, "In the boom period we established willy-nilly a higher education tracking system. Our upper track institutions tend to be better supported than lower track institutions—they tend also to have a much lower percentage of minorities and the poor within their student populations. They are more selective, tending to give greater weight or the illusion of greater weight to the SAT or ACT in the admissions process. Increasingly, employment opportunities for graduates of the upper track institutions have expanded in relation to graduates from lower track institutions, and graduate and professional schools—which open up yet additional opportunities—are more accessible."[24] When decisions about which college track you will be placed on are based on SAT scores, the potential for error cannot be overlooked; and as we have seen, error here can be compounded over the years. Althea Simmons of the NAACP told Congress, "As a former college teacher, I know of a number of instances where students were turned down by one school because of scores on standardized tests and were admitted to another institution and performed creditably."[25]

Peter Wells, the dean of students at Hopkins Grammar Day Prospect Hill School in New Haven, comes at the bitter aftertaste of SAT misuse from another angle. He wrote: "The most damaging effect of the SATs stems from the belief that they really mean something about a person, that the 20 to 80 scale constitutes a definitive statement about intelligence and worth. Not so long ago I tried to comfort a girl clutching her College Board explanatory folder. 'I'm not that stupid, am I?' she asked, pointing tearfully at the 38–42 on the cover. In fact she had always performed near the top of her class, far better than such scores might indicate possible, yet while reassuring her that she was much brighter and we all valued her, I could not help thinking that it would be very hard indeed to convince most colleges that she was, in fact, brighter than the scores would indicate."[26] Given a chance, this student could outperform students with vastly superior SAT scores. We know the SATs are imprecise.

We don't know how many students are held back by low SAT scores because an admissions committee placed too much credence in the SATs over other factors in selection.

Defenders of the SAT often resort to the argument that the SAT is really needed because it provides colleges with one fair national standard of an applicant's abilities. After all, one high school is different from the next, and grading practices could be inconsistent. Maybe a bright student has to work harder at High High School to get a 3.4 GPA than he would to get a 4.0 at Low High School in a neighboring county. We can't expect every college to compile its own ranking of the quality of every high school in the country, but it doesn't follow that the SAT is necessarily the national standard its proponents would have you believe. The fact is that an SAT score of 470 may mean very different things about academic ability depending on who got that score. So much for the national yardstick; if colleges have to discount SAT scores by the background of the test-taker, the value of the SAT in reducing uncertainty takes a nosedive. The *New York Times* printed an editorial in early 1980 which criticized a passage from the Nader report on ETS with these words: "The report also fails to acknowledge that many educators already understand the limitations of these academic tests. For example, at some colleges, the S.A.T. is optional. At Brown University and many other selective institutions, the S.A.T. score is weighed against the applicant's background and schooling. If a student from a well-to-do family and a top prep school gets a good score of 600 on the verbal test, that, says James Rogers, Brown's director of admissions, 'is just not as impressive as a 550 from a small-town student in the Far West.' "[27]

Now, I don't know about you, but I don't find this practice of retroactively adjusting the SAT scores as comforting as the *Times* meant to indicate. If it is necessary for an admissions committee to sit down with a pocket calculator and see what a 600 or 550 really means by adding or subtracting a host of regional, economic, sexual, social, racial, ethnic, educational, and parental factors, one might say that the supposed national yardstick is more like a national yo-yo. To be fair in interpreting your SAT score, an admissions committee has to take a long look at who you are, and this can lead to the spectacle of your score being adjusted up and down and up and down because of variables beyond the capacity of the SAT to measure. If the practice the *Times* refers to is widespread, then we have a situation where scores on a supposedly scientific and objective standardized test, given in order to compensate for differences in background and high schools attended, are changed to reflect differences in the backgrounds of the test-takers. In order to perform this chore fairly, the admissions staff has to look at the application and pick out those factors which might affect the SAT score and make him or her unique. One might ask if all this tuning is not an indication that the SAT is not doing the job for which it was created—making life easier for the admissions people. One might further inquire how the admissions people decide whose SAT scores to adjust and by how much. Finally, one might ask is this not a reversion to the kinds of subjective judgments the SAT was supposed to reduce. I'm not criticizing admissions personnel for this practice—given what we know about the SAT it is desirable, if not mandatory. But the practice does undercut the yardstick argument, and leaves open the prospect that SAT adjustments will vary from college to college.

Adjusted or not, SAT scores leave a lot to be desired as an indication of how well an applicant will perform once admitted to a college. First of all, there are some technical difficulties with the indiscriminate use of SAT results. According to Chuck Stone, former director of minority affairs at ETS, the SAT is what is known as a discrepant predictor. This means that the value of the predictions about college performance varies (that is, there are discrepancies) according to the SAT score itself. On the SAT, Stone testified that the predictions are better for students with high scores than for students with low scores. Stone illustrated this point by saying that while the SAT-V validity coefficient is .48 for students scoring in the 90th percentile, that coefficient plummets to .17 for students in the 10th percentile.[28] Thus, the SAT has a different trustworthiness for students with different scores. Despite this fact, and the fact that high school grades by themselves are better predictors that SATs by themselves, Stone charged that, "hundreds of thousands of students are wiped out annually by the 'SAT Saturday Massacre.' "[29]

We've touched on the connection between SAT scores and

parental income. Twenty years ago Martin Mayer wrote: "The Scholastic Aptitude Test of the College Board tests reading and social-class background, and very little else."[30] Some defenders of the SAT claim that the SAT only mirrors the unequal educational opportunities available to the poor. But some evidence indicates that the SAT may act at times more as a magnifying glass than a mere mirror. David White testified at New York hearings on the Truth-in-Testing bill about a study of SAT scores submitted by applicants to the University of California at Berkeley.[31] Berkeley required applicants to take the SAT, but only used those scores in decisions regarding a minority of students. This study showed that for the entering class of 1973, the average high school GPA for black students was 3.47, almost identical to the 3.5 average for white students. But if you compared SAT combined scores, blacks fell some 200 points behind whites on average. Was this a mirror or a magnifier? If it was just a mirror, you'd think the SAT score difference would be roughly proportional to the high school GPA difference. But at least in this study, the SAT difference was proportionally far greater. In addition, the black students admitted at Berkeley turned out to be more likely to graduate within four years of matriculation than were the white students. There were some differences by sex as well. Women admitted to Berkeley brought a 3.58 high school GPA (greater than the average male GPA) and were more likely to graduate within four years than their male counterparts. But the males had SAT averages over 90 points higher than the females.[32] None of this is conclusive proof of anything, but it should serve to put admissions staffs on guard when using the SAT for decisions.

Of course, even if scores were perfectly in sync for all subgroups, there would still remain the question of just what is meant by the term "scholastic aptitude" anyway. Banesh Hoffmann finds the concept somewhat dubious. He wrote: "Why should there be a standard of 'scholastic aptitude' when, for all we know, there is no such specific thing as 'scholastic aptitude' in the first place? Is it not a numerical invention? If by 'scholastic aptitude' we mean some combination of relatively superficial, numerically measurable, verbal and arithmetical traits that are correlated with professorial grades with all their crotchets, idiosyncracies, and exceptions, are we not talking of a smoothed-out, carefully sandpapered, statistical monstrosity?"[33] To the extent that the SAT samples depth of vocabulary and skill at algebra, it is not getting at ability so much as preparation. The mere fact that you currently do not know what the word "aardvark" means, or how to solve simultaneous equations, does not mean you are incapable of learning these things if it should be deemed necessary as part of your college program. David McClelland compared the knowledge of the "words and word-game skills" used on the SAT with knowledge of Latin in the Middle Ages. He wrote: "Only those young men who could read and write Latin could get into [the learned professions] and if tests had been given in Latin, I am sure they would have shown that professionals scored higher in Latin than men in general, that sons who grew up in families where Latin was used would have an advantage in those tests compared to those in poor families where Latin was unknown, and that these men were more likely to get into the professions. But would we conclude we were dealing with a general ability factor?"[34] Not if we knew what we were talking about, we wouldn't.

Professor Woody Kelly of Cornell University testified that the use of SAT scores may be self-justifying in the sense that advantages conferred by virtue of the SAT may have a multiplier effect. Kelly asked, "What does the test do other than what we know it does because of the decisions we make based upon that test? Of course, if I admit a student to Cornell because of a better test score, a student at Cornell is likely to get into a good law school, medical school and so forth, so to some extent, the use of the test becomes itself a circular prophecy in terms of adequacy and in terms of performance in later life, but aside from that I can tell . . . nothing."[35] A number of studies by independent researchers have failed to uncover stable relationships between college grades and postgraduation achievement in the outside world.[36] This would indicate that the pursuit of predictive power on college grades bears little or no meaning for those concerned with aiding colleges to select those students most likely to make a future contribution to society. If SAT scores represent only a mediocre success at this very narrow task of predicting grades in college, and if those grades themselves are relatively insignificant in predicting anything else, then just how valuable can SAT results be to us?

David McClelland has written about a quick experiment he performed. In the early 1960s he looked at what eight of his best students from the late 1940s were doing, and compared that with what eight of his poorer students were up to. His conclusion? "The only difference I noted was that those with better grades got into better law or medical schools, but even with this supposed advantage they did not have notably more successful careers as compared with the poorer students who had to be satisfied with 'second-rate' law and medical schools at the outset. Doubtless the C-students could not get into even second-rate law and medical schools under the stricter admissions testing standards of today. Is that an advantage for society?"[37] Now, this study doesn't prove grades are irrelevant—it's a small, nonrandom group with an impressionistic evaluation. But the fundamental point remains. Simply stated, even if the SAT were 100 percent accurate in predicting grades, with nary a bias or scoring error in sight, we would still have to think twice about using test scores as a court of no appeal. If the response variable (college grades in the freshman year) has little significance outside of the college atmosphere, we would want to exercise great caution in enthroning a predictor variable (the SAT) atop the admissions process. As it is, the flaws revealed in the SAT to date make it far less than a 100 percent accurate predictor.

We turn now to those survivors of the SATs, those students who have completed their college years and now want to enter graduate or professional schools for further study. College students who want to go on to additional training find a very important obstacle blocking their path at the start of their desired journey.

CHAPTER EIGHT

Narrowing Graduate Opportunities

America's graduate and professional schools stand at the apex of the educational pyramid. One would hope that this level at least would be free of the test-related defects which impair admissions judgments lower down. This, after all, is where students are transformed into the doctors, the lawyers, the Ph.D.'s who play such a vital role in our society. Decisions made here have a profound impact on the lives of the applicants individually, and upon the nation collectively. If the "wrong" applicants are admitted, not only are the rejected candidates being treated unfairly, but the country as a whole suffers from the misuse of resources. Unfortunately, the flaws which mar the SATs and companion tests are at least as visible in these upper levels and are possibly even more constricting as they narrow graduate opportunities.

Applicants to most graduate and professional schools must take a standardized test geared to that particular area before being considered for admission. Similar in nature to the SATs, these tests are supposed to reveal an individual's true "aptitude" for study in the law, medicine, business, and so forth. The test scores are then supposed to be considered together with a person's college grades, interviews with admissions personnel, recommendations from personal and academic sources, and written responses to questions on the admissions application to form a rich mosaic revealing the total individual. That's the theory.

The practice, however, is different. Test results often predominate to such an extent that many admissions committees view complex individuals as one-dimensional creatures defined by their scores. While the exact weight of the test results varies from school to school, there is a greater general overreliance on the tests at law, medical, and business schools. This overreliance can, in effect, deprive society of the services of individuals who do poorly on standardized tests but who have the potential to do splendidly in the real world. Some of the applicants with poor scores will simply not be admitted. Others will get in, but only to institutions with less prestige. These people will find that with the incredible competition for professional jobs, especially in law and business, employers will come to them last if at all. Many would-be lawyers and business executives, all graduates of professional schools, are driving cabs or working as sales-clerks because their fields didn't have room for them.

Law boards illustrate the point. The Law School Admission Test (LSAT) is required for admission at every accredited law school in the United States, with only the smallest of loopholes showing. The American Bar Association states in Standard 503 of the Standards for Approval of Law Schools that any law school not using the LSAT must "establish that it is using an acceptable test."[1] The LSAT is administered by our old acquaintance, ETS, this time under the ostensible direction of the Law School Admission Council (LSAC). The Council, composed of one representative from each American law school, actually owns the LSAT although it delegates the work involved in its distribution and scoring.

The number of candidates taking the LSAT has exploded in the past fifteen years. In 1962, the LSAT was given 30,528 times as candidates fought for the approximately 20,000 spaces available for beginning law students. By 1977, the LSAT was given 128,135 times.[2] But while the number of test-takers had quadrupled, the number of available spaces at law schools had only doubled (to roughly 40,000 slots), increasing the intensity of the competition for admittance.[3] Even when you discount for repeaters in the total number of LSATs given, there are still at least two candidates for every seat in an American law school today. The ratio balloons astronomically at the most prestigious schools. Yale Law School, for example, had 3,389 applicants for 165 places in 1977, or better than twenty persons battling for each seat.[4] It has been estimated that some 200,000 students will vie after the approximately 48,000 first-year law school seats in the early 1980s.[5]

Students applying to law schools are aware of the bright side of the profession. The law can be exciting and challenging for a practitioner, and the financial rewards are considerable. The cream of each year's legal crop is often enticed by the starting salaries paid by Wall Street law firms—up to $37,000 a year to start in 1980.[6] But the legal job market is two-tiered. Graduates of the top law schools are in demand and can count on a number of high-paying job offers. Yet those at the bottom of their classes, or at the top of unknown law schools, face bleak prospects for any legal work at all.

To make matters even more difficult, the increase in applications to law schools has brought a marked improvement in the credentials of law school applicants. Some very bright and accomplished people are either not getting in or are being relegated to the bottom of the law school glamor hierarchy. For example, in 1961 only 8 of the then 134 American law schools had entering classes with a median LSAT score of 600 or better. By 1974, over 100 law schools (two-thirds of the total) could make such a claim.[7] Or, looking only at the LSAT scores and college grades of applicants to the University of Chicago Law School, less than 10 percent of the 1962 entering class would have been admitted to the 1974 entering class.[8] Bear in mind also that the 1974 entering class at Boston University Law School had a higher LSAT average than the 1967 entering class at Harvard Law School.[9] All but a few states require a law degree before allowing an individual to practice law.[10] So, with the staggering increase in law school admissions competition, many otherwise qualified future lawyers have been kept out of the profession of their choice by rejection letters from admissions committees.

Given the importance of the decisions of the law school admissions committees, one would expect the utmost care in dividing the admits from the rejects. Unfortunately, one would be wrong. The LSAT is relied on far too heavily, to the neglect of other important individual characteristics. Peter Liacouras, the dean of Temple University Law School, has said, "The admission process to law school has become a national disaster area."[11] Much of this disaster is attributable to the LSATs. ETS claims that the LSAT scores are "reliable indications of certain mental abilities related to academic performance in law school."[12] But that claim has come under increasingly severe attack, including persistent intimations of cultural bias in the LSATs. Liacouras delivers the indictment: "Too many gifted applicants with great potential for lawyering and community leadership are being rejected from law schools because, for some unfathomable reasons, they did not do well on this single, multiple-choice, four-hour test. Too many law schools for too long have surrendered admissions criteria to psychologists at the Educational Testing Service; they seem to have forgotten that law school admission is the critical first step in admission to the legal profession."[13]

How have law schools abdicated their responsibilities to ETS? For one thing, many law schools have done away with the personal interview. As Harvard explains in its prelaw handbook: "It is a rare school that even encourages applicants to have informational interviews."[14] The absence of supplementary information about a person that could be provided through interviews is serious because the LSAT is so limited in what it measures. As Dean Liacouras noted, "No one would claim that the LSAT measures motivation, judgment, practicality, idealism, tenacity, character and maturity, integrity, patience, preparation, oral skills, perseverance, client-handling, organizational ability and leadership—in sum, the lawyering process."[15] Even if the LSATs are accurate in predicting which candidates will receive the highest grades in the first year of law school, which is all they claim to do, we have reason to fear that these candidates are not necessarily those who will do best in the actual practice of law.

Applicants to law schools know full well that their fate will be determined largely by their performance during the hours they spend taking the LSAT. Law schools convey this message in unmistakable terms. Admissions grids are published annually showing the number of people applying with certain LSAT scores, along with the number admitted from each category. Law schools are quick to speak of the average LSAT score of their students, with a higher average assumed to be associated with a better law school. Experts explain that the LSAT score, taken in tandem with the grade point average, are the two most important factors. Joel Seligman, a professor at Northeastern University School of Law, has written that some law schools make admissions decisions solely on the basis of grades and LSAT scores, while "many other law schools . . . overemphasize these factors."[16] Henry Coleman, the dean of students at Columbia University, has been quoted as saying, "It's reached the point where students have to have a certain score on the entrance exam just to get their applications opened at some law schools."[17]

Students feel this pressure to ace the LSAT. They are afraid that their hopes may be dashed by a bad Saturday of testing, and this very determination to do well can lead to freezing up. Yale Law School Dean of Admissions James Thomas realizes how powerfully the pressure can affect students. "One need only observe an administration of the LSAT at a center to grasp the extent to which anxieties coalesce and surface on the day of the test. Clothing is mismatched and faces are drawn and worn. Many students appear stunned and dazed, as if they had been on all-night binges. Elementary instructions are botched and a steady stream of nervous people visit the rest-room facilities to seek relief for some of the symptoms of their anxiety."[18] The strain can lead to distorted results on the test. The *Occupational Outlook Quarterly* charged, "It is perhaps only a slight exaggeration to say that we may be measuring endurance or metabolism or blood sugar levels as much as we are testing abstract thinking ability and writing skills."[19] Is this really a sensible way to select our future lawyers?

Sensible or not, the LSAT remains very popular with law school admissions personnel. The reason for the popularity, according to Dean Liacouras, is that "administered and evaluated by ETS, the LSAT spares law schools the burden of carefully reviewing the total profile of the applicants."[20] A. M. Minehart, editor of the *National Pre-Law Newsletter,* agrees. He writes that "admissions officers of law and other schools . . . overemphasize the importance of test scores and neglect other criteria for considering a student's aptitude and potential. Understaffed graduate-school admissions offices are largely responsible."[21] Minehart's point is well taken. At the Georgetown University Law Center, for instance, some 7,000 annual applications in the mid-1970s were being processed by all of two full-time admissions officers.[22] That's a staggering burden for any admissions officer to have to carry.

Steven Brill, a former law columnist for *Esquire* magazine, wrote that "overemphasizing the Law Boards has proved to be a popular alternative to increasing the size of admissions staffs and emphasizing other admissions criteria."[23] Grades are waning in importance alongside the LSAT due to "grade inflation." One reason for this, according to the *Occupational Outlook Quarterly,* "is a loss of confidence in undergraduate grading systems and the difficulty of evaluating applicants who have taken a substantial number of courses on a 'pass-fail' basis. Law schools also point to the steady improvement of undergraduate grades as evidence of an erosion of standards."[24] Whatever the rationale, the relative importance of LSAT scores and grades can be discerned in the admissions patterns at New York University Law School. At NYU in 1974, 52 of 141 applicants were admitted who had grade points of 3.5 to 3.74 (on a scale of 0 to 4, with a 4 equal to an A) and LSATs of 599 to 649. But applicants with just a slightly better LSAT—between 650 and 700—with the same grade point average, were admitted at the rate of 120 out of 136. Even more surprising, an applicant with a grade point average of 2.75 to 3 and a LSAT of 750 had a three times better chance of admission than a candidate with grades of 3.75 to 4 and a LSAT of 550 to 599.[25]

This sort of reliance on the LSAT is worrisome. A major problem with the LSAT is that the signals it sends are consistently misinterpreted by admissions personnel. Warnings are published that LSAT scores "should be regarded as useful but approximate measures of a candidate's abilities as measured by the test, not as an exact determination of his standing."[26] Despite the warnings, LSAT scores are given a precision in analysis that is totally unwarranted. Some law schools, such as the University of Tennessee, are said to have automatically rejected applicants who scored below an arbitrary LSAT cut-off point.[27] Yet cut-off points overlook the explicit statistical teaching that there is a normal range of error in the results of a test like the LSAT. This is the standard deviation concept which we discussed in Chapter 5.

Former Harvard Law School Dean Erwin Griswold has been quoted as saying that "it is not known whether the Law School Admission Test has any real statistical ability to select accurately from among many applicants, all of whom have the minimum qualifications."[28] After all, when the LSAT was first developed in the 1940s, it was used solely to exclude those who scored very poorly and thus appeared highly likely to fail in law school. Now, however, the test has been perverted to serve as a screening device for the best applicants, almost all of whom could successfully complete their studies at any law school that accepts them. At Harvard Law School, for example, despite the skill and sophistication of the admissions staff, statistically insignificant gaps in LSAT scores may make all the difference between acceptance and rejection. Director of Admissions Patricia Lydon was quoted as conceding that a 60 point margin on the LSAT between two applicants can determine the outcome.[29] An assistant dean of admissions at Harvard went even further. He stated that while "a 10 or 20 point difference doesn't make much difference, anything more than that probably does."[30]

ETS tells you that spreads of 60 points or so are inconclusive, but admissions people may make decisions based on 20 points or so. If Harvard Law School with its professional admissions staff has commented on LSAT scores this way, then perhaps only a few law schools fully heed the ETS advice regarding the proper interpretation of test results. The scandalous thing about this is that not only do LSAT scores dominate all other factors in some admissions decisions, but LSAT scores are being misused in the bargain. Scores which in fact are so close as to be meaningless are being used to "objectively" sort out the winners from the losers in the admissions lottery.

Ironically, despite the enshrinement of the LSAT in law school admissions offices, the test does not have any clear relation to a candidate's probability of becoming a successful lawyer. Dr. Harold Hodgkinson, a former director of the National Institute of Education, has said that no correlation exists between performance on the LSAT and performance as a lawyer.[31] When you think about it, this makes sense. The LSAT does not look for intangibles like determination, common sense, and judg- ment, although these qualities have a great deal to do with the transition from student to being a lawyer. All the LSAT purports to predict is what grades a candidate will get in his or her first year at law school. But law school grades themselves—even for all three years of law school and not just the first one—are highly artificial approximations of a student's mastery of a subject. Law- yers who had received grades like B— in criminal law may be in practice the most brilliant counsel you could ever ask for. So a mere correlation between LSAT scores and law school grades, especially when it is as weak as at present, cannot justify putting so many admissions eggs in the LSAT basket. Edward Bronson, a professor at California State University at Chico, charged that, "ETS claims only that the LSAT score correlates to first-year law school grades. But that modest claim allows the LSAT to be used by the law school as a bar to thousands of students who could do well in law school and become competent attorneys."[32]

Officials have defended the LSAT with arguments that seem to have more surface shine than inner strength. For example, the head of the LSAC, Bruce Zimmer, told New York legislators that the reason LSAT scores aren't linked to competence as a lawyer boils down to cost and complexity: "The cost of an ef- fective study of occupational performance of lawyers may well cost millions of dollars. Even a working definition of lawyer competency is elusive. How shall we compare an effective street lawyer, a legal services lawyer, scholar, corporate bond lawyer, or legislative research aide?"[33] Exactly; the variety of legal tasks defies simplistic characterization. But so do the applicants to our nation's law schools with their unique attributes, personalities, skills, and weaknesses. The LSAT does not draw back at the complexity of comparing these individuals. It could be argued that law school grades are an available yardstick for the LSAT. Yes, but so is annual income for those practicing lawyers, and I don't hear anyone clamoring to use that yardstick to determine who is, and is not, an adequate lawyer. I for one would not ac- cept income as such a benchmark, but it's not obvious that in- come is intrinsically less related to competence than are first-year grades. There's another twist here. LSAT scores are already cor- related somewhat to income—the income of the parents of applicants. We've already seen how closely SAT scores follow parental income. Some correlation of scores to parental income continues even though you don't take the LSAT until you are well on your way through college.

Professor Jerry Schechter, of the State University of New York at Stony Brook, compared some LSAT rhetoric with reported studies. The information booklet for the LSAT, according to Schechter, stated: "While the correlations between test scores and grades are not perfect, these studies show that LSAT scores help to predict which students will do well in law school. Moreover, a combination of a students' scores and undergraduate average gives a better prediction that either alone."[34] This sounds rather impressive. But it turns out that when they say the correlations "are imperfect," they're not using false modesty. Schechter wrote that, "In one ETS study on this, Schrader and Pitcher (1964) found the average LSAT score to correlate .35 with grades. The ranges however went from .07 to .49, not as rosy a picture as ETS presents to law school applicants."[35] A correlation with law school grades of less than .5 is minimal (remember, our old height-weight relationship hovered around .5). What's more, college grades by themselves have a better correlation with law school grades than do LSAT scores by themselves.[36] While the gain from adding LSAT scores on top of grades may indeed "help to predict which students will do well in law school," that incremental help is rather feeble. If the money spent on the LSAT were spent instead on hiring more admissions personnel at the law schools so that more time could be spent looking at applications, the marginal improvement in the admissions process might dwarf the lost data from the LSAT in significance.

Zimmer also defended the LSAT on the ground that, "We have a good test—a fair test that over the last thirty years has contributed to a more reliable, open and democratic law school admissions system than existed before the test was developed."[37] But this is confusing correlation with causation. It is true that law school admissions are more "open" to various minority and ethnic groups than they were thirty years ago, but it is doubtful that the LSAT can claim much of the credit for that accomplishment. The past thirty years have seen a revolution in national attitudes toward discrimination as well as landmark court rulings

and federal laws. What's more, members of the same minority
and ethnic groups supposedly helped by the LSAT are among its
most bitter critics. This is not an instance of sheer perversity.
Rather, there are reasons to worry that the LSAT may be acting
more as a barrier to, than a champion of, nondiscriminatory admissions at law schools. David White, a lawyer and writer in
Berkeley, California, has done some work on this subject, examining the effect of various factors in admissions to law school.
He has testified that, "For law schools . . . you discover that
the LSAT has a greater discriminatory impact against black students at the five schools studied than either undergraduate grades
or law school grades."[38] White claims that you have a better
chance of guessing an individual's race by finding out his LSAT
score than you do if only the individual's undergraduate grade
point average or grades earned in law school are supplied.[39]

Dean Liacouras points out the specter which continues to
loom over the LSATs. According to Liacouras, "To this day
there has not been a single reported validation study of the LSAT
in relation to lawyering performance—that is, which students
will become the best lawyers."[40] ETS as much as admits the inherent flaw in the LSAT regarding their inability to measure all
the qualities essential to becoming a good lawyer. The LSAC
has directed ETS to conduct a study of legal competence and the
LSATs.[41] But surely this is asking the architect to evaluate the
building. ETS has undertaken to play the role of critic for its
own product, under heavy pressure. In the legal realm, where ap-
pearances count for so much, this has the appearance of a potential conflict of interest. In any event, the acknowledgment of the
twin LSAT problems (overreliance by admissions staffs and lack
of demonstrated job-relatedness) is a short first step that is long
overdue.

The crush for admission to medical schools is even more intense than the competition for law school slots. In 1976, for example, "some 41,648 individuals the country over filed over
360,000 applications for the 15,613 places open in American
medical schools."[42] That's almost three applicants for every medical school seat. The ratio skyrockets at the most desirable schools.
Harvard Medical School, for instance, turns down roughly twenty

people for every one applicant accepted to an entering class of 165.[43] Overall, only 35 percent of all male applicants to medical schools, and 38 percent of the female applicants, were accepted in 1976.[44] There's a catch, too. Most medical schools are state-financed and gear their admissions policies to favor in-state residents. For the 1975–76 school year, 76 percent of all medical school students were from in-state, and 93 percent of those attending state-owned medical schools were residents. To put those figures in context, only seventeen medical schools in the entire country gave better than 2 percent odds of admission to out-of-state candidates.[45] The chief admissions officer at the University of Michigan Medical School was quoted as saying, "We no longer run an admissions committee, but a rejection committee. We're not looking so much for the good things anymore, but for flaws, a chance to reject."[46]

Alfred Gellhorn, former director of the Center for Biomedical Education, estimated that only one in nine students who start out college intending to be premed actually make it as far as admission to a medical school.[47] He stated that for every medical school applicant at least two others have been driven away by the frenzied mass of premeds. Then only one of three applicants gets into any medical school at all in this country. Unlike a counterpart in law school, a medical school student knows that job opportunities will be bountiful upon graduation. This is partly because of the restricted number of medical school places. The Bureau of Labor Statistics estimated that the U.S. needs about 22,000 new doctors a year, but our medical schools only graduate 15,000 a year.[48] The excess of demand over supply makes it very profitable to be a doctor today. Federal officials have estimated that doctors enjoy an average income of $75,000, with an average of over $100,000 a year for some specialists.[49]

Whatever the reasons, admission to medical school is coveted by increasing numbers of the best college grads. The result? Dr. Carlos Pestana, Associated Dean for Student Affairs at the University of Texas Health Science Center at San Antonio, wrote that these pressures have produced a tremendously competitive situation where literally thousands of completely qualified candidates get rejected every year even though they would have been admitted without question as outstanding had they applied some ten years earlier.[50] To help wade through this tide of applications, medical schools have turned to the Medical College Admissions Test (MCAT).

The MCAT is administered by the American College Testing program (ACT), another previous acquaintance of ours, while a separate outfit has been in charge of writing the MCAT. The American Association of Medical Colleges (AAMC) owns the MCAT, which is an all-day test that runs from 8 A.M. to 5 or 6 P.M. and is required by almost all medical schools. The MCAT is supposed to be "an objective measure of specified science knowledge and its application."[51] A student taking the MCAT gets six scores on a scale of 1 to 15, covering biology, chemistry, physics, science problems, reading analysis, and quantitative analysis. These MCAT scores are then taken into account in the admissions process in a somewhat similar way to the use of LSAT scores for legal aspirants.

Just how important are MCAT scores to a premed student? Dr. Sanford J. Brown has written to premeds that, "Besides your GPA (grade point average) there is, probably, no single more important criterion for admission to medical school today than your performance on the MCAT. . . . It is a fact that your performance on this . . . exam will help or hurt you as much as that GPA you sweated for during your entire college career.'"[52] There is some evidence that the MCAT is on the way to even greater importance. The premed grade averages of admitted first-year medical students have risen phenomenally. For the medical school class entering in 1976, 46 percent of the students had A averages (a GPA of 3.6 to 4), compared to 29 percent just five years earlier.[53] The percentage of B students and below fell during that period. An official at the University of Pennsylvania Medical School delivered the scary message that "having straight A's doesn't really distinguish you any more.'"[54] What this means is that very high GPAs are virtually required of—and presented by almost all—medical school applicants. The MCAT with its fluctuations then becomes a decisive factor for many candidates, since there is little else differentiating the hordes of applicants with fine grades.

Dr. Pestana has done some calculations with the MCATs. According to his figures, a medical school reapplicant (i.e., one who was rejected the first time he applied) with a GPA of 3.3 to 3.9 has a steeply rising chance of success according to the MCAT score he is able to present. A MCAT average of 4 to 5 would yield about a 20 percent chance of success, but a 7 or 8 would double the odds to 40 percent. Should the candidate possess a 10 to 11 on the MCAT, the odds go up to 60 percent, with a peak 70 to 80 percent chance of admission for anyone with an MCAT in the 13 to 14 range.[55] The MCAT, clearly, is accorded considerable respect by medical school admissions people.

Martha P. Leape, coordinator of the Health Careers Advisory Program at Harvard, has written of the concerns expressed "over the use of college grades and MCAT scores as the primary selection factors."[56] Dr. Pestana has written that statistically grades and MCAT results seem to be the most important considerations in admissions although he states that other factors play a large role as well.[57] Regardless of its exact weight in decisions, with this heavy emphasis on MCAT scores in the minds of medical school admissions people, criticism of the failings of the MCAT have become more important. The American Association of Medical Colleges (AAMC), the owner of the MCAT, is aware of its shortcomings: "The new MCAT cannot and does not measure motivation, the nature or sincerity of interest in the study of medicine, or the personal characteristics that have basic importance in the practitioner or teacher of medicine."[58] That is a crucial point about the MCAT. A study conducted by Dr. John Rhoads and others at the Duke University School of Medicine concluded that, given certain minimum standards of intelligence, "motivation determines medical school performance."[59] Once you get past a certain basic level, higher MCAT scores don't make a difference. That's because the MCAT admittedly does not register anything about an applicant's motivation.

The MCAT essentially concentrates on scientific questions. But at a certain point, a physician needs human qualities more than an appreciation of abstract and highly esoteric concepts of physics. As an undergraduate dean complained, "Instead of narrowing to science scores their notions of what makes a good doctor, the American Association of Medical Colleges should expand them to what makes a good person."[60] In his book, *Campus Shock,* Lansing Lamont writes that of thirty-eight premeds he interviewed, only one was motivated primarily by the ideal of service.[61] The dean of Yale Medical School was quoted as saying that, "The desire to do good for humanity is not a very high motivating factor."[62] We might not expect every intern to have visions of Dr. Schweitzer at all times, but a desire to do good for humanity might not be a bad thing to have in conjunction with the other incentives to become a doctor.

Dr. Howard Hiatt, dean of the Harvard School of Public Health, has expressed the opinion that medical school admissions are skewed and has called for a committee to investigate. Dr. Hiatt said, "It is time for a reevaluation of premedical and medical education. . . . Such a group might help develop guidelines for new admissions policies for medical schools."[63] Committee or no committee, overreliance on any standardized test for admission to medical school is an ill to be avoided. For one thing, MCAT scores have a standard range of error analogous to that encountered with the LSATs. Unless preventive measures are taken, medical school admissions committees can find it all too easy to misapply MCAT scores.

We have already seen that LSAT scores do not predict ultimate success as a lawyer. In the medical field there is mounting certainty that MCAT scores do not predict ultimate success as a physician. Drs. H. Jack Geiger and Victor Sidel, professors of community medicine in New York medical schools, have written: "There is no evidence, to our knowledge, that admission test scores, grade point averages, or national medical-board scores are reliable predictors of the quality of clinical performance by medical graduates."[64] Indeed, Geiger and Sidel note that there is some evidence that the students with the highest MCAT scores are more likely "to become researchers, academics and specialists," and not the practicing physicians who are most desperately needed.[65] As Lamont wrote, "Medical schools too often continued to admit those applicants with the scientific acumen that all but ensured their pursuit of lucrative specialties or research at a university hospital."[66] Dr. Thomas Roos, a professor and premedical advisor at Dartmouth, said, "The kind of guy who went into real estate because he was bright and wanted to make a killing is now attracted to medicine, a sure money-maker."[67] Certainly not all—nor even most—of our medical school applicants fit this description, but it would be well if medical schools sought out the more admirable traits in their applicants. We need doctors who will go to rural areas and into general practice and community service to supplement the specialists.

The point is this—most people who can present grades and MCAT scores of a certain caliber are competent to practice medicine after completing medical school. Selecting the lucky few to enter medical schools on the basis of who has most exceeded the competence threshold of grades and MCAT scores is a manner of selection that is not dictated by the public need for good doctors. Or, as Geiger and Sidel put it, "Certainly, scientific biological knowledge and the mastery of technical skills are essential in the practice of good medicine. But we know of no evidence that intellectual or scientific attainment, beyond an acceptable minimum threshold, contribute to competence in meeting healthcare needs."[68]

This contention of Drs. Geiger and Sidel is borne out by the study conducted by Dr. Rhoads and mentioned earlier.[69] Dr. Rhoads and his colleagues studied the students at the Duke University School of Medicine from 1962 through 1970. They examined the performance of students in the basic science portion of the curriculum, and compared that performance with the results in the clinical (dealing with patients) portion. Dr. Rhoads discovered that most of the students who achieved honors in the science courses did not achieve honors in the clinical courses. Moreover, of this group, Dr. Rhoads observed: "Their performance with patients was subtly disturbing because they appeared to be uninterested in patients as people."[70] Dr. Rhoads concluded, then, that "the student who is a superior scientist may become a good clinician, but he is no more likely to be so than the student who is not."[71]

Why should we care? Because Rhoads and others are concerned that current medical school admissions practices are biased in favor of the "science" doctors against the "clinical" doctors. That's not hard to understand. The MCAT asks science knowledge questions exclusively, so the student who would be a good clinician has no chance to display his or her potential. While an optimal mix of medical students would include both those with talents geared toward pure science and those with practical medical ability, the MCAT serves to boost the former at the expense of the latter. If we are to weigh applicants on the basis of how well we expect them to do at some point in the future, that point should be their performance at the end of schooling when they are practicing doctors, not at the very beginning of medical school when they are still taking science courses.

Yet the MCAT measures expected performance at the start of the race, not the finish. You can imagine the quality our athletic teams would have if they were selected on the basis of who gets off to the fastest start, not who finishes first. John Conger and Reginald Fitz did a study of predicted success in medical school. Their conclusion: "As a student moves from the preclinical to the clinical years, academic ability per se (as evidenced by undergraduate grades and MCAT scores) becomes relatively less crucial for success, while personal qualities (as judged by interviewers) tend to maintain their importance."[72] In other words, the closer a medical student gets to becoming a doctor, the less meaningful the MCAT score becomes.

These findings are serious. The *Journal of Medical Education* editorialized that "the evidence is that our selection is primarily directed at finding individuals who are likely to survive the first year of medical school . . . where few of the characteristics of the effective physician are required for success."[73] Reliance on MCAT scores could actually lead to poorer health care if we generate doctors who are great in the abstract and inadequate in the flesh. Alfred Gellhorn, former director of the Center for Biomedical Education and vice-president for health affairs of the City College of the City University of New York, is one of many troubled by the way students are admitted by medical schools. He stated that "our current system for selecting students who are to assume the responsibilities of patient care should be carefully reviewed."[74] In light of the lack of a definite relationship between the MCAT and an individual's worth as a doctor, it would seem hard to argue with him.

Business schools in general, and the master of business administration degree (M.B.A.) in particular, have recently come into vogue. Some of the impetus behind this increased demand for the degree lies in its salary advantage. While the holder of a

M.B.A. could expect 27 percent more pay than the holder of a B.B.A. in 1965, by 1975 that difference had widened to 47 percent.[75] In practical terms, "M.B.A. students get $3,000 to $4,000 more than students graduating with advanced liberal arts degrees," according to Samuel Thomas, dean of Baruch College.[76] As of May 1978, Harvard M.B.A.'s boasted an average starting salary of $25,931, a decent wage indeed.[77]

More important than the initial wage advantage of the degree, the M.B.A. is usurping the bachelor's degree as the basic requirement for an executive job. It is possible that someday the M.B.A. will be required to get any executive position, whether or not there is a salary differential compared to what new executives with only bachelor's degrees used to receive. Robert Turner, a business statistician, wrote: "But whereas fifty years ago a high school diploma was the ticket of admission to the managerial job market in business, and twenty-five years ago it was the bachelor's degree, today it is rapidly becoming the M.B.A. degree."[78] Turner's view was shared by Dena Rakoff of Harvard's Office of Career Services. Rakoff wrote, "The M.B.A. is beginning to replace the B.A. as the sine qua non of entry-level management positions. . . . It is beginning to be seen by some high-powered corporate employers as the first step in the employment-screening process."[79] There is no consensus whether the rise of the M.B.A. stems from a recognition on the part of employers of the value of what is taught in business schools, or because a tougher job market enhanced the competitive advantage of higher degrees.

In any event, some people are advancing the idea that the bloom is off the M.B.A. rose. Elizabeth Fowler of the *New York Times* wrote that despite the M.B.A.'s great reputation, "the fact that the 2,000 graduates a year of twenty-five years ago and the 4,600 in 1960 have grown to 50,000 annually now has been arousing some fears that maybe there are too many M.B.A.'s."[80] There are too many M.B.A.'s now in the sense that there are too many law school graduates—with supply outstripping demand, only graduates of the top schools will continue to reap the rewards of the advanced degree. Jeremy Main wrote that M.B.A.'s "face a two-tiered job market. . . . Graduates of the top business schools are still in great demand . . . but M.B.A.'s from

little-known colleges entered a different job market. They were
more likely to find work starting at $12,000 or $14,000 a year—
not much better than an ordinary bachelor of arts."[81] The outlines
of a two-tiered market can already be glimpsed. Rakoff has found
that while M.B.A.'s do have higher median starting salaries than
bachelor of arts graduates, that median might range wildly from
$14,000 to over $20,000, depending upon the business school.[82]
Not only does a difference in the value of an M.B.A. vary from
school to school in terms of starting salaries, but the very ability
to get a job interview at all may be at stake.

Business school admissions decisions are apparently becoming increasingly dependent upon a standardized test, the Graduate
Management Aptitude Test (GMAT). Just as with the LSAT,
ETS administers the GMAT, this time under the direction of
the Graduate Management Admission Council (GMAC). The
GMAC, like the LSAC and the AAMC, is composed of one
representative from each member institution, that is, each business school in the nation. The GMAT is a three–plus hour test
intended to measure certain "mental capabilities" in the study of
management in business school. Once more the test format is
composed of multiple-choice questions, and GMAT scores have
the same normal range of error encountered on the LSAT and
MCAT. GMATs are scaled from 200 to 800.

The student demand for admission to business schools can
be seen in the rising arc of GMAT-takers in the mid-1970s.
While the GMAT was given 124,584 times in 1974–75, some
147,000 GMATs were given in 1976–77.[83] Part of this surge
comes from students who were interested in law but thought the
field too crowded, according to Carol Stasinos, director of career
counseling and placement at Occidental College in Los Angeles.[84]
Any students switching for that reason presently have little to
gain. The heat is on for M.B.A.'s now, just as it is for law
degrees. Stanford Business School reported 3,300 applications
for 300 places in 1976, a ratio of eleven to one. Applications at
Stanford were up 60 percent in a period of two years. The
Wharton School of Business at the University of Pennsylvania
went from 1,400 applications a year in 1972 to 3,300 in 1976.
Harvard Business School had 2,900 applications in 1973, but
4,300 in 1976. By 1978, Harvard Business School was getting

over 10,000 requests for application forms a year for the 750 available seats, and over 5,000 actual applications.[85] Even with some signs that this frenzy for admission to business schools may have spent itself, the competition at the best schools remains tough.

Business school admissions policies are in a transitional period. The lengthening lines outside business school doors are leading to alterations in the selection process, alterations that seem to be leading to increased clout for GMAT scores. Interviews are falling by the wayside as schools like Harvard no longer grant them. Shortcuts are being found. Rakoff put the pieces together this way: "Before business schools' recent surge in popularity (and hence surge in applicants), the GMAT scores were not a very important factor in the admissions process; as the number of applicants rises, and as people who might have previously gone on to Ph.D. programs and law schools now turn toward business education, scores take on greater importance."[86] So far there are no indications that business schools have rigorously examined the traps their legal and medical relations have fallen into. Instead, the business schools seem to be marching straight ahead into the pitfalls of overreliance on standardized tests and possible misapplication of the test scores.

At least until now, one of the features that saved business schools from overreliance on GMATs was the greater age of the accepted students. Business school students tend to be older than law or medical students because admissions committees have placed great weight upon recommendations for candidates who have been working in the world of business for several years after college. Detlev Vagts, who teaches at both Harvard Law and Business schools, has detected differences in student bodies as a result of such a policy. He wrote: "Another consequence of the application and admissions process is that it generates a class that is not as bright and clever, particularly on the verbal side, as a law school class. The business school admissions policy depends heavily on organizational or managerial experience reflected in recommendations or other records. A high performance as measured in those terms can counterbalance a less than impressive college academic record and a mediocre set of test scores."[87] This willingness to look at real world abilities has been a saving grace of business schools, even at the cost of students with somewhat less facility in manipulating the English language. Whether business schools have the determination or resources to continue to evaluate applications on more levels than GMATs and grades remains to be seen.

What is currently clear for all to see is that the GMAT has no more relation to success in business than the LSAT has to legal skill or the MCAT to medical competence. Lois Crooks, in a study prepared for ETS, lays the question to rest. She wrote that success in the real world of business is not related to long-standing admission factors such as undergraduate GPA and test scores, even though undergraduate GPA and test scores are related to success in the narrow confines of graduate school.[88] And J. Sterling Livingston, a professor of business administration at Harvard Business School, has written the following: "Academic achievement is not a valid yardstick to use in measuring managerial potential. Indeed, if academic achievement is equated with success in business, the well-educated manager is a myth."[89] If business schools should elect to take the road more traveled by, at least by the law and medical schools, they surely would be hard pressed to defend the decision to make the GMAT of paramount importance by claiming it is related to executive performance.

There is another well-known standardized test for students who hope to go on to further study after college. This test is called the Graduate Record Examination (GRE). The GRE is yet another test which bears the ETS imprint. Many graduate departments at universities across the land use GRE scores in their admissions decisions. In the 1977–78 admissions season, approximately 314,000 people took the GRE.[90] This test supplies three scores to interested graduate programs for each test-taker: a verbal, quantitative, and analytical score. How good is the GRE? According to Bernard Feder, "The GRE isn't even in the same league as the SAT; in fact it's a notoriously bad predictor. Yet despite the fact that grades are a much better predictor, graduate school officials continue to place more weight on GRE scores than they do on college grades—even when the grades are from the same university and the same department!"[91] This seems to be the whole fallacy of the "overachiever" in yet one more guise. To begin with, the correlation numbers for the GRE and graduate school performance are sometimes dismal, even in comparison to figures for other standardized tests. Feder concluded that "use of the GRE is essentially an act of faith."[92] If a graduate admissions committee leans on GRE scores so heavily that demonstrated ability by an applicant on courses in that same department is overlooked, then this might more appropriately be deemed an act of bad faith.

Why should we care? After all, graduate schools now seem to be a buyer's market for applicants, at least in comparison to law, medical, and business schools. And many of the better graduate departments are known to take the time to carefully weigh an applicant's recommendations and other qualities which may offset the GRE scores. But not all departments exercise that care. And with the job market for Ph.D.'s so unbelievably tight, the prestige of the school awarding the degree can make the difference between a job in that field and a stack of letters expressing regret. For example, it has been predicted that over 35 percent of social science Ph.D.'s will be unable to find employment in that field by 1985.[93] Lamont wrote that while there will be approximately 14,000 faculty openings in 1980, there will also be around 60,000 freshly minted Ph.D.'s fighting for those slots.[94] And that excess of applicants to positions is expected to grow in the coming years. The moral is that mere possession of a Ph.D. is not going to be a guarantee of employment. While there will be many exceptions, odds are a graduate of an influential school and department with access to the alumni network will be favored in the job hunt over an equally talented graduate of a less-known school. If GRE scores have even a small potential to tip the balance in admissions decisions, the long term repercussions can be severe for those students who lose out on the test.

Having explored the admissions terrain at law, medical, business, and some graduate schools, it is time to draw back a little and record some general impressions. Some illustrations are in order to show what an unquestioning faith in standardized tests can lead to. To get a feel for the pervasiveness of LSAT-mania, and by implication, test-mania, consider a joint program of the

City College of New York (CCNY) and the New York Law School. According to a student quoted in the *Harvard Law School Record* in 1978, under the terms of this program, fifty CCNY sophomores were allowed to take classes at the law school.[95] The fifty were guaranteed admission to the law school at the end of their junior year if they attained grades of B or better in the college classes and C or better in the law school classes. There was one other condition. The fifty also had to score above an LSAT cut-off figure used by the admissions office. That's terrific. It meant that as long as these terms for the program were in existence, even though these students could prove their ability to handle law school work, they would not be admitted without a certain score on the LSAT.

Remember, the LSAT is at most only a test of potential ability in first-year law classes. Yet here we had an admissions committee elevating an attempt at prediction to a higher status than actual performance. This is just one incident of overreliance on the LSAT. As a result, it's hard for any law school applicant to ignore the impact the LSAT could have on her life. As James Thomas, the dean of admissions at Yale Law School, wrote: ". . . the law schools themselves broadcast the importance of the LSAT in loud, clear, and sometimes devastatingly forthright prose, aided by the use of admissions grids and prompted by the notion that the higher the LSAT median at a law school the better the student body.[96] All this concentration on the LSAT was taking place at a time when the correlation Harvard Law School was able to obtain with first-year grades and the LSAT, even when the undergraduate GPA was mixed in, hovered between an r of .5 to .62, and an r^2 of .25 to .36.[97]

To take another example of a prevalent misunderstanding of the limits of the LSAT, consider Dean Liacouras's charge that "even law firms interviewing senior law students for jobs began asking the student who completed three years of law school with academic honors what score he or she received on the LSAT which was taken before entering law school."[98] The absurdity of these actions can be readily seen. To be consistent, the American Bar Association should require all lawyers who graduated before the LSAT was a requirement to take the test. Those who don't master the LSAT should then be disbarred on the assumption that failure on a predictive test outweighs years of demonstrated proficiency. More seriously, if the mystique of the LSAT has such sway over admissions personnel and employers when confronted with students who have passed law school courses, imagine the impact of the LSAT or other standardized tests on the fate of applicants who have not had the opportunity to prove themselves through performance in school.

Dean Thomas wrote the story of one person who tried to circumvent the rules in securing such an opportunity.[99] In the fall of 1975, he discovered a "Ms. X" who had bluffed her way into the first-year classes at Yale Law School by pretending to be enrolled. She was able to carry out her charade for about a month before being caught. Ms. X had hoped to make it through to exams in order to show she could indeed do the work despite her mediocre LSAT scores. She just might have been able to make her point. When exposed, she was rated by a professor as "somewhere in the middle of an excellent class of law students."[100] This is not meant to condone the ruse, but the episode raises doubts about the ability of the LSAT, or any of these graduate level standardized tests, to predict even first-year grades when such a key factor as determination is completely overlooked.

You may recall that in Chapter 1 we discussed the way ETS changed the content of the LSAT between the July and October 1977 administrations of the test.[101] Basically what ETS did was to increase the portion of the test devoted to math questions. But the rationale for that switch is controversial. The addition of more math to the LSAT made the test easier for those with a strong math background, and harder for those without math training. Thus it is hard to see how the LSAT is now more geared to helping potential top-notch lawyers score well, unless somehow advanced mathematical skill is essential to the profession. James Fallows of the *Washington Monthly* did not buy that argument. He wrote that standardized tests such as the LSAT shunt applicants aside on irrelevant grounds: "If we must still make judgments and exercise discrimination—as we should—it should be on standards that do justice to the range of talents we want ultimately to reward. Those who don't have a talent for, say, math, should not be made to suffer lifetime exclusion from the law or government service because of it."[102] One could ask why

ETS didn't add more sections on reading comprehension or reasoning ability, skills which are important to law and which might have greatly altered the scores of test-takers as well.

What it boils down to is that there are only a very limited number of spaces available for graduate and professional school applicants. With the excess of applicants, the schools look for ways to keep people out as well as reasons to admit them. Alfred Gellhorn has posed a question for medical schools that is applicable across the board. "Are present competitive medical school requirements essential to the making of a good physician or do they merely serve to reduce the number of applicants?"[103] At a time when Columbia University Law School accepted only 300 of 5,000 applicants, and Columbia Business School took only 400 of 1,900 suitors,[104] Columbia President William McGill warned in his 1975 commencement address: "After a long regimen characterized by remarkable academic success and accomplishment, these ill-fated students are discovering themselves to be failures after all. We must correct such distortions or face a revival of social unrest from frustrated students who feel that their society actively opposes them in realizing their destinies."[105] The objection to the standardized tests we have explored at this level is not that they are part of a process of screening out applicants who cannot do the work or would have the effect of slowing the entire class. Rather, the objection and the injury arises whenever the tests overstep their limited function in the screening, especially when the scores are not directly related to the qualities we as a society want in the graduates of our institutions of postgraduate learning.

We turn now to look at the role standardized tests have been able to carve for themselves in determining who can become a licensed member of a profession, or who can be certified to hold particular jobs.

CHAPTER NINE

Blocking Access to Licensed Professions

No longer are standardized tests solely creatures that leap out at you from the confines of educational institutions. In America today, these tests often are used to determine who is granted a license to practice their livelihood, and who will receive a coveted promotion. What's more, the roster of jobs which fall under the category of "licensed professions" grows longer almost by the day. What are some of the areas that force you to take a standardized test before you are admitted to the field, or granted a job promotion? Of course, doctors and lawyers have to take these tests. But they're not alone. Here's just a partial list of the workers who are now required to take a standardized test to "prove" their fitness for employment or advancement: CIA agents, auto mechanics, barbers, architects, policemen, firemen, plumbers, cosmetologists, realtors, insurance agents, exterminators, teachers, principals, school superintendents, civil servants, dentists, Peace Corps recruits, stockbrokers, actuaries, military personnel, and TV repair workers. Then there are the individual tests required by a host of private employers for whom no detailed statistical compilations are known.

The testing industry has been sharing in the surge of revenues generated by the booming requirements for tests. ETS, for example, has boosted its income generated by occupational testing from $2,100,000 to $11,200,000 in the period between 1969 and

163

1979.[1] One official of the College Board told an audience in the summer of 1979 that some 40 million American adults go through a career transition of some type each year and that CEEB was looking at the potential market created by all these transitions.[2] What's going on here? Depending on who you believe, the current wave of states requiring licensing tests for more professions is either a consumer protection move or the result of pressure from within these fields to limit competition by holding down the number of new people allowed into the field. Either way, some individuals who are fully capable of meeting the performance levels of their chosen professions will be hurt. They will be frozen out because they can't handle standardized tests as well as they can handle a broken carburetor. Paul Pottinger of the National Center for the Study of Professions told Congress that "tests are a major regulatory device in the professions, and we are concerned about the effects tests have on the freedom of competent citizens to pursue work of their choosing."[3]

Many serious objections have been raised about the appropriateness of using standardized tests to limit access to professions. There is, first of all, the economic argument that the consumer is actually hurt when the number of potential competitors is held down. The theory is that competition reduces prices and provides an incentive for quality work. If the number of professionals is lowered while the demand for their service remains the same, then prices will go up, and incompetent people may be able to stay afloat because their services will still be better than nothing at all. Pottinger was quoted about a study which showed that when TV repair workers were licensed through standardized tests, the quality of their work stayed the same, but their charges to consumers went up by about 20 percent.[4] That's just one study, not conclusive proof. But you do have to wonder why it takes an ability to test well to be qualified to repair TVs. When you take your business to a TV repair shop, it is probably because you want your TV set fixed and not because you are looking for someone who can fill in the slots on a standardized test.

Another objection to standardized tests in the workplace revolves around the potential for misuse. Until the spring of 1978, for instance, various agencies of the federal government were requiring job applicants to list their LSAT scores on their application forms.[5] As we have already seen, the most that can be claimed for LSAT scores is that they are partial predictors of law school grades. But when you are dealing with someone who is already a law school graduate, it seems silly to look at the predictor when the actual results, the law school grades, are readily available. The Federal Trade Commission (FTC) reached this conclusion as part of an out-of-court settlement in a race discrimination suit, and the Justice and Commerce Departments then followed the FTC's lead.[6] Other lawsuits have been filed challenging the accuracy of some of the standardized tests used for licensing. Without judging each suit on its merits, it does seem fair to say that some tests come up with startlingly different passing rates for minority groups. One recently used test, for example, when first administered, gave passing scores to 76 percent of the white test-takers, but to only 23 percent of black test-takers.[7]

Even in the complete absence of discriminatory intent or effect, the use of standardized tests to regulate entrance to jobs is a serious business. On many of these tests there is no recourse from the test score. You can't take a state examiner with you to work and then prove that you really can do the job regardless of what the test says. All you can do is study and hope and take the test again. State licensing boards may acknowledge that the tests don't measure all the knowledge and vital qualities essential for your profession, but that doesn't get you over the hurdle of beating the test itself. To this extent at least, job competence in fact is considered less important than mastery of the tricks of test-taking. Licensing tests don't do any better than all the tests we have seen at every step of the educational ladder when it comes to measuring those "little" things like an applicant's integrity, determination, and compassion. One of the leaders of an organization fighting the use of standardized tests for certification of school principals in Chicago said: "A paper-and-pencil test is one of the poorest ways to select an administrator. Our association has been pushing for a performance-based method of certification, that is, the proven ability to do the job that's required of an individual on the job while working with parents, students, and teachers."[8] A test might make more sense if we wanted to select principals who sat in their offices all day taking even more standardized tests for the greater glory of the school, but if we want principals who can deal with people, we'd better take that skill into account in our selection procedures.

Or take the use of standardized tests to pick our future auto mechanics. If this is the sole criterion, then it is an appalling prospect. The skills required to spot trouble in a car and then fix it are very different from what it takes to do well on a paper-and-pencil set of questions about spotting trouble in a car and then fixing it. Some people may have both these skills in equal measure. But as far as my car is concerned, when I go to the garage I am much more interested in getting a mechanic who can fix my car in his shop than someone who can fix it on paper. To be sure, a good mechanic is going to have to keep up with the latest technology, and to do this she has to be able to read repair manuals or get the information in some other way. But book learning is a far cry from mechanical ability. There are folks who don't read Proust on the weekends, but who sure can put a car together. There are other people I know who are superb on paper-and-pencil tests and who can work on my car anytime they can get past me, a sledgehammer, and a guard dog. The point is simply that we want our mechanics to be people who can fix cars. Using standardized tests to license those mechanics may lead us away from that goal rather than closer to it.

This is like the way many high school physical education classes used to be run. The boys would play basketball while the girls would take tests on the rules of basketball. The boys would wear gym clothes that in themselves constituted particularly noticeable offensive fouls, while the girls would be graded on how freshly laundered their uniforms were. If the goal was to have kids who could play the sport, who got exercise and an appreciation for team effort, then the boys' program had it all over the girls' program. This is true even though the girls undoubtedly would have scored higher on a standardized test about the fine points of the rules of basketball. You can't play a sport well, or perform in a job, unless you know the rules of the game.

But just because you know the rules, and can pick them out on a standardized test, doesn't mean you know how to play or how to do the job well.

We rely on standardized tests for licensing at our peril. There is the risk that we will end up running the real players off the court, and the real mechanics out of the garages. Can't you just see Richard Petty asking an applicant for one of his racing crews to take a standardized test on internal combustion engines? Or Red Auerbach telling Larry Bird to quit the Celtics until he scores well on a standardized test about passing lanes in basketball?

What's more, the questions on at least some of these tests for job certification don't always relate directly to the particular job involved. Sometimes the questions ostensibly reveal preferences common to people already in the field, so your chances of getting a job might depend whether you have the same attitude as a majority of your fellow workers supposedly do. Without additional criteria these sorts of questions might lead to a homogeneous work force, but it is far from clear that such a development would be desirable. David White, a lawyer and researcher, testified in New York hearings about one such test that had been challenged in court and ultimately thrown out. "Candidates in Bridgeport, Connecticut, for the position of firefighter were asked the question, true or false, 'I hate to read books.' True or false, 'I don't understand how intellectuals can discuss philosophical questions.' The answer is true in both instances and if you said that, you'd be more likely to be a firefighter today, until the test was made public to that judge and until he decided that that had no business in a decision as to whether to be a firefighter."[9] Would you really mind if one or two of the firefighters who respond to your call for help actually like to read books or discuss philosophical questions? That doesn't seem to be the kind of character flaw that should be held against an individual.

Sometimes the results of a standardized test can hinge on a dispute over the correct response to just one question. This is what happened on a 1978 test in Prince Georges County, Maryland, to determine who would be promoted to police captain.[10] Twenty-six police lieutenants had to take a test which included this question: "What is the deficiency to be found in routine command systems during emergency conditions?" The alternative answers were:

a) There is no emergency-oriented command in hierarchy.

b) There is no practice for training in command under emergency situations.

c) The routine command system has too long a chain of command for emergency situations.

d) All of the above.

Have you figured out the right answer? If you have, then you reached that decision with more ease than the promotion board for Prince Georges County. When the test was first scored, "c" was the correct answer. But then one of the lieutenants appealed that "d" was the correct answer. It turns out that some police manuals preferred "c," while others sided with "d." A four-man review board sided with "d" and then an appeal of the appeal was filed. In the meantime, three police lieutenants—let's call them Rich, Ted, and Carol—were caught in the middle.

The problem was that if answer "c" was kept, the lieutenants would be ranked in this order: Rich first, Carol second, and Ted fourth. But if "d" is right, then positions change: Ted would now be first and Rich and Carol would both drop a couple of notches. In short, a very arbitrary decision as to which of these answers would be designated as the correct answer would determine which of these individuals make captain, and which are denied a promotion. (A decision to drop the question entirely would also affect the outcome.) Is this really how we want our police captains to be selected? Might we not be at least somewhat interested in actual managerial competence as opposed to the ability to memorize lines from police manuals and spot them on a test? Wouldn't individual demonstrations of bravery in the line of duty, of incorruptibility in the devotion to the law, and of the willingness to work with community groups be valuable attributes for any police captain? The ability to spot "c" or "d" as the "right" answer doesn't seem to have much relation to the reality of what our police captains will be called on to do. What's even worse, at least in this case, is that the selection boiled down to little more than a matter of luck since strong support could be found for both "c" and "d."

This same type of problem can also surface in the tests given to select rookie police officers. David McClelland has written: ". . . suppose you are a ghetto resident in the Roxbury section of Boston. To qualify for being a policeman you have to take a three-hour-long general intelligence test in which you must know the meaning of words like 'quell,' 'pyromaniac,' and 'lexicon'. If you do not know enough of those words or cannot play analogy games with them, you do not qualify and must be satisfied with some such job as being a janitor for which an intelligence test is not required yet by the Massachusetts Civil Service Commission. You, not unreasonably, feel angry, upset, and unsuccessful. Because you do not know those words, you are considered to have low intelligence, and since you consequently have to take a low-status job and are unhappy, you contribute to the celebrated correlations of low intelligence with low occupational status and poor adjustment. Psychologists should be ashamed of themselves for promoting a view of general intelligence that has encouraged such a testing program, particularly when there is no solid evidence that significantly relates performance on this type of intelligence test with performance as a policeman."[11]

The long and short of it is that for police work as for most professions, there are other skills that matter as well as marking the "right" answer on a piece of paper. A police officer must be able to speak clearly and to understand what the people on the street are saying. A talent for investigation would be a tremendous plus, as would that thing we call "street smarts." A police officer will have to read and understand the law, take notes, and fill out reports, so some measures of writing and reading skills make sense. But there is far more than literacy involved in being a good police officer, and it is those additional skills which are totally ignored in selection systems that rely on standardized tests. In many police systems, new officers are chosen on the basis of their ranking on the standardized test given to recruits. Period. There is no explicit recognition of the things a kid growing up on the street might have learned while a more favored counterpart was hitting the books. It would make more sense to set the minimum required for reading and test-taking ability, and then evaluate all applicants who can make that minimum on the basis of how they do on the other skills essential to good police work. After all, if you're being mugged, or your life is in danger, do you really care how good the officer was at multiple-choice questions as long as he has the special talent to react properly in these crisis situations? Selection should be grounded in the bedrock of job performance, and not in the shifting sands of fluency with the language of the test publishers. A mistake in selection here could have grave consequences for all concerned.

Let's shift our focus now and put one of these tests under a microscope to see what turns up. We'll put what is called the Multistate Bar Examination (MBE) on our specimen slide for close inspection. The MBE is a six-hour standardized test used to help determine who will be allowed to practice law. When the MBE was first unveiled in February 1972, thirteen states used it for some 5,000 candidates. Use of the MBE expanded rapidly, with approximately forty states now under its sway and about 40,000 candidates taking the MBE each year. The MBE was developed by the National Conference of Bar Examiners (NCBE); it is now written and administered in conjunction with ETS and the local bar associations.[12] The MBE consists of 200 multiple-choice questions: 40 each on Contracts and Torts, with 30 apiece for Constitutional Law, Criminal Law, Real Property, and Evidence. The time pressure on this test is intense—candidates have an average of only 108 seconds to answer each question.

Although there are variations from state to state, here's a general description of what you have to do to pass the bar examination. In most states, the bar exam takes two full days. One day is taken up by the MBE. The other day is devoted to an essay examination which probes your knowledge of local state law. The MBE, as its name implies, only asks questions about what is deemed to be "national" law. The MBE is scored on a scale of 0 to 200. ETS has a formula which takes the number of right answers you have selected (your "raw score") and converts that into a score that is supposed to correct for any differences in difficulty between tests (your "scaled score"). The local bar association is in charge of writing the essay questions and grading those answers. Once both parts of the bar examination have been marked, the local bar association decides how much weight to give to the MBE and how much to the essay, and adds the scores together. Then all the candidates with combined scores over the designated cut-off score are admitted to the bar (provided they pass the morals check), and those below that score are told they can try again next time. Some states have an elaborate appeals process for those failing the bar exam, but too often this right to challenge is limited to the essay exam. In some jurisdictions, the MBE is entirely unavailable for scrutiny by the rejected candidates. On the other hand, some states pass candidates who score above a "trigger" score on the MBE. In these states, if your MBE score is high enough, the local bar won't pay any attention to your work on the essay exam. If you are incapable of writing a legal memorandum or a brief to a court, but can take multiple-choice tests well, you may have a friend in the MBE. Of course, if you are represented as a client by such a lawyer, you might not feel so warmly toward the practice of using MBE trigger scores.

How important is the bar exam? Professor Victor Schwartz of the University of Cincinnati Law School has written: "Your forthcoming bar examination may be the most important test that you have taken in your entire life: your entrance into the profession of your choice will depend on the outcome. All of your efforts in college to get into law school and the hundreds of hours of study in law school itself will mean little, as a practical matter, if you do not pass the bar. Of course, in every state you have the opportunity to take the bar exam again, but the process is costly, both in terms of time and in regard to employment opportunities."[13] That's pretty strong stuff. When you figure that the MBE often counts for at least half of the bar exam score, it becomes clear that this test can not be shrugged off.

Certainly the test is not shrugged off by the people who have to take it. The financial costs are considerable. Not only do you have to pay for the privilege of taking the MBE, but there is the additional matter of paying for a bar review course. There is no requirement that you take a review course, but most law school graduates (who, by the way, are the only people allowed to take the bar exam in most places) sign up anyway. It has been estimated that 85 percent of those preparing for the bar exam take a review course.[14] These review courses generally run to several hundred dollars. Then there is the income that many law school graduates lose while they devote their time to studying for the bar exam.

People taking the bar exams most recently are also under pressure because they are aware of the national trend toward a lower percentage of candidates passing. Despite the rise in LSAT scores needed to get into law school in the first place (as we saw in Chapter 8), despite three years at a law school, despite the heavy investment in bar review courses, the national passing percentage has gone down from 76 percent in 1973 to 67 percent in 1978.[15] It is possible that law school graduates are of poorer average quality than they were ten years ago, although what little evidence there is on this issue points in the other direction. A number of critics have charged that the downturn in passing rates is not entirely coincidental at a time when a glut of lawyers threatens to flood the legal marketplace.

Bar committees deny that there is any conscious effort to reduce competition by placing a ceiling on the number of new practitioners admitted to the bar. They are probably right. But perhaps a subconscious raising of admission requirements is being stimulated by the hordes of applicants at bar committee doors. Certainly it is hard to explain such swift changes in passing rates on the basis of a sudden decline in the quality of law school graduates. When a state such as New Jersey goes from passing 83 percent of bar exam candidates in 1974 down to 47 percent in 1979, applicants to the bar have reason to worry.[16]

The situation is aggravated on the MBE because the test-takers know the arbitrary nature of the test. The MBE is blissfully unaware of your writing skills and whether you can utter an entire sentence on your feet without the use of note cards. The MBE does not concern itself with whether you can gather facts, research the law, arrive at reasonable conclusions based on this research, and then synthesize your work into a forceful argument on behalf of a client. These abilities would seem to have some bearing on one's competence as a lawyer, not to mention the ability to counsel clients. What the MBE does test is a narrow kind of memory for what is often legal trivia which a practicing lawyer would look up. Of course, mixed in with these narrow questions on the MBE are some admirable questions which we want all future lawyers to be able to answer without exception. But most law school graduates know the incontrovertible basics, so if the MBE stuck to them exclusively it would be unlikely to make any appreciable dent in the number of qualified individuals seeking admission to the bar.

Many of the questions on the MBE concentrate on esoteric areas, on the footnotes to the law. Some legal areas which very few lawyers actually have to deal with during their careers receive an inordinate amount of attention. One favorite of the MBE seems to be the manipulation of historical legal rules which have extremely limited application in modern practice but are readily convertible into multiple-choice questions. These are rules of law which were of great importance to members of the legal profession in medieval England but have long since ceased to be dominant in this country. This is not to say that it isn't nice for lawyers to know the history and sources of modern law—indeed, all things being equal we'd prefer lawyers with that background as well as ones who know biblical stories and can expound on the symbolism of the great white whale in *Moby Dick*. But the bar exam is supposed to be a measure of the minimum requirements for competence in the legal profession, not an excuse to exclude people who aren't up on their history but who know how to interpret and use the modern legal codes.

What's more, the MBE can penalize test-takers by what it neglects to cover just as surely as it can by what it includes in the way of irrelevant material. There are a number of important branches of the law that don't get even a passing nod on the MBE. Candidates who would excel on questions about labor law or antitrust law or environmental law or energy law or poverty law don't get a chance to shine, since these areas are off-limits for the MBE. It is at least arguable that a working knowledge of these areas is more vital for an American lawyer at the end of the twentieth century than a familiarity with the feudal system of property division, but that doesn't seem to be the MBE approach. Granted that the NCBE had a difficult task in weaving together a test that could be sold to the bar associations of most states as a worthwhile venture, there is still the question of whether the subjects on the MBE bear much relation to contemporary legal practice.

Even if you're entirely happy with the choice of subjects included on the MBE, and the list of areas kept off, and the relative proportion of these questions and the level of detail required, you still have to wonder if the actual questions sort out the knowledgeable from the pretenders. The only complete MBE ever released at one time to the public as far as I know was the February 23, 1972, version. When those questions and answers were disclosed an uproar followed. The problem was that learned experts in the law disagreed vehemently with many of the answers that the MBE writers claimed were correct. In fact, law professors from several law schools in D.C. were said to have disagreed about which of the alternative answers were the right ones on some 25 percent of the questions.[17] The MBE officals conceded that 5 of the 200 questions had more than one correct answer and adjusted scores to that extent.[18] Having been burned by the controversy over the accuracy of the designated answers, the MBE overseers have apparently been reluctant to expose entire tests to view. Bar review courses acquaint their charges with this sorry history, which tends to produce cynical test-takers who are trained to see the trick aspect to MBE questions, and to wonder if they should look for the right answer or the answer most likely to be designated as "right" when the tests are scored.

Another remarkable aspect to the MBE is that it does not make even the slightest claim to predicting which test-takers will make better lawyers. You will recall that the LSAT pegged itself to predicting law school grades, so there was at least some way of telling whether the LSAT was doing well on that minimal task. But on the MBE you just have high scorers and low scorers and no comparison point to see if the MBE is doing the job of sorting out the competent from the incompetent. People's entire careers are at stake, and we have no definitive way of saying whether the signals the MBE sends out are accurate or likely to put us on a collision course with the goal of protecting the public from hacks. We know that committees of distinguished people have given the MBE questions their approval, but we also know of the disputes that arose the one time an entire MBE was released. With all respect for the individuals involved in the process of designing the MBE, it is still asking a lot of the public and the rejected candidates to take it on faith that the MBE is as good as it can be, and that that is good enough. Most people would be horrified if America adopted a system of determining criminal guilt or innocence where the defendant could not confront his accusers. But in some ways that's what the MBE does. A failed candidate is sentenced to exclusion from the practice of law unless and until he passes the bar. And in many jurisdictions this "guilty" test-taker cannot directly challenge the worth of the MBE questions or argue the value of his answers.

Just how closely is the MBE related to the job of performing legal work? We can't say for sure, but the fit is clearly far from exact. Not only does the MBE exclude skills essential to being a good lawyer (skills such as oral facility and research ability) and include questions largely irrelevant to modern practice, but most practicing lawyers would be hard-pressed to do well on the MBE if they were suddenly required to take it with no preparation. If the MBE really measures the knowledge which is an absolute minimum to the decent practice of law, then decent practitioners in the field might be expected to do well on the MBE just on the strength of their years of experience. But I submit that the depth of experience and the wisdom of decades possessed by such lawyers might actually hinder their performance on the MBE. Knowing too much on a multiple-choice test can sometimes be as disastrous as knowing too little, especially if you haven't brushed up on your test-taking techniques. I doubt that even the most ardent supporters of the MBE would embrace the proposition that practicing lawyers should regularly be required to retake the MBE, to make sure that despite their satisfactory performance as lawyers they still meet the hypothetical essentials embodied in the MBE. And what about the host of competent lawyers who were admitted to the bar prior to 1972 when the MBE was begun? Should they be required to prove their competence on the MBE on pain of disbarment? I wouldn't expect many lawyers, even the best, to take the MBE even on an experimental basis, for fear that a poor score could leak out and place an unfair aura of incompetence around them.

Another interesting aspect to the MBE is that the score re-

quired to pass it varies from state to state. Each state bar committee has the power to set the score needed by an applicant to
pass the MBE portion of the bar exam (or to pass the bar exam
entirely in states which use MBE trigger scores).[19] If the MBE
truly measures a lawyer's knowledge of the essentials of national
law, does this system of differing score requirements by state make
sense? Are lawyers somehow undeniably more "competent" in
states with higher MBE requirements, or less competent in states
that set lower MBE minimums? Just what does it mean to say
that Adam had a 118 on the MBE, and Eve a 107? Will Adam
therefore become a better lawyer than Eve? Are they both assuredly more qualified to practice law than the individuals who
scored just under the MBE minimum for that state? Since the
MBE, like most standardized tests, has a standard deviation and
is susceptible to coaching, the validity of using either cut-off or
trigger scores must be open to serious question.

There is one aspect to the MBE that makes it particularly
unsuited for the selection of lawyers. This aspect involves the
MBE's penchant of asking candidates to select not the "right"
alternative answer, or even the "wrong"' alternative, but rather
to identify the "best" or "worst" of the alternatives listed. If you're
at all familiar with law school, you know that students are trained
to see all sides of an issue, to examine the possibilities of arguments that may look to be losers on the surface. A law student is
taught to see the potential in just about any answer—it is the
quality of her reasoning in reaching a conclusion about the alternatives that is constantly stressed. Now it is one thing to ask
applicants to the bar to pick out an alternative that experts agree
is clearly the right answer. But it is a far different thing to tell
a candidate that she must decide what is going on in the mind of
the test writer in deciding which of several plausible responses
will be marked as correct. This leads to a renewed emphasis on
test gamesmanship, and gives an edge to those who take coaching
courses where favorite MBE red herrings are vividly displayed
and test-taking tricks are mastered. A candidate may know her
legal subjects, but she isn't allowed to explain her answer on the
MBE or to point out why a given question is dumb. The MBE
asks candidates to ignore all the legal skills that have been instilled during three years of legal education, and to demonstrate

a test-taking skill most lawyers will never be called on to perform during their entire practice. Your legal reasoning could be superb, but if it doesn't follow exactly the meandering stream of thought of the writers of the MBE, you're out of court. What's more, even though you might have picked an alternative generally conceded to be at least the second best of the alternatives on a given question, there is no partial credit. On the MBE, it's whole hog or nothing, with able candidates running the risk of picking a pig in the poke on their answer sheets.

It doesn't have to be this way. We could construct a system where applicants to the bar could show their proficiency in real legal work as opposed to the games on the MBE. To begin with, some states do allow failed candidates to challenge the grading of their essays. It is hard to see why marks on a legal essay are within the scope of criticism while the arbitrary aspects of the MBE are kept from view in many states. David White wrote about one advanced state, Michigan, which "not only allows candidates to review their failing answers, it actively encourages candidates to challenge their score, to prepare researched memoranda supporting their answers, and to present their case for review by the bar examiners. In a sense, Michigan makes the challenging of a failing grade part of the examination—the challenge entails a demonstration of legal research and oral persuasion."[20] An applicant who can go through these steps and convince the bar examiners of the worth of his arguments has shown concrete legal skills, not the secondhand surrogates revealed on tests like the MBE. I'm not saying that the MBE is necessarily any worse than many of the other tests used to license professionals; I have concentrated on the MBE largely because it is most familiar to me. But it does seem that the mania for standardized tests at the professional level may be trading away real safeguards for the public for the false economy of relatively inexpensive and rapidly scored tests. Why deprive individuals of a legal career—and members of the public of adequate representation—on the basis of a test that is only indirectly related to legal competence when there are tools better suited for the task? Of course, there are problems with the traditional straight essay bar exam as well, and a return to the past is no solution. But approaches such as Michigan's must be encouraged.[21] Until those efforts bear fruit, the MBE should be subjected to strict scrutiny in the hope that its questions will become less likely to produce confusion and more concerned with areas of everyday importance to our nation's lawyers.

Standardized tests have such a hold on the public imagination that we sometimes force candidates to possess skills not clearly needed for success on the job. In denouncing standardized tests, Pottinger put the argument this way: ". . . these tests currently have no validity with respect to work and life skills required outside of academia. They are sometimes poor predictors of academic competence, but they are always poor predictors of competence in the real world."[22] For all this, standardized tests show little sign of loosening their stranglehold on the admissions process to the licensed fields and regulated professions we have touched on in this chapter. We now turn to a search for answers to the question of how these tests could obtain and maintain such a strong grip.

PART THREE

Why Have
We Allowed This
to Happen?

CHAPTER TEN

A Frankenstein Story

Once upon a time, a good-hearted doctor who wanted to help humanity gave life to a strange new creature. This creature did not look like anything that had ever come before—indeed, in some ways it was misshaped and had a terrifying effect on many who saw it for the first time. The thing did have great power, a power its creator meant to be used to serve people. When the creature was approached with understanding and a firm insistence that it do the bidding of human employers, all went well enough. But there was tragedy on the horizon. Few people outside the small group of the creator's close friends really understood what it was that made the creature work. And one day some people came and took the creature from its home in Europe and transported it across the Atlantic to America. Once in America the creature was able to get free of the restraints which had served to harness its strength, aided by some people who thought they would be able to use the thing for their own purposes. But soon the creature was out of control altogether, roaming the countryside virtually at will and gathering power over the awe-struck populace. Some people fell under the creature's sway because they were impressed with the technical accomplishment of bringing such a thing to life in the first place. Others saw it as a monster, but felt they would be crushed if they challenged the creature in open combat. Soon the creature was bold enough to give orders openly to the very people it had been intended to serve. Its creator was no longer around to rein it in.

This may sound a lot like a version of the familiar story of Dr. Victor Frankenstein and his monster. But it's not. This is a rough story of the birth and rapid rise to power of another creature, the standardized, group-administered intelligence test. The intelligence test (or IQ test, as it is called) got its start in France in the early 1900s.[1] Alfred Binet was the person who first came up with the IQ test, at the request of the French government. At the time, the French were looking for a test that would help find those children with low ability who would be aided by programs designed for their needs. Binet's test was a way to sort out these children with special needs, and he made no claims about the reasons behind the difficulties the children were encountering or that the test had any broader applications. What's more, Binet explicitly rejected the notion that his test measured permanent intelligence levels in children or adults. Binet was of the conviction that we must "react against and protest the brutal pessimism of those who regarded the test as measuring some fixed and unchanging quantity."[2] Rather, he saw the test as a step on the path to "remedying" whatever problems the children were having. First the problems would be spotted, then treated, and then the children would be ready to rejoin their classmates free of their old disadvantage. This test of Binet's, then, had the potential to do great good. But Binet died in 1911, before he could be sure his philosophy would be respected, and before he could see what havoc his creation would wreak in America.

The monster known as the IQ test was set loose in this country when the Binet test was translated into English by Lewis Terman and Henry Goddard, among others. Along with this translation came new and more dramatic claims for the Binet test. No longer would it be called a mere tool to help schoolchildren. Now it was claimed that this test would inexpensively and swiftly allow scientists to determine with fantastic precision the innate intelligence of every person in America. Those with a high IQ would be rewarded; those with a low IQ would be branded as likely criminals, mental defectives, and people who would be banned from having children for fear they would produce stupid children. The fact that the citizens who scored high on the IQ tests seemed to be the same people who were the wealthiest and longest-established in America did not create skepticism. Instead, this fact was considered one more proof of the accuracy of the IQ tests and not an instance of social and economic advantages asserting themselves. The first widespread IQ test in America was published in 1916. Known as the Stanford-Binet, it was the product of Terman's adaptations of Binet's original test. The IQ test, freed of its shackles of limited claims and narrow use, soon went on a monstrous rampage, and Binet was no longer alive and able to cut the test back down to size.

Judge Peckham has written of Terman's claim that "his test could be employed as an objective tool to learn the identity of the 'feebleminded' and 'borderline feebleminded' and hopefully to discourage them from breeding."[3] And where might such kinds of people be found? Well, in 1916, the same year he brought out his IQ test, Terman was ready to declare that "borderline feeble-minded" people "represent the level of intelligence which is very, very common among Spanish-Indian and Mexican families of the Southwest and also among negroes. Their dullness seems to be racial or at least inherent in the family stocks from which they come."[4] A rather remarkable assertion for a man of science to make, especially when based upon tests given in English to populations not always brought up in that language.

Henry Goddard enriched society by coining the term "moron" to label people who scored at the "12-year" level on his IQ tests. Goddard had an intricate classification system for "feeble-minded adults." He would deem certain people as "idiots," others "imbeciles," and still others "morons," according to their scores on the IQ tests.[5] As far as is known, Goddard did not come up with a name for people who were quick to denigrate others based on the flimsy evidence of IQ tests.

An unfettered belief in the ability of IQ tests to label both individuals and entire races as "feeble-minded" for life is scientifically unjustified. This goes double when you realize that some sixty years after Terman's IQ test came out, there is still no agreement on a detailed definition of "intelligence." And Americans of pure "racial or family stocks," if they exist at all, are a tiny subset of our population.

Be that as it may, once Terman brought out his test, once Goddard had established his footing at Ellis Island, once it was clear that these new tests could be used to certain political ends such as limiting immigration and promoting eugenics, the testing genie was out of the bottle. World War I army recruits were subjected to the Army Alpha test which was used to separate the leaders from the cannon fodder. What was the basis for this separation? Well, some of the questions which supposedly sorted out the intrinsically intelligent from the inferior were on the order of asking what city the Dodgers played for, and what company manufactured revolvers.[6] It didn't seem to strike a lot of people back then that one could possibly be ignorant of the answers to those questions and still be intelligent. Or that a formerly unintelligent person could magically become intelligent by talking to a gun owner who liked baseball. After World War I, the IQ tests spread wildly throughout the educational field, somewhat in the manner of crabgrass in an open pasture. Then came the "ability" and "achievement" and "aptitude" tests which are offshoots of the basic IQ test idea. There is an argument as to whether modern tests of this sort are the children, grandchildren, or great-grandchildren of the IQ test. But it is hard to dispute that they are direct descendants, no matter which generation you decide to place them in. As to eugenics, that notion became rather unpopular in this country when Adolf Hitler became associated with the concept in the public mind. You should be clear in your mind that none of the contemporary tests or testers that I know of would have anything to do with the sordid applications initially envisioned for IQ tests by some proponents. By and large they feel they have cleaned up the unsavory aspects of the past, and maybe they are right. But that is no reason to shroud the origin of the IQ test in a fog of forgetfulness.

Of course, the search for the key to human intelligence is not a passion of the twentieth century alone. Probably the earliest recognizable attempt at enlisting science in this quest for a quality as elusive as the alchemist's stone goes back to Britain in the eighteenth century. That was when physical anthropology was all the rage. People who were considered scientists in their day went around claiming that the size and/or shape of your head could explain differences in intelligence among individuals.

The funny thing is that back then the scientists, largely drawn from the ranks of the affluent and privileged, were finding that it was the affluent and privileged who were the most intelligent members of society.[7] Some of these observers based this "impartial" conclusion on research which showed that the skull of a deceased member of the upper class would hold more buckshot than the skull of a deceased member of the lower class. The reasoning was that a greater skull capacity for buckshot meant a greater head volume which meant more room for the brain, and, hence, a superior intellect. The assumptions here were that a large brain was connected to intelligence, and that a large skull was associated with a large brain and not just an empty wilderness. From findings such as this, pressure gradually built to sterilize or prohibit the "inferior" from reproducing their genes in the form of children. Of course, modern science tells us that these notions were and are preposterous, and modern science is right. But shouldn't this history make us very hesitant to leap to any bold conclusions about the perceived shortcomings of people based on today's tests? Will people two hundred years from now look back on our practices with horror, amusement, and outrage?

Something strange has gone on here. Even as the reputation of the IQ test as a measure of fixed, innate, unchanging intelligence has plummeted within the scientific community, the idea of IQ as a valid summary of a person is still widespread. It's hard to get over the assumption that a high IQ score goes hand in glove with being smart and vice versa. We can take to heart statements like Judge Peckham's that "IQ tests, like other ability tests, essentially measure achievement in the skills covered by the examinations."[8] We can realize that the skills covered on the IQ tests can only be a small part of all the things that go into true intelligence, and that even then the tests may be subject to error or bias or misscoring and so forth. But even so, it almost takes a conscious act of will to separate a reported IQ score from our assessment of someone's intelligence. What has happened is that even as the claims for the IQ test have been scaled down, the effects of decades of indoctrination linger.

For example, you may say that if IQ is such a challengeable concept, how is it that geniuses like Beethoven and Newton and

Galileo and Da Vinci all had high IQ's? We all seem to have read at one time or another stories ranking these geniuses of yore in terms of their relative IQ: who was smartest? Well, there's a little hook here. None of these people took an IQ test in their lives. We don't know if they would have gotten high, medium, or low scores if they had been given an IQ test as we know it today. What has happened is that writers have estimated how smart they think these people were based on their work, and then assigned them an IQ score out of the air. But unless you are careful, it is easy to read these stories as supporting the basic precision of IQ scores, as opposed to a retroactive hunch as to what IQ score these acknowledged geniuses might have received had they taken a modern IQ test. Of course, if we followed the example of some who have given the IQ test in America, Newton would clearly have registered the highest IQ score in a group with Beethoven and Galileo and Da Vinci. Why is that so clear? Only because Newton is the sole native English speaker of the bunch, and the IQ test would be given in English. Perhaps that test would even "reveal" how shockingly overrated the other three had been.

Nonetheless, there is a common feeling that IQ tests do measure intelligence and that this measurement is precise and fixed. The tenacity of this belief brings to mind the following discussion between Alice and the Queen in *Through the Looking-Glass:*

> "There's no use trying," she said: "one *can't* believe impossible things."
>
> "I daresay you haven't had much practice," said the Queen. "When I was your age, I always did it for half-an-hour a day. Why, sometimes I've believed as many as six impossible things before breakfast."

The Queen doesn't go on to specify whether she practiced believing that it is possible in a matter of a few hours to pinpoint scientifically something as grand and elusive as human intelligence. All that the responsible publishers of IQ tests even claim for their product is that it reflects a person's ability on some specific skills at a specific time. One official of the company which publishes

the Stanford-Binet IQ test (which has become much more sophisticated in the sixty-plus years since its introduction) put the idea
to rest that IQ tests are eternal in their results. This official was
quoted in testimony as follows: "It is safe to say that . . . no
one in aptitude testing today believes that intelligence tests
measure innate capacity."[9]

What does an IQ score mean anyway? Well, an IQ score is
supposed to be an indication of your ability at certain tasks relative to all other persons of your age. IQ scores are built on normal curves such as we discussed earlier, but this time the mean
(or average) score is set at 100, and the standard deviation is
15. So, if your IQ score is 100, in theory you are average for your
age. An IQ score under 100 is considered below average for an
age group, while a score above 100 is thought of as above average. With the standard deviation of 15 points, we know that
about two-thirds of all people will have IQ scores that are above
85 and below 115 (that is, within 15 points, plus or minus, of
100). Some 95 percent of people will have scores that are within
two standard deviations of the average, which is to say greater
than 70 and less than 130. Over 99 percent of test-takers are expected to be within three standard deviations, or between 55
and 145 on their IQ score. Now this is all very interesting, and
the IQ score can be of some value for diagnostic and other purposes when kept in perspective. But there is also something
buried in what I have just told you that is a dead giveaway that
an IQ score is by no means the same as pure intelligence. Did
you spot it?

The catch is this: since IQ scores are computed on the basis
of your age group, they may tell you something, however limited, about your standing relative to your peers. But you can't
equate that score to what your intellectual ranking would be
among all adults or children.[10] Look at it this way. A five-year-old
child can be sharp as a whip and do tremendously well on the test
questions asked of him. Let's say for his efforts he pulls down a
135 as his score on the IQ test. Let's say further that this particular score is relatively accurate in terms of the child's real
abilities on the skills tested, and wasn't distorted by testing error
or bias or any of the other problems we've run into with standardized tests. Now let's say the child's thirty-three-year-old

mother also took the test, and also got a more or less "true" score in the high range, but a 125. Who is more intelligent, the child or the mother? If you're tempted to choose the child with the 135 IQ over the mother with the 125, think again. The mother has twenty-eight years more experience than the child; she is familiar with many aspects of life that the child has not even begun to dream of. So the comparison would be ludicrous if it weren't for those three-digit IQ numbers. IQ tests don't even begin to tell us if someone can drive a car, read great works of literature, balance a checkbook, display social and emotional maturity, and survive if left to their own resources. The most these IQ numbers say is that the child may be more advanced *for his age* in certain skills than the mother is for her age group. But it is not possible to rate child against parent by a straight comparison of scores. A five-year-old is just not more "intelligent" in any common meaning of the word than a thirty-three-year-old woman, even if she were way below average intelligence for her age.

Why, then, is it that the IQ test can have such a great impact on people? The answer comes in three parts. First, the IQ test does have some positive value, and this is the foundation of support which keeps it in use. Second, for a number of reasons, there are many people who want the IQ test to be able to perform the magical feat of a quick and accurate peek into people's brains. Many of these reasons are perfectly understandable. If IQ tests could really do all the things people want them to do, then the burden of difficult personal judgments would be relieved. To some extent, as Walter Lippmann wrote years ago, complete reliance on IQ scores is a "conclusion planted by the will to believe."[11] Third, the magic of numbers is well-nigh irresistible. Compare two statements that may be equally valid (or invalid) assessments of a child's abilities. "Charles seems to have a little better than average talent in reading, at least for his grade level." "Charles has been tested and has an IQ of 110." Even when you know the limits to IQ tests, it is tough to keep from giving the latter statement more credence than the former. Listen to the testimony of a former school official in California: "There is a magic, I think, involved with the IQ test that has been trained into us in our schools of education, whether we be regular educators or special educators and I think we seem to see that as some sort of a final, solid piece of data that we can use to make judgments."[12] The problem is that this apparently solid piece of data has the power to overwhelm common sense and become the sole information used in evaluating an individual instead of just one of many.

The IQ test has been shown to be correlated with various measures of success in a variety of reports. Yet we know that correlation does not necessarily mean causation. It could be that IQ scores are really reflecting the importance of some other factors. For example, in discussing intelligence tests, David McClelland has written: "Certainly they are valid for predicting who will get ahead in a number of prestige jobs where credentials are important. So is white skin: it too is a valid predictor of job success in prestige jobs. But no one would argue that white skin per se is an ability factor."[13] One of our national goals is that education and opportunity be made available to people on the basis of merit and not on the basis of human prejudices. A theory called Social Darwinism, which used to be in vogue, held that the people at the top of society are there because they have earned their places through talent and hard work, while the less fortunate (at least materially) have earned their position through inability and indolence. But nonetheless we can look at society and see many bright, hard-working poor people and others who are lazy and slow and rich. It may be self-satisfying for those on top to say those on the bottom are there because they have low IQs and couldn't work their way up, but it is far from justifiable as a blanket claim.

If "intelligence" as measured by IQ tests were the sole determinant of success in our society, then we would expect that the children of the poor who get high IQ scores would be more likely to get the higher education which is often a gateway to economic progress than the children of the rich who get low IQ scores. But McClelland has written, "It appears to be no more likely for the bright children (high IQ) from the lower classes to go to college (despite their high aptitude for it) than for the 'stupid' children from the upper classes. Why is this? . . . now we have an alternative explanation of college-going—namely, socioeconomic status which seems to be as good a predictor of this type of success as ability."[14] Even to the extent that the IQ test score can be shown to be correlated with certain types of later success, we must be very careful not to leap to the conclusion that the high IQ score "caused" the later success. It could be that IQ tests have the tendency to pick up the signals sent off by children who have been exposed to affluent environments. What is registering on the IQ screen then may be qualities connected as much with wealth as "intelligence." If this is so, it would be difficult to prove that it was a child's own qualities of intelligence, and not the wealthy background, which "caused" success. In a way that would be like saying that because signals bounce off an airplane and show up as blips on a radar screen that it is the blips on the screen which "cause" the plane to fly.

Sometimes a kind of circular reasoning is used to bolster the position of standardized tests such as the IQ test. The logic would go something like this: high IQ scores tend to be related to high reading test scores which can be followed by high SAT scores, and so forth. This tendency has been noted and has a certain appeal. But the thing to remember is that most of these standardized tests are as closely related to each other as macaroni shells are to spaghetti noodles. The tests may come in different shapes and forms, but by and large they are made of the same elements, and they tend to test the same types of mental gymnastics. If you do well on one form of standardized test, you might be expected to perform highly on most other forms of standardized tests. This is by no means proof that you're extraordinarily bright or dim, but rather reflects whether you have mastered one very specialized kind of behavior. The idea is much the same as the fact that someone who's skilled at solving crossword puzzles is likely to be a good Scrabble player, or that a tennis pro could put up a respectable fight the first time out on a racquetball court. But this doesn't mean the crossword puzzle buff will take to chess or that the tennis star won't be a lousy bowler. In other words, as Lippmann wrote, "The fact that the same people always do well with puzzles would in itself be no evidence that the solving of puzzles was a general test of intelligence."[15]

We might have more confidence that we were getting a fair picture of intelligence if we gave a variety of tests instead of constantly repeating the paper-and-pencil multiple-choice tests. If intelligence is the ability to adapt to surroundings and to learn from experience, we might ask youngsters to take some IQ tests or equivalents, but we could also insist that the person demonstrate an ability to get around on the New York subway system, and to write an essay on what the economics of inflation means for financial planning, and to show survival skills on a program patterned after the Outward Bound model. Mastery of this wider range of skills is surely preferable to an exclusive preoccupation with the important but not all-important skills that standardized tests attempt to measure. You may object that we already have a range of standardized tests in the ability (or aptitude) tests and the achievement tests. The names of these two different kinds of standardized tests make it sound as though far different things were being measured. But this is misleading. All standardized tests are achievement tests, because they can measure only what you have learned prior to taking the test.

An achievement test sounds as though it is designed to reveal what you have achieved so far, while an ability test (or aptitude test as it is sometimes called) sounds as if it will show your future potential to learn regardless of your present level of achievement. In fact, both kinds of tests measure, or try to measure, achievement levels. The difference is that ability tests then attempt to predict what this level of current achievement means for your future propects for achievement. Judah Schwartz, a professor at MIT and testing expert, has written, "The notion that one can construct an ability test that will not be influenced by the child's experience is not a thoughtful notion. . . . The ability-achievement distinction is one that, in practice, cannot be made. . . . Group achievement tests and group ability tests are sufficiently similar that, without labels, one has difficulty telling which is which. If these group ability tests are used to predict, and group achievement tests are used to confirm these predictions, why should anyone be surprised?"[16] The crystal ball of standardized tests does not really show the future; when it is working, it may give a clearer view of the past. This is then used as a trend to project into the coming years. But notice what this means. A change in your achievement levels may have great repercussions on your measured ability forecasts. If you are a poor reader, most standardized aptitude tests will jump to the conclusion that you have low ability to learn whatever subject is being examined.

That may be true, of course, but it may be you are just a poor reader. If you were to improve your reading skills, your ability test result might jump as well. What seemed like a steady assertion about what you can—or cannot—do in the future turns out to be a changeable omen based largely on what you have done in the past.

According to Arthur Laughland, "No people on the face of the earth have been bitten quite as hard by the testing bug as the American people."[17] What is it about the standardized tests, and the way we think about them, that has made us so susceptible to the testing bug? One student who talked to Thomas Cottle, an education writer, had a theory. He said, "You got to have money and you got to have IQ points and PSAT points and SAT points. Americans love numbers, and quantities. . . . Inches, pounds, dollars, points on tests, that's all anybody cares about—even the minority students in our school. Nobody asks them whether they're happy. All people want to know is whether their achievement scores have gone up, or how many points they scored in a basketball game."[18] It's true that numbers are big in our society. They make it seem easier to describe a person's performance, whether in school or on the basketball court. But they can never be a substitute for judgment. Just as the highest scorer in a basketball game is not necessarily the most valuable player to a team, so the highest IQ scorer is not necessarily the person who will contribute most to society in the intellectual realm. But there is much more to the testing movement than just an American preference for numbers over some more complicated forms of assessment.

There are some idealistic reasons for using standardized tests. In theory, these tests are supposed to be more accurate and less biased than personal judgments by individuals. There is a genuine desire to get away from inequitable selection systems. Ironically and sadly, the standardized tests have been able to avoid old problems only at the price of creating new sources of unfairness. We have seen how various biases and scoring errors can creep into these tests and sap their capacity for treating all test-takers fairly. What's more, at the same time that schools and employers have turned to standardized tests for some praiseworthy reasons, they have also resorted to these tests for less laudable motives. Standardized tests are inexpensive compared to more thorough methods of evaluating candidates. And the tests can serve as lightning rods for criticism of schools or employers. Instead of being called to account for the reasoning used concerning a particular applicant, the decision maker can lay all the blame on the tests. Tests pose the temptation for officials to shirk their responsibilities on the hard cases, and at the same time provide a convenient scapegoat for any objection to decisions made on their say-so.

Not surprisingly, many of the institutions which rely most heavily on these tests in making their decisions can be found in the ranks of the staunchest defenders of standardized testing. Paul Jacobs, director of test development at Thomas Edison College in N.J., testified that, "Historically, the use of standardized testing in college admissions developed to ease the burden of colleges in selecting new students. From a college's point of view, the system works. A college can, for example, require its applicants to take the SAT exam, and in this way the college obtains comparable scores on all applicants at no charge to itself. But the present system lacks responsibility and accountability to the students themselves, the very people who are paying for the service."[19] Even though it is the students who are paying the tab, they have precious little say about how the tests are administered, interpreted, or designed. By a strange quirk, the use of these tests with all their imperfections can confer a certain status on the organizations which depend on them. Instead of using their own fallible judgment, now there is a "scientific tool" which will do all the work.

This particular attitude thrives whenever the people depending on the tests are not particularly knowledgeable about them. Oscar Buros has written: "If these test users were better informed regarding the merits and limitations of their testing instruments, they would probably be less happy and successful in their work. The test user who has faith—however unjustified—can speak with confidence in interpreting test results and in making recommendations. The well-informed test user cannot do this; he knows that the best of our tests are still highly fallible instruments which are extremely difficult to interpret with assurance in individual cases. Consequently, he must interpret test results cautiously and with so many reservations that others wonder whether he really knows what he is talking about."[20] It is a cruel irony that the more sophisticated test user can be made to look less skilled than an unquestioning follower of the tests. Buros also wrote that even the most careful of the test users can fall into new traps when they run from one standardized test to another. "Even the better informed test users who finally become convinced that a widely used test has no validity after all are likely to rush to use a new instrument which promises far more than any good test can deliver. Counselors, personnel directors, psychologists, and school administrators seem to have an unshakable will to believe the exaggerated claims of test authors and publishers."[21]

On top of this, standardized tests have been helped to multiply by explicit testing requirements that have been written into various laws authorizing federal and state support for education. The legislators who vote for these programs have often turned to standardized tests to provide a measure of whether the programs are working. The desirability of program accountability is beyond dispute. Unfortunately, the ability of standardized tests by themselves to tell us whether a program is deserving of our tax dollars is very much open to question. Here's what often happens with this type of legislation. Sponsors and supporters of a bill will have different goals in mind when they think about the results they'd like to see from legislation. As the bill moves toward becoming law, various compromises in language and structure paper over the cracks in the wall of support behind it. Many provisions are purposely left ambiguous to head off potential conflicts among legislators who intend to vote for the bill. Everyone agrees, of course, that the program should have to prove its worth in practice, but the exact definition of satisfactory progress, and how it will be measured, are only vaguely indicated at best. The bill then becomes law, and one day someone charged with administering the law sits down to determine how program performance will be measured. Whenever a standardized test is chosen, or required by law, the crucial question is still to be resolved, namely how the test will be written and given. Unless the test perfectly matches the full scope of the program, these decisions will affect the public perception of the worth of the program,

Along the way, something subtle yet disturbing has taken place. The responsibility for deciding whether a particular program is working, whether a given method of dealing with educational problems will be continued or discarded, has slipped out of the hands of our elected representatives. What's more, unless the educational bureaucracy is extremely diligent, that power will end up in the hands of the people who write the tests and interpret the results. Testers who had no part in the passage of the law may be called on to determine retroactively what the goals of that legislation were. Then they use their tests to show "scientifically" whether the goals, which they themselves may have defined, are being achieved. This is not necessarily the fault of the testers: if Congress and the executive departments pass the buck on setting performance standards, someone's going to latch on to it. The dirty little secret is this: the decision of what aspects of a program to test, and how to test them, is a matter of policy, not sheer science. Testers will acknowledge this in scholarly papers and conferences, but the message has not gotten to our legislators. It is irresponsible to pass a law calling for program evaluation without coming to grips with how that program should be evaluated and what level of performance is adequate. Testers will make up their own standards if none are provided for them, and this will usually lead to measuring the things that are easiest to test, not necessarily what is most important. The outcome may be an oversimplified representation of reality. The fate of the program, and of the people being served by it, will hang in the balance. To voluntarily surrender this power of making or breaking laws to testers on the basis of their institutional prestige is a mistake.

The fact is that the very same program can be rated as a success or a failure according to the questions that are asked in its evaluation. For example, a program might be established to help children of impoverished families to learn to read better. If you ask about results, you may find that the average reading level (however defined) of poor children in the program has gone up, so the program looks like a success. But you might also find that the average reading of affluent children in the same area has gone up as much for a number of different reasons. If your goal was a program that would close the gap in reading abilities between the two groups, the program looks like a disappointment. Different approaches to program evaluation may be warranted in different situations. But in view of the great impact these different approaches can have on future programs, the public should have a say in the process. When the decisions about testing methodology are made behind the closed doors of the testers, the public can be shut out. Certainly the testers should be expected to use their expertise once the decision has been made on what we really want to see measured. But testers should not be allowed to tailor our views of what is important to fit their particular preferences for ease of measurement. Look at it another way. It is at least as important that we ask the right questions in evaluating programs, or individuals, as it is for those programs or individuals to come up with the right answers. If we yield to the tendency of standardized tests to depend on paper-and-pencil exercises over real life competency, disasters can result.

All of this runs against the notion of a meritocracy in America. Under a truly meritocratic system, people would be evaluated on the basis of who best met the requirements of a job or the demands of an educational institution. Everything else would be extraneous—race, sex, religion, family background, and friends in high places would have no part in hiring or admissions decisions. Standardized tests were heralded as agents of the meritocracy. Yet these tests do not live up to the role expected of them when they inadvertently incorporate some of the flaws in the old system of selection. As James Fallows has written, the close correlations between family incomes and scores on some standardized tests "strongly suggest that what the tests measure is exposure to upper middle class culture—perhaps even the culture of the professional class of the east coast."[22] A meritocracy is supposed to get away from influences such as class and inherited wealth. To the extent that tests incorporate these factors, they can hardly advance the meritocratic ideal. Of course, it is true that a child of the affluent is likely to be a better reader by the tenth grade than a child of the poor, if only as a consequence of better schools along the way. But can we really feel comfortable about using tests to pick up this discrepancy in opportunity and then using that finding to label the poor child as unworthy to compete in further educational contests? Would we be willing to make our children wear weights in a race and then calmly abide by the results when their futures were at stake? Fallows writes: "For all its other claims, the testing industry finally rests its defense on 'equity.' . . . But it is impossible to ignore the evidence that, in most instances, the tests simply ratify earlier advantage—that, as engines of mobility, they have sputtered and died."[23]

In some ways this has given rise to a worst-of-both-worlds situation. We profess to use a meritocratic system, so the "losers" in our schools and businesses must bear the stigma of being incompetents rather than people who didn't have an even chance at the start; while the standardized tests, those prime tools of the meritocracy, give us results that in many instances look suspiciously like those generated by a system of selection by privilege. In the words of James Fallows in the *Washington Monthly*, "The fairness of the meritocracy today . . . is a phony. We deal from a stacked deck, and then treat the losers as if they had misplayed a full hand."[24] If standardized tests are thought of as the dealers in the game, an eagle-eyed observer would spot them giving most of the high cards to the favored of society. Even worse, that observer could see that the tests weren't always dealing from the entire deck of skills related to jobs or schooling, but instead had picked a few familiar cards and skills to recycle constantly. We'd question a card game that left out kings, jacks, tens, sevens, sixes, fives, and threes, but somehow standardized tests can cut character traits and sophisticated intellectual skills from the deck and continue to operate. Fallows writes, "Even the professions themselves realize that there is more to life than answering multiple-choice exam questions. Those who get into medical schools are largely the ones who are good at taking tests, but those who end up leading the professions—or becoming chief executives in business, or excelling in government or law or academics—are the ones who possess a mixture of the other, untestable qualities, too."[25] It is fair to ask if any system which devalues the worth of these intangibles, and the harder-to-measure scholarly skills such as research and writing, can truly be called meritocratic.

Standardized tests have been exalted to the point where they are likely to reverse the outcome of the race between the tortoise and the hare. Fallows thinks the hare would win today, "because, in our version of the meritocracy, the competition is over before it really begins. Our system is one in which people's 'merit' is judged quite early on, using standards of dubious accuracy that emphasize inequalities of rearing and birth; and then people are channeled on to their fated designations, with few real tests of performance to distract them as they go. The first step is the aptitude test, given in the grade school years. The test may be arbitrary, it may measure the household vocabulary of the child's parents better than it measures anything else, but on the basis of the results, the children with 'promise' are placed on a different academic track from the rest, the better for their own abilities to be developed. . . . The tracks . . . become self-fulfilling systems, making it as difficult for those on the upper level to fall as for those on the lower level to rise."[26] If you get off to a fast start with the tests, you're likely to have your lead protected rather than be subject to challenge down the road. That's not what a meritocracy is supposed to be about, especially when the fast start is based on family circumstances to a significant extent. Mark Twain wrote a poignant story about a gathering in heaven of all the most capable human beings who ever lived.[27] Their names were unfamiliar because they were the people who never received a fair shake in life and could receive the recognition that was their due only after moving on from earth. If Twain were writing today, he'd surely include some poor standardized test-takers among his gathering.

The trend toward selecting the likely winners at the start of the race, and then working to see that they do win, is not limited to the worlds of education and business. The realm of amateur sports seems to be embracing this practice as well. I have a friend who is an Olympic-class rower. When he first took up the sport over seven years ago, physiological testing on hereditary traits such as maximum oxygen intake was not a big part of the program at his college. But now these tests of "potential" are all the rage. When my friend is tested in the lab, he doesn't score well on several of the physiological factors supposedly vital to success at rowing. When he is tested on the water in competition, he is rarely beaten, even by those who outperform him in the lab. My friend might be compared to "overachievers" in school; his performance makes liars of his tests. He told me that if he had been subjected to all these medical tests when he was just starting to row, if he had been informed that he was genetically "unsuited" for rowing, he wouldn't have known enough to fight that judgment but would have quietly switched to a different sport. That would have been a waste both of his talent and of the potential of the American Olympic rowing program. Overreliance on tests in sports, as in other fields, could lead to overlooking completely those with few of the talents recognizable by standardized tests, but great talents for winning at what they set out to do. Someone may object that this is how the East Germans pick their Olympic athletes, and they do very well indeed. But the East German system misses out on individuals like my friend. It also narrows participation by those not deemed to be biologically "fit." At least in education, our national goal has been to try to teach all children rather than to pick a small elite at the start and concentrate all our resources on them. We used to sneer at those European systems which restricted educational opportunities to a few, believing we were better off if education were provided to all who could benefit from it. Are we now ready to follow the lead of a country like East Germany by preselecting our athletes and scholars, reducing the flexibility to accommodate late bloomers and squeezing out those who don't test well?

Let's move on and look at the way tests affect various minority groups through cultural biases, through decisions such as the Bakke case, and through the increased use of minimum competency testing in our high schools.

CHAPTER ELEVEN

Bias, Bakke, and Minimum Competency

Just what does "test bias" mean? The phrase is really shorthand for two kinds of situations. The first instance of test bias takes place when the skills measured by a test differ significantly from the skills actually needed at school or on a job. This lack of fit can occur either because the test includes items that are not relevant, or because the test fails to include items that are relevant. In that sense the test is biased because it is skewed toward a combination of abilities very different from the set of talents directly related to performance. Test results will favor those who are strong in the tested skills at the expense of those who are strong in real life achievement. For example, say we gave a standardized test to license accountants. If all the questions on the test dealt with the history of opera, and none of them asked about interest rates, we'd have a biased test. An abysmal prospective accountant could pass that test because he was an opera buff, while a mathematically gifted test-taker could fail because she couldn't tell an opera from a barbershop quartet. This kind of test could lead to admitting people with no feel for numbers into the accounting field, while keeping many talented individuals off the books.

The second type of test bias takes place when the test scores are influenced by irrelevant characteristics of the test-taker such as race, sex, family wealth, religion, and so forth. In these cases, test-takers get sorted by which group they belong to as opposed to their relative capabilities. Since standardized tests must often resort to measuring surrogates for skill instead of the desired skill itself, whenever the surrogates selected reveal exposure more than aptitude, then the validity of the test is in jeopardy. How can this happen? The heavy reliance on vocabulary questions on many standardized tests is a case on point. Vocabulary is assumed to be a surrogate for verbal ability. There is some correlation, but a knowledge of the definition of every single word in the dictionary is not the same as an ability to use words properly and effectively in communicating. Some people do possess both an extensive vocabulary and a gift for expression. But we all know people who use eight syllables when two will do and generally manage to mangle English both in writing and speaking. We also know people whose vocabulary is much less diverse, yet who demonstrate a mastery of the language in the clarity of their speech and the precision of their writing. While we may feel that the latter group has a greater command of English, the former will tend to score higher on standardized tests. When acquisition of specific words to your vocabulary is a function of class and race as much as intelligence, we run into an example of the second form of test bias.

This kind of test bias is often called "cultural bias," which is another way of saying that test scores may feed back information about your cultural background instead of your ability. Professor James Loewen addressed this topic in testimony to Congress. He referred to the pattern of lower scores received by members of minority groups and residents of rural areas on some tests: "Items based on words like Thucydides, Herodotus, chianti, argentum, Hera, ambergris, Cather, cuneiform, Runnymede, minotaur, and Latinate test exposure, not aptitude, and America's residential and cultural segregation limits the exposure of minorities and rural children to this kind of information."[1] The main idea here is that standardized tests have less trouble measuring some forms of ability among those with similar upbringings than they do with rating people from very different upbringings. Test publishers have tried to eliminate cultural biases from their tests, but that is no mean task. These biases may be largely hidden from sight, like an iceberg, but they can tear gaping holes in test validity nonetheless. We're not dealing with anything so blatant as asking different questions of different test-takers in order to rig the outcome. That would be easy to spot and stop.

Yet even when the tests ask everyone the same question it does not automatically follow that one group is not being given an unfair advantage over another. For example, if the word "environment" is used on a standardized test, that would not strike you off the bat as giving rise to problems of cultural bias. Environment is a fairly common word which we would expect most people to know and understand. Look at what can happen on a standardized test, though, when the test-taker cannot defend his choice from the given alternatives. Complete this analogy:

> Forest is to tree as environment is to _____.
>   (a) wildlife sanctuary
>   (b) family member
>   (c) ancient Egypt
>   (d) batting average

What did you choose? You probably picked (a) by reasoning that just as a tree is part of the forest which surrounds it, so a wildlife sanctuary is part of the environment which surrounds it.

That's a fine answer, splendid logic, and congratulations. I know that somebody is going to figure out why (c) or (d) could work, but offhand they don't seem to fit the analogy and I wrote them for that purpose. But look a little more closely at (b). That works just as well as (a) when you think about it. "Environment" is defined as "something that surrounds" and this need not refer to the great outdoors. Just as a tree is part of the forest which surrounds it, so a family member is part of the environment which surrounds him. Your choice between (a) and (b) depends on the clues you picked up about what the word "environment" was meant to mean in this context. Are you a "smarter" person for picking (a) over (b) or vice versa? Clearly not. But since this is a standardized test, there is only one "right" answer allowed, and you will be marked according to how the test writer thinks about these words.

The reason this can be a problem, apart from the essential arbitrariness of the selection, is that there are some indications that a test-taker's choice of (a) or (b) may fall along racial lines. Professor Loewen told of an experiment which suggested words have different primary meanings in the white and black communities even when we are not talking about various kinds of slang. This particular study showed blacks tended to think of "environment" in terms of people and home, while whites associated the word with open air and the earth.[2] Loewen explained, "Neither usage is wrong; blacks are centering on the social environment while whites center on the natural environment. Obviously, any syllogism, antonym, or other verbal ability item that used 'environment' would *have* to be slanted, purposefully or accidentally, against one race or the other."[3] Unless you were previously familiar with these varying response patterns, this analogy would appear entirely innocuous.

These are subtle concerns, perhaps, but they can have profound consequences when the same kinds of cultural bias are found in many questions on a given test. One of the side effects of cultural bias is called differential validity. Differential validity means that the test does a better job predicting performance for some groups than for other groups. Judge Peckham cited two studies of the relation of IQ scores to grades. The studies found a correlation (known as the r value) of IQ scores to grades for white children of .25 in one case and .46 in the other. Those are low r figures to start with. But the r values for the same test for blacks were even smaller: .14 and .20 in the two instances.[4] In other words, to the limited extent these tests were able to predict, they did a better job on white children than black children. Judge Peckham wrote, "Differential validity means that more errors will be made for black children than whites, and that is unacceptable."[5]

This form of cultural bias, differential validity, is unacceptable, because it evokes images of the bad old days when it was fashionable to allege that some racial and ethnic groups were hereditarily superior in intelligence to other groups. Test bias is unacceptable because it allows standardized tests by themselves to define "intelligence" or "ability." We have seen over and over again that the skills measured on a test are but a small fraction of the range of skills which constitute intelligence and ability. To equate all mental ability with test scores for the sake of convenience is neither scientific nor justifiable. We should have learned our lesson about these kinds of comparisons back in the 1920s after the attempts to portray immigrants as "feeble-minded." Back then all sorts of studies came out that "showed" the intelligence of those who wanted in to be defective. The average IQ score for Italian immigrants in one study was 16 points below the average for the entire country, a difference approximately equal to the reported gap on IQ scores between black and white Americans today. Princeton Psychology Professor Leon Kamin has written, "We see today that the psychologists who provided 'expert' and 'scientific' teaching relevant to the immigration debate did so on the basis of pitifully inadequate data. There is probably no living psychologist who would view the World War I army data as relevant to the heritable IQ of European 'races.' . . . There is probably no psychometrician today prepared to assert that that 16-point deficit was produced by inferior Italian IQ genes. That does not prevent the same mental testers from pointing gravely to the possible genetic significance of Professor Jensen's recent survey of the contemporary IQ literature. . . . This kind of finding, like Goddard's earlier report that 83 percent of Jewish immigrants were feebleminded, cannot be ignored by thoughtful citizens."[6]

I don't know what proportion of intelligence is inherited and how much is a response to environmental factors, but I'm certainly not about to jump to any conclusions on the basis of the flimsy and fallible figures supplied by standardized tests. About the only thing we can say with complete confidence regarding human heredity is that having children is hereditary—if your parents didn't have any children, you won't have any either. Beyond that we are treading on definitional quicksand. Does the currently lower average IQ score of blacks mean they are less intelligent as a group? That's a very dubious proposition. Did the lower IQ scores for the immigrants in the early part of this century mean they were less intelligent? Do indications that people of Oriental ancestry score higher on IQ tests than whites mean that whites are less intelligent? I think not. What's more, we've seen how changeable these IQ scores can be over time. If new IQ tests were to "prove" tomorrow that blacks are more intelligent than whites, what would that mean for individuals of each race?

Wouldn't we still be committed to equality under the law, or would the new motto be, "one more-intelligent-than-average person, one vote?" There is a range of intelligence in any group. Whether or not your basic assumptions about a group's average intelligence are correct, you can't just look at a person's skin color and predict his intelligence.

These kinds of comparisons of "racial intelligence" continue even though, in Judge Peckham's words, "The rather weak evidence on the record in support of the genetic explanation tends to rest on the disparities in IQ scores, which obviously overlooks any possible bias on the tests themselves."[7] And just what are the possible sources of bias on standardized tests? Some of these sources have already been discussed, but drawing on the work of Professor Sylvia Johnson of Howard University, let's take a quick jog through the bias neighborhood.[8]

First, bias may be built in by the test publishers' decisions regarding the content of test items, the test format, the response variable, the standardization group, and the item analysis techniques. Bias may also be imported into the test because of differences among test-takers. Significant differences in school experience, in prior test exposure and coaching, in motivation, in previous racial discrimination, and in family background can all affect test scores. Third, the circumstances involved in taking the test can lend bias to the results—characteristics and expectations of the tester as well as the physical environment may all affect test performance. Finally, the abuse of test scores through over-reliance and misinterpretation can contribute to test bias. In short, there are many openings for bias to slip into a standardized test. Constant vigilance is required to seal off as many ports of entry as possible, but the prospects of a total blockade of test bias are remote at best.

Consider the way IQ tests have historically been open to bias against blacks. For example, when the Stanford-Binet IQ test was first standardized on a group of test-takers in 1916, that group contained a grand total of exactly zero blacks.[9] Remember that for a standardization group to be most valuable it must be representative of the entire population of test-takers. A standardization group totally devoid of black test-takers hardly fits the bill. Not until 1972 was this particular test restandardized on a group that included significant numbers of blacks.[10] I do not mean to imply that the Stanford-Binet is worse in this regard than competing IQ tests—indeed it may be better—but its visibility and longevity make the point worth noting. What's more, this problem is not automatically rectified by adding blacks to the standardization group, as Judge Peckham makes clear: "The [IQ] tests were standardized and developed on an all-white population, and naturally their scientific validity is questionable for culturally different groups. Black children's intelligence may be manifested in ways that the tests do not show, so that the existing tests developed on the white population obviously would be inadequate. Testing organizations did become sensitive to the absence of minority children in the standardizing samples. . . . The problem with these efforts is that . . . mixing the populations . . . does not eliminate any preexisting bias. If the tests were inappropriate before, and, as the testimony indicated, the test items were not changed significantly after the mixing, the tests would remain inappropriate."[11]

Professor Loewen has written a standardized test to give people a feel for what it could be like to take a test that is dominated by different cultures. This "Loewen Low Aptitude Test" is an offspring of the "BITCH" test (Black Intelligence Test of Cultural Homogeneity) written by Professor Robert Williams. Here is a portion of the Loewen Test.[12]

> *Directions:* Answer every question. Do your best in the time allotted, for your entire future is at stake.

> *Analogies Test*
> 1. Spline is to mitre as _____ is to _____.
>   a) Love . . . marriage
>   b) Straw . . . mud
>   c) Key . . . lock
>   d) Bond . . . bail
>   e) Bond . . . paper
>
> 2. _____ is to sake as opera is to _____.
>   a) Pete's . . . many
>   b) Hit . . . run
>   c) Swordplay . . . chianti

    d) Attend . . . forego
    e) Her . . . star

Verbal Aptitude and Reasoning Test
3. Saturday Ajax got an LD.
    a) He had smoked too much grass
    b) He tripped out on drugs
    c) He brought her to his apartment
    d) He showed it off to his fox
    e) He became "wised up" (less dense)

4. Which of these situations is least congruous?
    a) An Eames in the dining room
    b) A Chippendale in the dining room
    c) An Eames in the living room
    d) A Chippendale in the living room
    e) All of the above

You may have noticed these questions seemed biased in favor of different groups. James Fallows has explained that question 1 is "biased toward the working class, toward students whose 'exposure' would have taught them that a spline is a small piece of wood inserted to keep a mortise joint tight. From there, reasoning takes over—spline adds strength to a mitre as straw adds strength to mud. (If you chose 'love . . . marriage,' you have not grasped the concept of the 'best' answer. . . . Here, any SAT veteran should recognize 'straw . . . mud' as the 'best' because, like 'spline . . . mitre,' it is tangible, not abstract.)"[18] Your guess is as good as mine on questions 2 and 4, although I think (c) is the correct answer to 2 if swordplay and sake are both thought of as culturally linked to Japan while opera and chianti have the same kind of link to Italy. The answer to question 3 is (d), which follows if the slang term "LD" for an Eldorado car is part of your vocabulary. As to question 4, while I know the cartoon characters Chip and Dale would not be congruous anywhere in a house, the rest is lost to me.

Although it might be fun to play around with these questions now, think about how you'd feel if your entire future did depend on answering questions that came from a different cultural background and did not seem to bear any direct relation to skills necessary for college or employment. How frequently do questions which reflect cultural biases get asked on standardized tests? It's hard to say for sure, unless you want to take the publishers' word for it that they've virtually eliminated the problem. The reason for this uncertainty is that the publishers hide many of their tests and test questions from free access by the public and identified critics. David White testified about some questions he had heard were on standardized tests based on reports from friends who had taken the tests. White criticized the reported questions for cultural bias, but added, ". . . the serious question I have is these are rumors. They're only things that people tell me. I don't even know if those questions are on the test. What position am I in? I have a B.A. in English. I'm a lawyer. I have to go to a testing company and have them make a unilateral unreviewable decision as to whether or not I am an expert in the testing field, and because of the biases that I seem to exhibit about standardized testing . . . I might fail that test."[14]

White is not the only person who has been frustrated by the wall of secrecy that has been built around standardized tests. Edwin Taylor wrote about another instance of test secrecy prevailing over the interests of public discussion. According to Taylor, "Three students in a graduate school of education take a national standardized test for elementary school principals. They are horrified by many of the questions, which they think are ambiguous, poorly phrased, implicitly racist, and inappropriate in content for certification of elementary school principals. The students write an article about this test for a national magazine, quoting twelve test questions from a copy obtained for them by the editor of the magazine. Before publication they send the article to the company that developed the test. The company threatens to sue the editor if the article is published since, they say, he violated an agreement of secrecy entered into when the test was sent to him. The article is not published."[15] Concerns about cultural bias are not going to be relieved if publishers of the tests insist on the privilege of choosing who will be allowed to review the content of these tests. It would not be inconsistent with human nature if at least some test publishers restricted access to "experts" who share a cultural predisposition in favor of the tests while giving a cold shoulder to those ruffians whose cultural background leads them to a tendency to criticize the tests.

Some of the most startling testimony on test bias was given at a hearing in the New York legislature in May 1979 concerning the Truth-in-Testing law which was enacted later that year. Dr. David Perham of the Admissions Department at Colgate University testified against the proposed bill, saying, ". . . the bill in front of us might very well harm the matching system that goes on in the admissions process."[16] What was surprising was that when he was discussing the SAT, Dr. Perham said, "In terms of the bias of the test, we all recognize that the test is biased. Sensitive admissions officers know that and make adjustments for it in terms of people's backgrounds and that's not just minority students but, of course, it would be foreign students, students of unusual backgrounds as well."[17] This is a remarkable position to take when you're opposed to test disclosure. Mary Ann McLean, a tenacious aide to New York State Senator Kenneth LaValle, a principle supporter of the bill, questioned Dr. Perham on this point.

> MS. MCLEAN: You made an interesting note about the seeming obviousness of the cultural bias in the test and that you make an adjustment for that.
>
> You contract for this service. Don't you feel some right to have the test constructed in such a manner that you don't have to make adjustments?
>
> DR. PERHAM: Well, they're trying to do that.
>
> MS. MCLEAN: Who is?
>
> DR. PERHAM: The College Board, ETS. They're aware of the fact that—that minority students, disadvantaged students have a hard time scoring high on that examination. I mean that's no secret so they, from my knowledge, they are working on it in the sense that they're trying to develop new kinds of examinations which might be more relevant to that kind of background. Now, someone from those organizations might speak to that point.
>
> MS. MCLEAN: They haven't made the statement that they believe they're culturally biased, but they may, in fact, be working on it.[18]

This dialogue raises some disturbing questions. To start with, it is somewhat confusing for SAT proponents to argue that the test is a valid national yardstick at the same time that a test supporter such as Dr. Perham is testifying that "we all recognize that the test is biased." What's more, if sensitive admissions officers such as Dr. Perham are making adjustments for test scores while other less sensitive admissions officers are not, what sense is a college applicant to make of the system? Dr. Perham is undoubtedly qualified to make adjustments in scores on the basis of his professional expertise and good intentions, but can we count on other admissions officers to always strike the right balance? After all, the SAT was supposed to relieve admissions staffs of the heavy burden of judging the individual intellectual ability of applicants on the basis of their background. To the extent that CEEB and ETS are working on developing tests more relevant to students from all walks of life, does that mean they should issue a warning that the current SAT form may be flawed with regard to certain test-takers? If the SAT is culturally biased as Dr. Perham seems to suggest in his testimony, exactly how well is it helping the "matching system that goes on in the admissions process?" At the very least, the perspective of Dr. Perham makes it imperative that CEEB and ETS attempt to ensure some uniformity in the interpretation of SAT scores. It won't do to have blanket statements defending the SAT from charges of cultural bias coexisting with statements from admissions officers such as Dr. Perham who feel a need to adjust SAT scores to reflect people's backgrounds. If the SAT is not equally valid for all groups of test-takers, then CEEB and ETS should issue guidelines for score adjustment, and make these guidelines known to test-takers and the general public.

Of course, there are some forms of cultural bias that are inevitable, and probably desirable, on standardized tests. The tests are given in English, for example, which is the language you need to know to operate in the mainstream of American society. We have seen how wrong it is to test a non-English speaker in English and then reach conclusions as to his innate intelligence based on poor test scores. You always have to look behind the test score to see if factors such as a lack of familiarity with the language are responsible. Yet if a student is applying to a college where all the classes will be conducted in English, and papers written in English, then we want to know that the applicant can use the language. If he can't, then special courses in English would be needed for the applicant so he can prepare himself to do the work required at college. Sometimes colleges will provide these courses, sometimes the individual has to seek them out on his own, but it wouldn't be fair to the applicant or the school to proceed without them. Still, this process can be carried too far when tests concentrate on laundry lists of vocabulary words which reveal the dirty linen of class and race more than a person's ability for learning. Then we are in danger of promoting tests which tell us that a test-taker is from a low income background and is less likely to do well for that reason and therefore a low score will be recorded. Is it right to tell students they won't get high test scores because they're poor, and that because they don't get high test scores they're likely to remain poor? Vicious is an understatement for that kind of cycle.

Some defenders of current testing practices argue that even if test questions don't look particularly worthy when examined one by one, test scores are still worthwhile because they are correlated with certain measures of success. While there are some correlations, we have already seen a number of cases where the strength of the relationship was far from overwhelming. And that still doesn't justify tests which mirror race and family income in their outcomes. Edwin Taylor made this point in an article about standardized elementary school science achievement tests. Taylor wrote: "Anyone who knows how these tests are constructed is aware that a large number of questions are composed and tested. The items retained for the published version are those that discriminate in the ways that test makers decide the items should discriminate. Typically, items that discriminate between boys and girls are eliminated, while those that discriminate between white suburban children and black inner-city children are not. Thus, the discrimination defense is perverse and self-serving."[19] In addition, even when test scores correlate somewhat with some types of success, that doesn't mean the tests are measuring intelligence or impartial ability. McClelland explains: "Since we . . . know that social-class background is related to getting higher-ability test scores . . . as well as to having the right personal credentials for success, *the correlation between intelligence test scores and job success often may be an artifact,* the product of their joint association with class status. Employers may have a right to select bond salesmen who have gone to the right schools because they do better, but psychologists do not have a right to argue that it is their *intelligence* that makes them more proficient in their jobs."[20] Just because a test claims to be measuring ability or intelligence is no guarantee that the test is actually measuring those qualities.

The impact of these tests on minority groups has been disputed. Defenders of standardized tests argue that the tests are opening up school and job opportunities because the "objective" test score overwhelms prejudice or an unfamiliarity with the educational background of an applicant. As a spokesman for the College Board put it with regard to the SAT, ". . . it would be a cruel anomaly if an association of educational institutions devoted to increasing access to college were in fact putting up, instead of knocking down, barriers to higher education."[21] By its very nature, the SAT can't help but act as a barrier, cruel anomaly or no. A higher SAT score means a better chance of admission, and a lower score means a lesser chance. If you don't get over the cut-off score, or the score considered competitive with the other applicants, you face a tough fight for admission. And if you are admitted despite your low SAT scores, odds are that your grades, personal qualities, and recommendations are all so outstanding that your admission would never have been in doubt but for your SAT results. It is true that high SAT scores may work to your advantage if you are from an unknown high school and an admissions committee isn't sure how hard it was for you to earn your high grades. But it is also true that mediocre SAT scores may blow you out of the water if you have high grades from an unknown high school. As we have seen, differences in SAT scores—as with differences in most standardized tests—can be caused by factors other than sheer brainpower. So the question is not whether the SAT is used as a barrier—after all, if the SAT wasn't used in admissions decisions there would be little reason to continue it since it doesn't focus on diagnostic concerns—but whether that barrier is equitable. If the height of the barrier goes up and down according to the person trying to surmount it, then there is cause for alarm.

Minority groups do not seem to buy the argument that most standardized tests have a beneficial effect on their prospects. Individuals and organizations representing these groups have pointed out that, if anything, standardized tests often have a negative impact. There is some strong support for that position. Vito Perrone told Congress that minority groups would do better at the college level if high school grades were given a greater emphasis by admissions officers, with a corresponding reduction in the weight of admission test scores. "What happens when test scores are made the *major* factor upon which admissions decisions are made? Those selected tend to be white, middle and upper class persons from families endowed with college and post graduate degree holders. If high school grades alone are used, those selected will come from a broader socioeconomic background, with more minorities represented."[22] Professor Loewen told Congress of his experiences while teaching at Tougaloo College, an institution of higher learning for blacks, located in Mississippi.[23] Loewen said that despite a strong sociology department at the college, seniors in the department regularly got GRE scores in the 200 to 565 range, which is to say the test scores were not overly impressive in general. Yet some students with GREs in the 400s managed to gain admission to graduate school programs because someone could be persuaded to ignore the GRE score in light of Tougaloo's fine reputation. Students admitted to graduate school in this fashion then went on to do exemplary work despite their low GRE scores. Loewen said this process led him to question the value of the GRE and to devise a strategy for dealing with it. He recounted, "We also learned to help some students develop reasons why they had not *taken* the GRE, for some schools found it possible to waive the GRE requirement for a believable excuse, while they would not have overlooked a 400 score on it if taken."[24] That's a pretty arbitrary distinction for a school to make, but it illustrates the power of tests. Schools sophisticated enough to understand the limits of tests and to waive them in some cases still have trouble putting them in perspective when the three-digit printout is in the admissions folder.

Chuck Stone, who served as the director of minority affairs at ETS between 1970 and 1972, delivered an impassioned critique of test scores in testimony before the New York State legislature in 1979. Stone said, "One very damaging aspect of ETS's standardized tests is the high correlation between income and test scores . . . the higher the median family income, the higher the test score. Thus, according to ETS's own table, the average pupil who comes from a family earning $16,890 a year will score between 500 and 549 on the SAT. A student whose family earns $9,865 a year will score, on the average, between 250 and 299, almost at the bottom of the scale. What is the significance of these two incomes? The median family income for white families is $16,865 a year and the median family income for black families is closer to $9,865 a year. When colleges and universities use an ETS SAT score as a single predictor for admissions, they wipe out the vast majority of black students. Even worse, the SAT doesn't predict as accurately for low-scoring students as it does for high-scoring students. For example, the SAT verbal validity coefficient for a student scoring in the 90th percentile range is .48. But a student scoring in the 10th percentile range has a validity coefficient of .17. . . . The reason standardized tests correlate so highly with income is that they are normed on middle-class white students. Black students don't have a chance."[25] While no one is saying that testers set out with the intent of producing these kinds of results, and good intentions abound, the fact remains that despite their best efforts, SAT scores may work against many members of minority groups.

What a lot of people don't realize is that members of minority groups are not the only ones who can be hurt by standardized test scores. To the extent that these tests reflect income levels, children from low-income white families are also at a disadvantage. It's not a strictly racial distinction, although race does play a part. A poor white child from Appalachia may score lower than a black child from a fashionable suburb, even though both are of equal intelligence. With more black families proportionately below the average income level than white families, the impact of the relation between test scores and income naturally falls harder on these blacks, as well as on members of other less-affluent minority groups. Yet minorities have company in shouldering this burden. For, as Professor Loewen testified, "Many members of the majority, particularly persons from the working class or rural areas, are similarly disadvantaged. Test scores are drastically lower in some parts of the country than others."[26] There is no reason to believe that children from farming counties are less intelligent than children from metropolitan areas, but some tests do show a noticeable difference in scores. The logical explanation for this difference is not that children from rural areas have less ability, but that the tests are geared to the culture and values of a more urban tradition. It would not be difficult to redress this inequity. A new group of test writers selected from the countryside could create tests with a more rural slant and thereby reduce the score differences. Short of this sort of fundamental rebalancing of the tests, which would respect the cultural diversity of America, the use of tests in selection must be tempered by a recognition that tests are not always fair.

All this brings us to what goes under the heading of the Bakke case. This case involved controversial questions such as the use of quotas and charges of reverse discrimination. It got its start in the mid-1970s when a white medical school applicant by the name of Allan Bakke was rejected by the University of California at Davis Medical School. Bakke brought suit because his Medical College Admission Test (MCAT) scores and grade point average from college (GPA) were higher than those of some other students who had been admitted under a minority group admissions category. The case went all the way to the Supreme Court which issued a complicated decision that confirmed Bakke's right to admission and apparently frowned on the use of racial quotas while saying race could still be taken into account as one of many factors.[27] It's not my intention here to engage in a legal analysis of the court's opinion, or to speculate on exactly what effect it will have on admissions in the years to come. Nor is any of this intended as the slightest criticism of Bakke as an individual or as a medical school student or as a doctor—all indications are that he is doing well in his chosen profession and will prove to be a fine physician. But it does seem that the court took one very important assumption for granted in reaching its decision, namely that the use of a strict admissions ladder based predominantly on a combination of MCAT scores and GPA is the best way to select medical students.

That's a big assumption, although it seems to be held by many people. One line of thought about the whole Bakke case was that it amounted to slipping some minority students to the front of a well-established line even though they didn't deserve to be there. That belief in the "justice" of using MCATs and GPAs as determining criteria lay behind many of the outraged cries of reverse discrimination. If MCATs and GPAs were perfect predictors of physician performance, then we would indeed be faced with the anguishing choice of either rejecting more qualified white applicants or turning our backs on minority aspirations. If the choice were that stark, then well-meaning Americans would find themselves facing a divisive issue and the historic conflict over equality of opportunity versus equality of result would rage once more. Indeed, that is exactly how many people saw the case and some of these people were tarred unfairly as "racist" when in fact they were merely upholding their principle of strictly resisting discrimination by race. Unfortunately, the Bakke case furor concentrated on the wrong question. Attention was focused on whether it was permissible to grant special privileges—or honor an outstanding debt, depending on how you looked at it—to members of minority groups in the context of an otherwise perfect system of admissions to medical schools. The crucial question of whether that system made sense at all, whether you were talking about any of the colors in the rainbow, tended to get overlooked.

The crux of the matter is this: ranking applicants in the order of their MCATs and GPAs alone is not the same as ranking them in the order of the best prospective doctors. This is not just an issue of racial preference or prejudice, but is more profoundly a question of selecting the best potential doctors to serve the needs of society. This point needs to be made explicit. I am not suggesting the use of quotas, racial or otherwise, in medical school admissions. It seems to me that if an applicant won't be able to do the work required in school or as a doctor, then you're not doing anyone a favor by admitting that applicant. It wouldn't be fair to the medical school, or to the classmates slowed down by this person, or to future patients, or to other members of the applicant's racial or ethnic group who would be unfairly stig-matized as less capable by such a policy. Ultimately, it wouldn't even be fair to the applicant, who could never live up to the demands of the field and who would have been better off in a different, more compatible line of work. But the judgment of who will be the best doctors must be based on broader and more meaningful information than is provided by MCATs and GPAs alone. If you're playing a game of five-card poker, you insist on seeing the entire hand of the winner of the pot, not just the two highest cards. If you're selecting applicants for medical school, you better look at personality and dedication and compassion, and not just test scores and grades. A straight or a flush should beat two of a kind whether the pot is cash or enrollment in medical school.

We are not safe in relying on the MCAT as a sole judge of future medical competence. Perrone put it succinctly when he stated, "The entrance examination—similar in format to other admissions tests—has demonstrated little relation to medical school grades, medical school grades have little relationship to practice, nor, for that matter, do scores on medical board exami-nations."[28] No good doctor would rely exclusively on one drug in treatment if that drug had demonstrated little relation to re-covery and if a more balanced form of treatment were feasible. In the same manner, the MCAT should be supplemented with GPAs, interviews, recommendations, background checks, and so forth, if we want a healthier system. As of now, many medical schools have resorted to using the MCAT not to establish that an individual is competent enough in science to be evaluated on the other dimensions important to a doctor, but rather as a device to make extremely fine distinctions. Professor Sylvia Johnson has written, "The problem arises when it is assumed that if a certain cutting score on the test eliminates potentially unsuccessful appli-cants, choosing a higher cutting score will be 'better,' thus auto-matically eliminating more of the potentially unsuccessful. When in fact, as that cutting score is raised, many potentially successful applicants are also eliminated. Given a group of qualified appli-cants, the fact that one student's test score or grades are somewhat higher than those of another does not mean that the first is more 'qualified' than the second. Some basic level of competency should be established, but beyond that many other factors should be used to determine success."[29]

Whenever I need a doctor, I want the best one available. Any reduction in selection or certification standards which would reduce the quality of health care is totally unsatisfactory. That is one reason why any narrow admissions policy which largely limits the competition for medical school spots to test scores and grades is so worrisome. Of course, we want doctors who are skilled in scientific theory and academic techniques, and to the extent that tests and grades are even imperfect measures of those qualities, they are useful. But we can't stop there. When you need a doctor, you want somone who can do more than take tests. Your doctor must be able to understand what you are saying when you describe symptoms and explain how you feel; be concerned about your well-being and willing to make some sacrifices if necessary to see to it that you receive proper care; treat you with respect and honesty; and clearly convey what it is that you can do to speed your recovery. These clinical aspects of being a doctor are at least as important as the classroom qualities. We are learning all the time about how significant a good "bedside manner" can be in restoring confidence to a patient and helping the body to fight illness. A technically perfect doctor can do a poor job if she neglects the human element in her diagnoses and treatments. And a doctor who is not as coldly brilliant can do a superb job if she can gain her patients' trust and speak to them in their own language so there is no misunderstanding. We are insisting on higher standards when we demand that much more go into medical school admissions decisions than just the numerical figures for MCATs and grades.

The aura of test precision which surrounds the MCAT as well as the other standardized selection tests has contributed to a public perception that high MCAT scores are identical with medical competence. As Johnson writes, "Such a meaning supposes that the test score is an implicit substitution for the 'real thing' that we want to measure."[30] In reality, MCAT scores fall far short of that standard since there is much more to doctoring than the material covered on the test. The use of criteria in addition to MCAT scores in determining who our doctors will be twenty and thirty years from now is not only a matter of racial justice, but also a critical component of the effort to produce excellent doctors. We need doctors who take an interest in their patients, who are devoted to preventive medicine and community health, who are effective in the office as well as the classroom. It is possible that when we use this more comprehensive definition of qualities we want in our doctors that the problems of racial and social inequities in admissions will be alleviated if not cured. The MCAT, for instance, has a history of connection between test scores and parental income. In 1975–76 one study reported correlation between MCAT scores and parental incomes as high as .95.[31] Now even if the test has been improved since then, and the correlation reduced, or if that study was on the high side, there's still an awfully long way to go. A lessened reliance on the MCAT, in conjunction with greater emphasis on meeting the needs of the entire spectrum of patients, may well have the incidental but beneficial effect of increasing minority representation in the medical profession. If we hadn't been so intimidated by standardized test scores, it wouldn't have been so hard to realize that opening up medicine and maintaining (or even raising) standards are not inevitably trade-offs, but can go together like doctors and stethoscopes.

As to the minimum competency tests that are sweeping the country as requirements for a high school diploma, we need to make sure that they do not become a trap for the unwary. The tests have drawn much of their support from the desire of parents to ensure that their children really receive the education they are entitled to. Few observers would deny that our public schools have not been able to meet all the demands placed on them. The clamor by the public for greater accountability by the schools is an encouraging sign if it indicates a greater willingness of parents to get involved in improving their children's education. But, possibly, the pendulum may have swung a little too far in the direction of understating the quality of education in the public schools in recent years. After all, at least one onlooker has noted that as a nation we have a higher literacy rate than ever before—an estimated 80 plus percent of adults are literate today as opposed to about 55 percent in 1941, about 35 percent in 1918, and about 15 percent in 1776.[32] Whatever the exact figures, a determination to push on to 100 percent literacy is a worthwhile goal. The controversial issue is not whether it is desirable to improve the education our children obtain—that's a tough ambition to argue against—but whether minimum competency testing will help us get there. The jury is still out on this question.

Although the system varies state by state, a typical minimum competency testing program involves administering standardized tests to high school seniors to determine whether they will be awarded a normal diploma. Some areas use these tests purely for informational purposes, but many either withhold high school diplomas from those who fail the test or award "second class" diplomas to students who score under the cut-off. There are two pitfalls to watch out for here. First, we must be sure that we are being fair to the individuals who are denied full status as high school graduates. Second, we must do our best to see that passing these tests is a meaningful statement of accomplishment of educational objectives, and not just a formal requirement which weakens rather than strengthens our schools. Individual injustices can occur if the tests measure family background rather than skill ōr if they are used to further penalize the very victims of years of neglect by the school system. Look at the Florida functional literacy minimum competency test for a minute. This test, which goes by the nickname of "funky lit," is a standardized test that was to be used to determine which high school students in Florida would earn full diplomas.[33] As mentioned earlier, a federal judge has suspended use of the test for this purpose for several years until all the students who started first grade while the state schools were still officially segregated have graduated from high school. The first time this test was administered as a trial, a very disturbing pattern emerged. Not only did 36 percent of the students fail the test, but 78 percent of the black students failed as compared with 25 percent of the white students.[34]

There are some obvious questions here. Are a full 36 percent of Florida high school seniors functionally illiterate? Just what does it mean to be functionally illiterate anyway? Well, that's the first catch, the first thing to pay close attention to whenever you're considering a minimum competency program. It seems that "functional literacy" is defined as being able to pass the functional literacy test. That line of reasoning should sound familiar from our discussion of intelligence tests. The test is not what you might think a literacy test would be—a student isn't asked to read a passage (to see if he can read) and then explain the meaning of the passage (to see if he understood what he read). Instead, the student is told to pick the "best" answer in a multiple-choice format regarding questions about skills deemed vital to survival in society. These may be questions involving unit pricing or deciphering timetables and the like. The rub is that the particular questions chosen reflect the opinions of the test writers as to what skills are essential to earn a diploma and which are merely optional. Reasonable people can disagree as to which areas should be covered and which left uncovered. So it is essential that the decisions about topics to be included on the tests be made in the open and that they reflect a public consensus about which skills are absolutely needed; otherwise the possibility exists that questions will be selected on the basis of personal and cultural biases, not out of any evil intent, but as a consequence of leaving the decision in the hands of a few professionals.

The staggering differences in passing rates between whites and blacks is another area that needs to be investigated. Does this really show such disproportionate skills in the two groups, or have sources of cultural bias crept in and done their damage? We know that some other standardized tests have demonstrated instances of cultural bias, so we should be dismayed but not shocked if the problem recurs on standardized minimum competency tests. And to the extent that the scores reveal underlying differences in what the two groups have learned, what conclusions are we to draw? What are we to think of a school system which fails to educate its pupils on skills needed to attain minimal levels of competency, and then turns around after twelve years of passing grades and promotions and blames the individual student for the problem? Presumably, that high school senior was well on the way to failure much earlier—maybe starting to go off the track in tenth grade or seventh or fourth. Why wait until the last minute to zap a student who has been getting passing grades, especially when the penalty is so great, with the consequences of not having a full high school diploma so severe for people looking for jobs. It seems, then, that for a minimum testing program to be fair, it must be based on community standards and consist solely of subjects that have been taught in the schools. There must be diagnostic testing at early stages of schooling, and serious classes designed to help those who have fallen behind on the objectives. The tests must measure achievement of the "minimal" skills and not whether the child's parents are of any particular race, religion, or socioeconomic status. And the tests must point the way to improving education, rather than providing an excuse for abandoning a costly, frustrating, and absolutely vital endeavor. That's a tall order to fill, but the attempt should be made, and we should be aware of exactly what is entailed in a responsible minimum competency plan.

Even if we succeed in meeting these requirements of fairness in minimum competency tests, we must still confront the question of whether the overall gains are worth the costs to the educational process. Once we dictate that passing a minimum competency test is required for graduation from high school (or even for promotion in the lower grades between kindergarten and twelfth grade), then we can be sure that schools will dwell on the test subjects first and foremost.[35] The school curriculum will be reshaped to emphasize what the test emphasizes and downplay what the test leaves out. What's more, there is a risk that students will be taught in such a way that their scores on the test go up while their mastery of the skills tested remains static or even drops. This could happen if the mechanics of basic skills were drilled over and over again to the detriment of explanations about the theory behind the mechanics, which are necessary for a full understanding of the subject. In sum, while the ideal of minimum competency testing is appealing, at least in the abstract, there remains uncertainty as to whether this ideal will—or can—be translated into practice. The public must have a chance to become involved in the test formulation stage if there is to be any realistic hope of making minimum competency testing work.

We turn now to a look at some of the connections between the testing industry and the academic institutions which require students to take standardized tests.

CHAPTER TWELVE

The Psychometric-Academic Complex

The relationship between test publishers (who are sometimes called "psychometricians," meaning people who attempt to measure mental traits) and academics can be found in the several meanings of the word "complex." A complex can be something that consists of two connected parts. Complex also means a matter is complicated. And, if you have a complex about something, you tend to get very touchy whenever that particular subject is raised. The worlds of standardized testing and educational institutions are linked; these links are sometimes quite complicated; and most individuals involved react defensively whenever this association is put in the spotlight. The existence of this complex (in all senses of the word) is one of the factors behind the rise of testing, and it also serves as a shield against outside criticism. Academics have lent their prestige to some members of the testing industry by serving on their panels, as consultants, and sometimes by sitting on the board of directors of a particular testing outfit. There is nothing wrong with this type of work—after all, educators have skills in this field which can be used to improve test quality. But it is important to remember this connection when you are evaluating testimony about testing. Not all professors are purely disinterested parties on the subject of standardized tests. This does not mean their comments may not be as valid, or even more valid, than those of someone outside of testing, merely that they should be put in perspective.

The most obvious connections occur whenever members of our educational hierarchy work directly with testing companies in either a paid or unpaid capacity. Certainly none of these academics is doing work he doesn't believe in just because it can be rewarding either in terms of salary or professional status. Yet once an educator enters this world of test development, it becomes difficult to turn around and go back outside. The community exerts a social force which helps to bind its members together, especially when faced with a barrage of criticism from those outside the circle. What's more, it is possible to become wrapped up in the statistical work devoted to refinements in the testing procedure to the exclusion of a careful examination of policy considerations. Some very fine work is being done at the margins of testing, and people who are making contributions in those areas could not be blamed for wanting to avoid the distractions of the distasteful quarrel over exactly what purposes these new refinements should be put to. Once within this sphere, attacks on some of the general concepts of testing, or specific forms of test abuse, can appear to be personal assaults on the dedicated professionals in the field. Much restraint is required to incorporate the best of the criticisms in new work rather than simply lash back at the hostile remarks.

The Board of Trustees of the Educational Testing Service has sixteen members. According to the *New York Times,* as of late 1979 nearly all of those trustees were educators.[1] Over half of them were college presidents, including the heads of Duke University and Vassar College. The president of the College Board and the head of the American Council on Education were also represented.[2] With this sort of makeup, it is not startling to discover that ETS tests seem much more concerned with the institutional desires of colleges than with the needs of the students who actually pay for the tests. As long as colleges can shift the burden of paying for these tests to students, who have no forceful representation on the Board, pressures for substantial internal reform will remain slight. While college officials are interested in issues of test fairness and other student concerns, there is no sense of urgency. That sense is largely restricted to the students, who have to bear the direct costs of standardized tests, both in dollars and opportunities foreclosed. This, at least, is my conclusion about the relative priorities of that segment of testing which falls under the jurisdiction of ETS and the College Board. It is also the conclusion of Layton Olson, the vice-president of the National Student Educational Fund. In testimony before the New York legislature in 1979, Olson said: ". . . standardized tests or services are required—or endorsed—by educational institutions and public agencies. Normally, a student does not have the option *not* to take the test. Nor does he or she have the option to shop around between testing services. As currently organized, tests and services are designed to meet the admissions and other administrative needs of testing services' primary constituents, or clients—administrators in postsecondary institutions, in public education agencies, and high schools."[3]

These tests, then, in the first instance are designed for the convenience of the colleges which require them as opposed to the students who are judged by them. While the interests of institutions and students do overlap at times, they also diverge at important junctures, and when they do, it is the students who lose out. As Olson testified, "The testing services are designed only *secondarily* in their operating standards, in their information materials, in their investment in improving services or developing new services, in their research activities, or in their corporate structures to meet the needs of their consumers—test-takers and their families. Yet, test-takers have the most at risk—and they pay for testing services."[4] Moreover, a commission on test practices sponsored by the College Board itself came to a similar conclusion in its report: "As the commission's work proceeded, it became apparent that in its members' opinion, the Board's traditional services reflected primarily and purposefully the interests of the Board's member colleges."[5] The report went on to recommend that "While in reality no one can solve anyone else's problems of choice, the College Board can give the students faced with the difficult decisions surrounding the transition out of high school support equal to that which colleges receive. In short, the Commission thinks that a symmetry or balance should obtain between the services that the Board offers to potential entrants and those that it offers to colleges."[6] The academics who sit on the panels of the testers are being asked to wear too many hats. It is tough enough for them to respond to the needs of the test companies while protecting the interests of colleges in general without expecting them to act as guardians for students as well.

Academics do have a lot at stake in the preservation of some scheme of standardized testing, if not necessarily the present arrangement. If tests were abolished, then the positions these educators hold in testing companies would disappear. More importantly, the work of admissions committees would be thrown into confusion until some substitute methods for evaluating candidates were found. Academics would not be the only ones affected. The people who run coaching schools for standardized tests would suddenly find that their services were no longer required. Educational systems which relied on tests for ranking schools and children would be forced to reevaluate their policies. And a few computers might get lonely if they were no longer needed for scanning millions of test answer sheets. Few critics are calling for the outright abolition of standardized tests as we know them, and fewer still think there is any realistic chance of such an event in the near future. But the mere prospect of such an apocalypse is enough to scare some of these interested parties into an inflexible opposition to modifying the current setup. When reform is proposed, the cry goes up that this would be a giant step toward the horrors of a world without any standardized tests and with but a fraction of the number two pencils currently available. What is overlooked is that tests are far from perfect now, and that it is only through a concerted effort to improve them (and our use of them) that pressures for their abandonment can be channeled into more productive ventures. Academics should be in the forefront of efforts to bring about a superior version of testing programs if they are intent on protecting the advantages that come to them with the use of tests.

There is some controversy as to how independent the academics who serve as overseers of the industry—as members of the governing boards, as temporary staff, or as directors of the client bodies which represent specialized schools—are able to be. Some of these positions do not carry any salary with them (being on the Board of Trustees of ETS, for example, is not compensated financially), while others offer only moderate pay compared with what a professor could earn with a different employer. And yet the public positions, at least, of the supervisors and the supervised seem to be constantly crafted of the same clay. Part of this may be explained by an understandable reluctance to express grievances in public, and part may reflect a mesh as the interests of the two groups become increasingly entwined, so that it is hard to tell where one stops and the other begins. For instance, the people who run the Preliminary Scholastic Aptitude Test (PSAT) now sell the names of students who have taken the test to interested colleges at eleven cents a head.[7] Some 21 million of these transactions took place in the 1979–80 year, with names, ". . . presorted by zip code, race, sex, intended major and test score."[8] But surely with the instances of scoring error, computer breakdowns, and public turmoil, one would expect more internal discord to surface if the representatives of educational establishments were exercising a tight check on the testers. With some exceptions, it's fair to say that the bodies set up to control the test companies have become identified in the minds of many with the testing industry itself. By and large, the testers don't have to face skeptical groups of potential consumers who demand constant reassurance of the quality of the product. Instead, many of the sponsors are already so sold on the tests that they function as auxiliary sales representatives to the groups which appointed them. There have been precious few instances of a test-sponsoring body deciding to switch from one testing company to another in search of better tests. You could explain that on the basis of excellent performance, perhaps, but the track record of some of these tests falls short of that standard. Moreover, in any truly competitive field, there is occasional movement which is caused not by dissatisfaction with the old product, but by greater promise shown by a new one.

Just as sponsors of particular tests have grown resistant to change, so have the forces which helped usher in the overall reign of testing become loath to subject it to periodic scrutiny. Except for the people who have to take the tests, things are comfortable now, so why change? Tests have become so firmly entrenched in education that some leaders appear unable to imagine that they might take any other shape or form. Perrone put it this way: "We have constructed a mechanism and related support systems clothed in the language and mystique of science with restricted accessibility being a major by-product. Testing has become so much a part of our educational structures—the conventional wisdom—that its purposes do not receive sufficient challenge and any significant examination of how well those purposes match use is left wanting."[9] Conventional wisdom is sometimes true wisdom, in which case it will withstand questioning. But when conventional wisdom goes too long without a rigorous rethinking, odds are it is no longer wisdom, even if it once was. The fit between the purposes of standardized testing and the uses tests are put to can grow poorer and poorer over time when changes taking place in the system are ignored. What's more, we may also reach a stage where the balance between attention directed to test improvement and that to test advertising dips sharply in the wrong direction. We may even be there today. Allan Nairn, for instance, told the New York legislature that the 1977 ETS budget showed that $390,000 was spent on test item writing and examiner committees. That's less than half of the over $810,000 ETS was spending years earlier (1972) on publications, public relations, and company representatives in D.C.[10] You can re-arrange budget figures to make them look better or worse, but the question remains as to whether the proportions spent on research and promotion are satisfactory.

The ironic aspect of the wholehearted embrace many educators have given to standardized testing is that the tests constitute a violation of the autonomy which these same educators have been scrupulously guarding for years. Of course, this surrender by academics is not unique—we have seen many professions such as law and medicine virtually trampling over each other in the stampede to deposit responsibility at the doorsteps of standardized testing. Still, as Bernard Feder has written, "It's somewhat amusing that so many teachers and professors—who resent and resist the intrusion of outsiders trying to enter their disciplines without proper credentials—assume that test makers are qualified to give tests, to grade, evaluate, categorize, and screen other people without knowing which side of a bell-shaped curve is up."[11] Professors who would hit the roof if another professor attempted to tell them how or what to teach in their courses seem to be content to let test publishers, with the aid of some of their colleagues, set the standards for evaluation of their students. Sherwood Kohn, a journalist, may have touched on an explanation for this phenomenon. He wrote that, "Educators, as well as the general public, tend to be overwhelmed by the sheer weight of numbers offered by the testing industry, the enormous influence that test publishers wield in the field of education, and the claims of 'scientific measurement' that test publishers have made in the past."[12]

As for the present, test publishers sometimes respond to specific criticisms with arguments which may appear plausible on the surface, but have contradictory cross-currents underneath. For example, a spokesman for ETS testified in 1979 to the effect that the strong correlation between SAT scores and family income was not as distasteful as it looked. The spokesman said, "The fact that SAT scores are related to students' family incomes is often misinterpreted or misunderstood. The relationship is far from perfect and shows up only in the averages for groups of students. Many individual students from low income families attain high scores and many individuals from affluent families attain low scores."[13] True. The relationship between scores and income which shows up on the average does not mean that there is absolutely no chance for a poor person to score well or a rich person to score poorly. But if we are to draw much comfort from this fact, we do so only at the expense of the prime justification of the SAT itself. For the relationship that the SAT detects between test performance and first-year college grades, weak as the relationship is, also shows up only on the average. A high score on the SAT does not mean there is absolutely no chance an individual will flunk out of college, nor does a low score mean an individual won't graduate Phi Beta Kappa (unless of course the individual was refused admission on the basis of the low score). If ETS would have us discount the unease about test score–income relationships, then they should similarly have us downplay the worth of the SAT. The spokesman then went on to repeat in essence the argument that the standardized tests are simply mirroring society, which doesn't explain why disadvantaged groups do worse on the test "mirror" than on other supposed mirrors, such as school grades.

This same spokesman in the same statement went on to attempt to assuage Congressional concerns that standardized tests had overstepped their rightful bounds. A quick reading, or a quick hearing, gives the impression that this statement is both modest and soothing. After claiming that tests like the SAT are "a great strength to a fair selection system," the ETS official said, "Nevertheless, most colleges and universities are properly reluctant to rely exclusively on admission tests and grades in selecting students. Admissions officers appreciate that even though these measures are the best predictors of academic performance, the relationship is certainly not exact."[14] Subdued as this may sound, it still makes the case for tests stronger than it would otherwise be by linking them with grades. As this spokesman noted, even when grades and test scores are used in tandem, "the relationship is certainly not exact." It is not exact in much the same fashion as crossing your own twenty-five-yard line or even the fifty-yard line is not the same as scoring a touchdown. More importantly, when taken by themselves, high school grades have a greater predictive value than the SAT scores. As David White has testified, "If we're interested in validity, we should recognize that the consistent finding in research is that the most valid predictor of future academic performance is previous academic performance."[15] Putting that in terms of the SAT, White explained that the correlation coefficient of high school grades (the r value) is .5, while the r for the SAT verbal subtest is only .42, and for the math subtest only .39.[16] As White noted, "When the SAT and the high school grades are combined, the correlation goes up from .50 with high school grades to .56 in combination. So what we're really talking about is a six percent solution."[17] Sherlock Holmes might have had an interesting time with a six- or seven-percent solution, but that's hardly an awe-inspiring figure for standardized tests. Even if this way of looking at the tests understates their value somewhat, it should put the marginal improvement in prediction with even the best of standardized tests into context.

Industry officials have revealed a paradoxical attitude about their tests in public statements. On the one hand, they try to be cautious now in their claims for the tests. Yes, they have flaws. Yes, they are imperfect. No, they should not be relied on too heavily. They assert that tests really have much less of an impact on decisions than the public has been led to believe by scare stories. But as soon as these ritual incantations are finished, the other hand juts forward. These tests are vital, without question, to provide an unchanging measuring rod for people from all walks of life. Without these tests only students from the big-time high schools could ever hope to get into the select colleges. The poor and minorities would be hurt the most if these tests were touched (even though these are the same groups who have often been in the vanguard of the movement to reform tests). In short, the spokesmen seem to be saying that the tests are both moderate in their virtues and positively indispensable in their worth. Arguing both positions simultaneously requires a certain dexterity.

This nimbleness has also been apparent in certain responses by test publishers to critical evaluations of some test questions. The argument goes something like this. A test question is criticized because it is ambiguous and could be answered reasonably in at least two ways. But because this is a standardized, multiple-choice, "objective" test, the student can't explain her answer, so if her perception of the ambiguity is different from what the test writer was thinking of, she gets the question marked wrong. The publisher may then claim that the ambiguity was planned, and that it is the superior student who can think the way the test writer thinks. In his classic work, *The Tyranny of Testing,* Banesh Hoffmann wrote with regard to a question he had criticized earlier that "the Educational Testing Service conceded the presence of ambiguity, and even sought to suggest that it was a virtue, by pointing out that a certain amount of ambiguity is part and parcel of tests of sensitivity to the reactions of others to written communication."[18] But when ETS was defending other questions that had come under attack, according to Hoffmann, "it does not stress this matter of the presence of ambiguity. Yet it and other test makers are ready to plead for just enough special laxity in the interpretation of words to allow them to escape from an awkward position even though they deny the candidate equivalent latitude on the ground that the test is objective."[19] In all fairness, it seems that a student who has to take a standardized test should be allowed to explain (and receive credit for) his insight into a problem on the test if test publishers feel free to indulge in the same "right of explanation" in responding to concerns about given test questions.

The secrecy which surrounds the use of test questions may serve the purposes of the psychometric-academic complex, but it does little to satisfy the hunger for information on the part of the public and test researchers who are not granted access by the publishers. The test publishers' claim that their policy of releasing some of the questions from some of their tests some of the time is sufficient runs into serious challenge. The contention is challenged by Lewis Pike, among others. Pike has a doctorate in educational psychology, with a concentration on educational testing and measurement. He also worked at ETS for fourteen years, with two of those years spent on test development and the other twelve on research. What's more, he is a supporter of the continued use of standardized tests.[20] And he is troubled by the limited release of test contents. Pike testified: "I have long been and continue to be an advocate for the use of standardized tests for appropriate purposes. . . . However, the very importance of such testing suggests to me that no reasonable effort should be spared to insure that both constituencies, the colleges and the students, are well served."[21] Essential to this goal of serving colleges and students well, according to Pike, is ready availability of previously used tests to the public. In his words, "There is no substitute for direct access to test copies. . . . While . . . descriptive information is good to have, I feel that it simply cannot replace seeing the test itself. As a researcher, I have consistently found that my work with tests such as the SAT and GRE and tests of English as a foreign language could be most fruitful only after I had spent considerable time reviewing and reacting to direct test copy, interacting with individual items, relating those items to the directions that they come with and so on. If I were a consumer, that is, a person having to take the test or a legislator charged with representing consumers, I would not willingly settle for less."[22]

Why should we have to settle for less? The testing companies don't want to allow open access to the contents of their tests. They claim that they are already releasing tons of information and, therefore, see no reason to expand on present opportunities for test review. An official of ETS has testified that student concerns about tests can be met more effectively if "the products of the testing programs and the admissions processes of schools and colleges are open, fully understood, and stripped of whatever unnecessary vestiges of mystery may yet obscure them from students and the public."[23] This sounds fine, but then this same official draws a line for an "open" and "fully understood" standardized testing program which is way short of full disclosure to the public. Further, not all members of the testing industry always live up to even the minimal guarantees of openness. Paul Pottinger of the National Center for the Study of the Professions testified: "Test companies will tell you that many people have access to their tests. But in a case I was closely associated with, it took court action to be allowed to see a test that was disputed, and even then the courts agreed to a test company's stipulation that we only be allowed to view the tests for a limited amount of time. No notes could be taken."[24] Jon Haber of the United States Student Association complained that testing agencies "claimed that test research is routinely published and available to the public, academic, and research libraries, and to any individual who may request it. This is simply not true. Many important studies are not disclosed by the testing agencies."[25] To be sure, there are issues of ownership and privacy protection that need to go into the balance. But if there is to be any error in striking that balance, shouldn't it be on the side of better information for the public?

What happens now is that the same companies which could be hurt if test inspection revealed glaring faults are in charge of determining who is allowed to inspect many of the significant facts. Shouldn't this determination be made by some group other than the members of the testing industry? Certainly the experiences of David White indicate the potential for scholarly anxiety when the intricate mechanisms of standardized tests are screened off from the public. White told New York State legislators that he had read a paper published by one of the quality testing companies.[26] This paper analyzed a test which was supposed to establish a minimum competence level in a field related to health. Five experts had been called in to look at the 126 test questions. The experts were asked to eliminate all the alternative answers which were obviously and blatantly wrong. The analysts then were to look at each question and see how many of the alternative answers for that question had been eliminated by the experts as clearly wrong. Questions which had alternative answers which were mostly eliminated by the experts would be considered easy for the people taking the test. Questions that had few alternatives which were spotted as completely wrong would be considered hard for test-takers. On those questions a process of elimination wouldn't do much good since it was more difficult to sort the clearly wrong alternatives from the possibly correct ones. That was the plan.

What was not expected was that the experts would eliminate as clearly wrong some of the alternative answers that the test writer had designated as correct. After all, the experts were only supposed to weed out alternatives that couldn't possibly be correct. It turned out, according to White, that of the five experts, none picked fewer than 9 of the 126 "right" answers as clearly wrong, and one expert singled out 26 of the "right" answers as obviously false. It's not entirely certain what caused this problem, whether the flaw was in the test questions or in the experts, but it is clear these results don't increase confidence in the precision of that particular test.

While this discrepancy between the observations of the experts and the selections of the test writer is a source of concern, of greater concern is the erratic availability of this sort of information about tests to the public. White said, "The name of the test, the questions and answers involved in the disputed instances, and the remedies undertaken by the test publishers, all remain secret."[27] White thinks that at least some of "the disputed questions in the test remain and are now being used to test individuals on their minimum competency in a health-related area."[28] It may be that all of these disputed questions have been replaced, and that the new questions are free of the confusion about right answers that plagued the older version of the test. Perhaps. But we have to take it on faith that the needed corrections have been made by the testers involved. Test-takers are at the mercy of test publishers who control the kind and quantity of information about their tests available to the general public. This may all have been a misunderstanding, the test may have been fine to start with, or it may be fine now, but we have no way of knowing. And we have no way of knowing how many problems of this sort are not even published in a paper where a diligent researcher such as David White can find them.

You would think that with all the shortcomings in standard-ized tests that have been cited in the media, the industry might be eager to dispel exaggerated notions of test inaccuracy. Some-times fear of the unknown proves to be much greater than the reality of a problem. The industry could have much to gain by inviting outsiders in to show them that their worries are at least overstated, if not groundless. If the testers had as much confidence in their tests as they proclaim, that wouldn't seem to be such a drastic step. If the tests are good, opening the books to all (with appropriate safeguards) at least has the potential to calm some fears and maybe even stimulate some cooperation that could lead to test improvement. As things stand now, however, standardized tests not only have to take the rap for actual flaws, they also have to carry the additional heavy baggage of being secretive. Paul Pottinger thinks this secrecy contributes to test abuse through mis-understanding. He said: "Admissions officers often do not seri-ously question test validity. Or they use tests as convenient decision-making devices regardless of the validity, i.e., they accept the utility of the tests without understanding them. Accurate data and information about the meaning of these test scores is so hard to obtain that practically speaking learning about the true value of tests is not worth the effort for most test users."[29] If publishers are concerned that tests are relied on too heavily because officials have an inflated view of their worth, why not release all test data—warts and all—to bring test presumptions under control?

Representatives of student groups think such a move would yield gains. As Abby Helfer of the Student Association of Syra-cuse University stated, "In addition to giving all test-takers the opportunity to study the same material . . . disclosure may also lessen the effects of cultural and socioeconomic bias in these tests by allowing minority persons to familiarize themselves with these often unfamiliar contents."[30] James Stern, a legislative assistant with the Student Association of the State University of New York, remarked, "As students we do not believe that standardized tests can be accepted as fair and accurate indicators of an individual's capacity to learn if their contents are withheld from public scrutiny."[31] In short, secrecy actually works to undercut the proper use of tests as much as it protects them from additional criticism. Even if the charges leveled against the tests are totally untrue, they are nonetheless provided with a hospitable environment in which to thrive in the culture of secrecy. Skepticism regarding content fairness will be difficult, if not impossible, to overcome as long as the public cannot see the actual tests which gave rise to the charges. Be that as it may, test publishers continue to embrace the charms of secrecy even as they loudly proclaim their passion for the beauty of public understanding of the tests.

Important as they are, the support of some powerful members of the academic community and the continuance of test secrecy by themselves do not account for all of the testing industry's ability to resist reforms. There is also an institutional dynamic at play. After decades of virtually uncontested dominance, it's difficult to turn an institution around. Tests, and the testing industry, have grown influential through the use of certain procedures and operating techniques. Even as the atmosphere around the testing industry evolves, the tendency inside the industry is to continue today what was done yesterday because "that's the way it's always been done." In the absence of strong competition, it's much easier to hold your ground than to pioneer new advances. Paul Jacobs has mentioned this phenomenon. He said, "When a testing agency is set up or a government agency or any institution, it has a particular mission, but as the world changes, the institution doesn't necessarily change with it and the institution often is concerned with expanding itself, perpetuating itself. I think this happens particularly with testing agencies."[32] Martin Mayer detected some of this drive when he wrote years ago about his perceptions of the ETS philosophy: "If 'guidance' is in the air, ETS will prove that standardized tests are the heart of guidance; if reform agitates the schools, ETS will demonstrate the 'need' for tests which match the new programs . . . ETS has even hooked its wagon onto the star of 'creativity.' "[33] The problem is that an institution can become so caught up in advancing its own agenda that it loses sight of the importance of other considerations. When the institution or industry has been able to insulate itself from serious checks on its independence, this tendency toward self-absorption becomes more serious.

Beyond the industry's understandable interest in expansion of markets while maintaining the status quo in its prestige and basic tenets, we come back to the magic of numbers as a bulwark of the testing domain. Like magic, statistics can be used to produce good or bad results. Yet there is a presumption that someone who uses statistics is invariably a scientist and never a scoundrel, wittingly or not. Kohn wrote, "In our technologically oriented society, where many people place their faith solely in quantitative evidence of reality, and are unable to trust qualitative or subjective data, the individual who can support his contentions with numbers is infinitely more acceptable as an authority than the one who can only voice an opinion, no matter how well informed."[34] We have seen that it is possible to punch holes in many of the statistical arguments made on behalf of standardized tests. But it's hard to get people to stay and watch the statistical counterpunching for an entire fifteen round fight. Part of the audience leaves the hall after seeing the champions of testing throw the first statistical punch; their assumption is that the challenger won't be able to respond in kind. And if the challenger should prove reluctant to mix it up with statistics, then some view it as a technical knockout on behalf of the tests, even when the statistical battle is by far the least important subject of contention. Banesh Hoffmann warned that criticisms of standardized tests "coming from responsible people, should not be lightly brushed aside as the opinions of outsiders or as idle thoughts lacking a basis of statistical evidence. Statistics are no substitute for intellectual standards, nor are they a shield against all types of criticism. Their use by people who lack insight can have disastrous consequences."[35]

Discussion of test statistics should be just the start of the debate rather than the conclusion, because statistics can be used to hide the errors in the system as well as to find the virtues. To quote from Hoffmann, "Because the statistics usually cited as justification for the use of multiple-choice tests ignore the nonnumerical aspects of both testing and its side effects, they are, in fact, far from being accurate measures of the whole merit or lack of merit of current test procedures."[36] We know that the theory behind the use of statistics in the construction of standardized tests is not that hard to master, but the mere mention of the word "statistics" is enough to scare some people off. And the use of a testing jargon which defines words differently from their everyday meaning undoubtedly contributes to this effect. The effect, of course, may be unintentional, but it is pronounced. Bernard Feder writes, "Outsiders are kept away by a number of devices, including the use of an arcane language (a test maker with his or her professional costume on is a 'psychometrician' for example). The fact is that, while some of the manipulations may be quite complicated, the basic ideas are really simple and understandable."[37] Until this notion takes hold, the testing experts will maintain the upper hand in keeping their turf an exclusive preserve with only minor trespassing by the "nonexpert public." Such an outcome would be most unfortunate. Professor Kelly of Cornell has said, "What seems funny . . . is that we talk about this as if testing is the purview of testing organizations and not, in fact, the appropriate purview of citizens or parents or students."[38] The sad fact is that the joke is on us.

Why have the people subjected to standardized tests been so slow to revolt over their exclusion from the testing structure? Part of the answer can be found in the esoteric level of many of the published reports about testing and its ills. Reports written in statistical symbols and "educationese" are not designed to reach a general audience. It takes awhile for news from these technical publications to reach a wider readership. And it took the courage of testing insiders going public with their concerns before test criticism attained true respectability, spreading beyond the preoccupations of a small fringe group. The work of people like Banesh Hoffmann, Paul Houts, Vito Perrone, and others in putting the problems with testolotry into readable form for a broad spectrum of the public is just now beginning to pay off. The great weight of the testing industry has been used to slow down the growing public awareness of these insurgent ideas, but they are gathering force. Of course, if you are one of the people who have always done well on standardized tests, you aren't instinctively endeared to test criticism. Why question a system that has worked to your own advantage? Isn't it more comforting to believe that the very fact that the tests were able to spot your talent is yet another proof of their desirability? That's certainly a tempting thought, and not without at least some substance, for the tests can be effective in limited roles. Boat rocking is rarely comfortable in the boat. But a studied indifference to the plight of those trying to stay afloat in the ocean of tests could return to haunt a son or a daughter or niece or nephew who ends up in the same predicament. And too great a belief in the "justice" of your successes on standardized tests may one day come to look as absurd as the supposed "divine right of kings" or the precepts of Social Darwinism appear to us now.

The hardest struggle is faced by those who have been hurt on the tests. I think we underestimate the size of this group because many of them choose not to make an issue of it publicly. It can't be a simple decision to "come out of the closet" if you're a standardized test "underscorer." If you have been able to carve out an impressive niche despite low scores, you'd have to be reluctant to draw attention to yourself. The risk exists that your colleagues would come to the conclusion that your accomplishments have less meaning than your scores. People might start thinking that you're not really as able or as intelligent as you've been able to present yourself. And if you haven't been able to overcome the stigma of being a low scorer, your comments may be dismissed as "sour grapes." You may even have called your own competence into question because of these tests, and if you're capable of falling into that trap, how can you be confident others won't make the same mistake? People who have failed various standardized tests don't have support groups where others who've had the same problem can reassure them. They carry the doubt inside, and feel that their experiences are unique, more connected to some unusual personal weakness than is really the case. This is starting to change as some organizations begin to speak up for those unfairly or inaccurately branded by the tests. But progress in test reform, in placing the tests in perspective, in teaching people how to surmount their difficulties with standardized tests, in weaning other people from their dependence on these tests will come much faster as test victims add their voices to the call for constructive change.

We have now examined fully the assorted pitfalls associated with standardized tests. We have discussed what is wrong with the tests, explored how the tests have come to dominate our lives, and speculated about the reasons why we have allowed tests to wield such influence. So, what we can do about the tests that have become so important? Chapter 13 sketches some methods for preparing for major standardized tests if you (or your child) have to take one in the near future, and suggests some places you might look for further help.

PART FOUR

What Can
We Do?

CHAPTER THIRTEEN

Beating
the System

What if you—or your child or family member or friend—have to take an important standardized test in a few months? What should you do to get ready for it? Obviously the answer varies according to who you are and what test you have to take. But there is some advice that is generally applicable if you're trying to beat the testing system or to keep it from beating you. Most important, you must not be content just to follow the strategy suggested in this or any other book, but must instead exercise your own independent judgment. You know much better than anyone else what kind of experiences you've had with standardized tests, what works for you and what doesn't. Spice everything you hear with healthy doses of salt, and be the final judge of what tastes right and what seems wrong. There are no guarantees, but the following suggestions should at least give you some ideas about what you should be considering and where you might go to get additional, and sometimes conflicting, opinions.

Before you get caught up in test preparation, get a broader perspective of the test and the particular situation you are in. Try to stay as calm about the whole thing as possible, maybe by thinking of it as a mental game. The challenge is to play up to your abilities. The trick is to know the rules of the game, to be familiar with the court it is being played on, and to have an idea of how the referees tend to react in certain circumstances. Probably one of the hardest things in the world to do is to maintain a sense of relaxation or composure when everyone is telling you not to be nervous. Staying cool is fine if you can manage it without going to the extreme of falling asleep in the middle of the test, but if you're a little nervous don't worry about it. Not only is it natural to be somewhat on edge, but that extra adrenaline might help you to think a bit faster. And no matter what the test is, or how experienced the people around you taking that test are, there will be about as many completely calm test-takers as there are banks offering loans at 2 percent interest. If you can keep from getting nervous about the fact that you are nervous, then you're off to a good start.

You want to keep two balls juggling in the air at the same time. The first ball has a message on it which reminds you to do as well as you can because, all things being equal, a high score is nice. The second ball has a slightly different message emblazoned on it. That message is that no matter what happens, no matter how badly you might goof up, this is still just a stupid test. You should not latch on to this as an excuse to quit trying if the going is difficult, or to do less than your best; just think of it as a commentary on the ultimate significance of this test as far as your worth as a human being is concerned. You won't become more or less intelligent once your score has been reported. A high score does not make you any smarter than you already are, nor does a low score turn you into a dullard. You've read about the many ways these tests can go wrong in arriving at your reported score. And you know that even when the test is accurately measuring what it claims to be measuring, those skills which the test focuses on are but a small part of the total picture of your abilities, intellectual and otherwise. If you're a good student and you just don't do well on the standardized test despite your best efforts, then take it as a reflection on the limitations of the test rather than as a conclusive, negative statement about you. By the same reasoning, if you get a great score on your test, by all means celebrate your fortune, but don't get to thinking that you are a superior being. You handled the test well, which is an accomplishment, but that is just the beginning of your labor, not the final product of it.

If you're a parent, the task before you is more difficult in some ways, because you must encourage your child to prepare for the test, but you don't want to overdo it. Unless your child is unusually indifferent about these tests, he or she is already feeling more than enough pressure about the outcome. If you push hard, you take the risk that the child will be overwhelmed by the added tension and will choke on the test. Or the child may decide that a poor performance on the test would be just the way to rebel against parental "interference." You know your child best, so you will have to decide where the line is between encouragement and nagging. Try to be especially sensitive to the anxiety your child may be experiencing as the test date draws nearer. Sometimes people who are most concerned with a test are the ones who cling to a mask of nonchalance most ferociously. Your assurances that you will not disown your offspring if their SATs are lower than the block average may be shrugged off at the time, but will be appreciated. Since you're a parent, you're used to trying the nearly impossible in helping your child. So try to convey a sense of the importance of the test and your willingness to be of assistance without blowing up the event to global dimensions.

In any event, don't let the test put a roof on your ambitions or assume that it is a floor which will always keep you elevated. The one way that the tests will get you is if you let them tell you what to do. There are realities, of course. Not everyone is going to become a brain surgeon, and not everyone should try. Knowing your strengths and weaknesses is a big part of being an adult. But your knowledge of those strengths and weaknesses must be formed by much more than just test results if it is to be reliable. The point is this: if your test scores are markedly different from the other indications you get about your talents (such as grades, peer and teacher responses, recommendations from employers, and personal accomplishments in a variety of fields), don't believe the test scores are automatically right while all these other indications are to be ignored. If anything, it is the test scores which are likely to be in error. You may end up trying for a goal you can't quite reach, but better that you try than miss opportunities just inches away because a test says you can't extend yourself that far. There are too many people who are underrated by the tests to justify any resignation on your part. And if you are gifted at taking tests, don't count on your skill in this one area alone to get you past all obstacles. Good guidance counselors, or older friends who have been through the tests, may be able to help you interpret test results without incorporating them as part of your image of yourself.

Now, what should you do to get ready for your test? The first thing is to read all the information available about the test. Many test publishers distribute pamphlets containing general information about their tests, and some include sample test questions. Study this material and look especially hard for the following facts: What are the rules on scoring? How much time will you have on average per question? What types of questions are likely to be on the test? These are important questions because the answers will largely dictate your test-taking strategy. First, as far as the scoring rules are concerned, you want to know if there is a penalty for guessing, and if so, what that penalty is. If the test score is simply the number of right answers you make, then you know that you must not leave a single answer blank. Since you will not lose points on this type of test for making wrong answers, you have nothing to lose on even the wildest of guesses. If you are taking this kind of test and you run out of time with twenty questions left blank, quickly fill in one space for each question at random. The odds are that you will get some answers right by pure chance. Even if you had the amazing bad luck to be wrong on all twenty of your guesses—which is unlikely on the more common kinds of standardized tests—you haven't lost anything by trying.

However, some tests try to discourage this sort of gambling by exacting a penalty for each wrong answer. The theory is that the penalty will either discourage guessing entirely, or at least substantially reduce the potential gain from filling in the blanks at random. If you are taking one of the "penalty tests," you should know how severe the penalty is for wrong answers. Once you know that, you can follow a simple formula to determine when to guess and when to leave an answer blank. Let's say you are taking a test where you have five alternative answers for every question, and a penalty for wrong answers. The penalty is that one-quarter of your wrong answers will be subtracted from the number of your right answers in arriving at your raw test score. So when should you guess? You want to play by the house rules on a standardized test, so play it safe. If there are five alternative answers and you have no idea whatsoever which of them is right, or which is definitely wrong, then don't guess. The odds are that if you guess wildly you will get one out of every five such questions right. But you will be losing a point for every four you get wrong, so, on average, there is no gain to you from guessing. Better to take those last frantic minutes and devote them to working on a few of the remaining questions and getting them right than to guess and break even. Here's the breakdown. If you have five blank questions and just guess, the odds are you will get one right and four wrong. You gain a point for the right answer, but lose a point for the four wrong answers (one-quarter times four wrong equals one), so it's a wash. If you concentrate instead on one question and get it right without guessing on the other four, then you gain a point and don't have to worry about the penalty for guessing wrong on the other four.

In short, on a test with these characteristics (five choices and a penalty amounting to one-quarter of the wrong answers), you simply break even on wild guesses. But the setup shifts in your favor dramatically for every alternative answer that you can eliminate as being wrong beyond a doubt. Anytime you can eliminate even one of the alternative answers on a question, make a guess among the remaining alternatives. The odds are now that you will gain more from your guesses than you will lose from the penalty. If you've been able to get rid of one alternative, then you should now get the right answer for one out of every four questions on average just by guessing among the remaining alternatives. Say you are able to eliminate one of the alternatives on sixteen questions and then guess among the rest. The odds are that you will come up with four right answers and twelve wrong answers. This will produce a net gain to you of one point on your score (four right minus three penalty points, that is, one-quarter of the twelve wrong answers). The more alternatives you can eliminate, the more this system works for you. So now you know ahead of time when to guess, and when to hold your pencil still. The rub is that you must be sure of yourself when you eliminate alternatives as obviously wrong. Usually at least one alternative will stand out as totally off the wall, but don't get reckless here.

If all of the alternatives appear plausible, then just leave them be and go on to the next question. And if you don't know what the penalty is for guessing, because the publisher makes a point of withholding that information, then be very cautious. Different people have different attitudes about what to do when the guessing penalty is unknown. Some will go ahead and guess freely, figuring that the penalty is probably low. I would be worried that the penalty is high and tend not to answer unless I had eliminated all but two alternatives. This is a situation you have to call for yourself.

Second, the matter of average answer time per question will be important to you. One of the things you don't want to do on a standardized test if you can possibly help it is to run out of time. In order to prevent that, you should set a strict time budget for yourself in advance. If there are 180 questions on the test and you have to finish in three hours, then you know you can't spend more than an average of one minute per question. Devise a set of signposts to check along the way to see that you are not falling behind your schedule. One method is to check your watch every time you finish a batch of thirty questions. Since you know you have an average of one minute per question, if you find you're spending more than thirty minutes on thirty questions, you'll have to pick up your pace. This doesn't mean that you refuse ever to spend more than one minute on a question. Sometimes you'll find that it takes two minutes to crack one question, while another question comes to you in a flash. That's okay, since you're making up time on the easier question. But if you find yourself going round and round on a question for four minutes without getting anywhere, forget it and move on to the next. It's not worth spending all that time on an obscure question when you can be making points on some of the questions ahead of you. You can come back and guess on that hard question at the end of the test. Before moving on, though, cross out (on the question booklet, not the answer sheet) all the alternatives you've been able to eliminate in your four minutes on the problem. That way, when you come back to guess (or work it out, if you've finished the rest of the test ahead of time), you won't have to waste time trying to remember how you had analyzed the question. And if you skip a question, be careful to answer the next one in the appropriate blank on the answer sheet.

Third, if you know what types of questions you are likely to encounter, then you'll have an edge on the test. It bolsters your confidence, if nothing else, to be able to recognize certain kinds of questions when you see them in a testing situation. What's more, you will save time in figuring them out if you've already had some experience with them. Some test publishers are fond of questions interpreting bar graphs and line graphs and the like. This type of question is not terribly difficult to answer if you know the technique for reading the graph, so it's worth your while to find out about it ahead of the test. Otherwise, even if you are able to puzzle out the correct approach during the test, you will have spent time that could have been put to better use. If there is a sample test available, and you've never taken this particular standardized test before, it is definitely a good idea to take the sample test. Try to do this several weeks before you have to take the real test, and try to take the practice test under test conditions. You want to take the practice test early so that you will have time to go over your answers and see where you went wrong. Then you can study the suggested answers for the questions you had trouble with in order to find out what the test publisher is looking for. If you totally bombed out on the practice test, don't panic, you still have time to learn about the various questions and maybe even retake the sample test later to give you a feel for how much you've been able to pick up in a few short weeks. You want to take the practice test under test conditions so you will be more confident when you have to take the real test and find it's not an entirely new adventure.

How much more you will want to do in preparing for a test is up to you. Obviously, if the test is going to be very important to you and you're completely unfamiliar with it or have a history of difficulty with standardized tests, then a little extra work could be a big help. Don't wait until three days before the test and decide to cram 5,000 vocabulary words. Unless you have a photographic memory, that kind of work is unlikely to do you much good. If you stay up late the night before the exam feverishly studying, your efforts are probably going to be counterproductive. A good night's sleep before the test can be worth weeks of cramming, so don't push it. In fact, no matter how you prepare, I would recommend that you stop at least three days before the test. That way your mind can recuperate a little from the onslaught of knowledge you've been subjecting it to. You'll be fresh for the test, maybe even a little eager, and whatever you've forgotten in the space of three days isn't likely to stick with you overnight either. So if the test is on Saturday morning, make Wednesday night your last big push. Thursday and Friday should be a time to catch your breath and relax a bit if you can. If you feel a need to skim some notes, or to review the Pythagorean theorem, or to read flash cards on vocabulary on Thursday and Friday, okay, but don't spend too much time on that work. If you find it easier to relax while occupied with studying, you're better off doing what feels natural, so go ahead. But don't sacrifice sleep, and don't forget that it takes longer to fall asleep when you're wound up than it usually does. So go to bed a little early the night before the test.

What about going to a coaching course for the test? That's an extremely hard question to answer without knowing all the details about your situation. The short answer is that if you can afford the time and the money for a coaching course, it's probably worth doing. If it's a reputable course, you could push your score above the level you'd get without taking the course. And you will acquire at least some substantive learning, even if it's not directly related to a higher score. At bottom, a good course could help you score higher than you would otherwise, and, unless something is really botched, a course won't leave you in worse shape than when you started. The harder question is whether your prospective score increase is worth the cost of the course. That would seem to depend on three factors you must weigh for yourself. Those three factors are: One, how likely are you to gain points? Two, how important would a score gain be to you? And three, how important is it that you score well on the test, taking your other achievements into account? Let's look at these factors one by one.

First, how likely is it that the course will boost your score? There's no way to know for sure, but there are some rules of thumb. If you're new to the test, or have had trouble with standardized tests before, or are unfamiliar with the subject matter being tested, it stands to reason that you have the most to gain in a coaching course.[1] Conversely, if you've taken this particular test a number of times (or tests very similar to it), and have always done well on standardized tests, and know your trigonometry and whatever else is on the test, then a coaching course would have to do a lot to raise you above your starting point.

Second, how much do you stand to gain by getting a top score on the test? Clearly, if the test is used for hiring and only the top 5 percent of candidates are eligible to go onto the selection list, the test score you receive is very important to you. This is an all-or-nothing test, which means you want to go all out in preparing for it. Or if you're applying to schools with cut-off score requirements, a difference of even five points could be enough to switch your name from the list marked "reject" to the list marked "accept." On the other hand, if you've already received a 770 on a test, even a successful drive to push yourself to the 800 level probably isn't going to make any practical difference since your score was so high in the first place.

Third, how important is it that you score well on the test, taking your other achievements into account? Maybe you have such impeccable credentials beside the test score that you will fare well as long as the score is not absolutely abysmal when compared with those of the other applicants. For example, if you're applying to college and are a straight-A student with athletic abilities that have earned recognition on at least a statewide level, with a winning personality and demonstrated leadership abilities, you can afford to present less than a super score in most cases because all these other qualities will get attention. On the other hand, if your strong suit consists of your academic promise alone, a poor test score could be more damaging. Test scores do not necessarily count the same for all applicants in all circumstances. Just as it is not prudent to disregard the impact test scores may have on your chances for selection, neither is it wise to become obsessed with test scores if you are in such a strong position that you could survive a mediocre performance.

After you've sifted through these factors you should have some inkling whether a coaching course would be worth your time and money. If you think it might be, then it's good to shop around. The education section of your local newspaper will probably carry advertising for coaching courses, and you can also check with the Yellow Pages and friends for additional courses. You could also contact your education department or vocational counselors for more courses to add to your list. Some local school systems run their own review courses which would save you money. Once you're convinced that you've located all the coaching schools within your area, the next step is to call them for some specific information. Look especially at cost, length of the course, total hours of the course, philosophy of instruction, and any guarantees for students who take the course. As to cost, you don't want to spend any more than you have to, but remember that an inexpensive course is no bargain if it's unreliable. Length of the course and total hours of instruction can give you some guides to the value of a course. While there may be exceptions, look in general for a course that is spread over an appreciable length of time (say a month or two) and that offers a substantial number of classroom hours. The longer period of time should allow the skills you are learning to sink in with practice and reinforcement. And if you aren't getting individual attention in the course because classroom time is meager, then you might do just as well by purchasing a review book or cassette program and studying with some friends. The philosophy of instruction should stress two things in particular: one, practice with questions similar to those asked on the test, coupled with feedback on your reasoning process in answering questions so you know why you are getting questions wrong or right;[2] and, two, emphasis on teaching the underlying subjects as well as the particular "test tricks"—the former might do you some good long after you've completed a given test.

Guarantees, if honored, are an indication that a course at least thinks highly of itself. A guarantee may take the form of a refund if you don't achieve a target goal after faithfully attending all the sessions. More likely is some sort of discount on a repeat course if you fail the test or don't register certain score gains. But just because a course offers guarantees doesn't mean it's right for you—after all, if a course is constantly honoring the guarantee because it isn't doing a great job for its students, you shouldn't be in any rush to sign up. Moreover, the guarantee may be written so restrictively that it only comes into play under very unusual conditions, which is no break either. And you might find a coaching course that looks fine in every other respect, in which case the absence of a guarantee alone should not scare you away. But if the other signs of respectability are present, the existence of a reasonable guarantee policy is a definite bonus. You should be careful in picking out a coaching course because the field has attracted its share of enterprising operations that may or may not give you value for your money. Remember that even at the best of the test schools there is no certainty that you will boost your score by a specific amount. You could take a good course, work hard, and actually see your test score go down. That's just how it works. All you are doing in searching for a good course is finding an organization that will make a decent effort to show you the ropes. If you exert yourself, the course may pay off, but you can't count on that as an absolute fact. And if you end up in one of the less satisfactory courses, you are reducing the odds that your preparation will lead to higher test scores.

The difficulty arises because even when a particular coaching school is able to demonstrate test score gains on average for its pupils, not everyone will achieve that average gain. Some will do better, some will do worse. In discussing the merits, or lack of same, of coaching schools, a representative of ACT testified: "Logic dictates that 'test preparation courses' that are of sufficient length and content to be considered *instruction* need little investigation, since their worth is obvious. They will help some students and they won't help others, as is the case with any instructional program."[3] You can't be 100 percent sure of success in advance with any coaching school, so what you are doing involves a calculated gamble. The ACT official went on to state: "Telling students that 'some preparatory courses may be helpful to some students for some tests' is hardly helpful, but it is the only reasonable statement that can be made given present knowledge of the topic. To state otherwise would be misleading."[4] So what are you to do? Shop around, check out the qualities of coaching courses we've talked about earlier, and ask friends and counselors for their advice. People who have already taken a course can tell you whether the tutors were competent and as interested in helping students as in receiving their payments. It isn't possible to make a blanket recommendation or condemnation of specific coaching schools without inspecting all of them and obtaining more data than is presently available. Moreover, there is always the possibility that a branch office will be working above or below the national standard for the chain. And the form of instruction that is most effective for one person may be very different from what best suits the next person.

Having said that, and with the explicit warning that you must not take my word for it, but have to explore the options yourself, my opinion is that a Stanley Kaplan course would be the safest bet in general. In the unofficial FTC reports which found coaching could help, it was the Stanley Kaplan course in particular which achieved that result. The philosophy of instruction and the duration of training subscribed to in the main by Stanley Kaplan are in accord with the principles which make the most sense to me, even though we disagree on other matters of testing policy. Kaplan himself is an energetic and sincere individual with a wealth of experience in the coaching field. A close inspection may reveal a number of coaching courses as good as—or even better than—Kaplan's. That is exactly what you should do: make a close inspection of the courses in your vicinity. If you find courses which meet your criteria other than the Kaplan centers, by all means sign up with them. Your knowledge of the alternatives will be much superior to that of any distant observer. All I am saying is this: the Kaplan chain merits your attention if you are near one of their offices. If you use them as a benchmark and find a course of higher standards, or if you go with the Kaplan course because you didn't find a course of comparable worth, then you are probably entitled to the satisfaction that goes with being an intelligent consumer.

You may detect a note of unease in this discussion of coaching. In the first place, there are some coaching schools which seem to be rip-off joints, and they inevitably take a certain cut of the business. At the same time, use of a good coaching school is in some sense a way for individuals to gain an advantage without addressing any of the larger problems of standardized testing. Since coaching courses cost money, and since not having money is the prime attribute of being poor, the widespread use of these courses may be just another way of heightening the competitive disadvantage that the poor suffer on standardized tests. Further, it is at least arguable that your gain from taking a coaching course is inversely proportional to the number of other people taking such courses: the more of your competitors who take coaching and boost their scores, the less impressive your test improvement looks. If everyone were to take a decent coaching course, average scores would probably go up, but other than that, the effects on the system might be minimal. If anything, the problem of over-reliance on the test might be worsened since some would feel the inequalities in background had been compensated for under such a regime.

Cramming for a test is a dubious proposition. Unlike coaching, which is spread out over an adequate interval before a test, cramming is the attempt to swallow huge portions of information whole in just a couple of days before a test. Maybe this is better than nothing for some people who can keep that knowledge down until they need it on the test, but most people would suffer severe indigestion—or worse—if put on such a crash program to gain intellectual weight. Since there is such a short time to work with, cramming stresses drills and tricks over instruction in the basics of a subject. Even when it produces score improvements, the up-swing in personal knowledge is ephemeral. If you manage to wear yourself down by trying to stuff in all this material just before the test, the net effect of cramming could be to lower your score rather than raise it. Unless you are immensely talented, you don't become a champion sprinter by practicing the hundred yard dash only for the two days before a race, and you aren't likely to become an overnight sensation on a standardized test by trying to do it all at once either.

What should you do if you can't afford a decent coaching course and you're convinced that you are one of the people who stands to gain the most from that kind of instruction? To begin with, don't assume that the course that looks best is inescapably closed to you. Some coaching courses offer scholarships, although they don't always go out of their way to advertise that fact. You should ask the people who run the course whether they have such a program, and what is necessary to qualify. You might have to get a school counselor or someone else to recommend you, but if you're eligible for a scholarship, follow through on the requirements. Short of a full scholarship, there may be opportunities for partial subsidies or deferred payments, if you are persistent. If all these avenues are blocked, try to enlist the aid of school counselors, teachers, or the PTA; or a civic group of some sort; or members of the clergy. If you have some success with these groups, you might be able to get a permanent fund established so that others who come after you will also benefit. Maybe all this effort will be in vain and you just can't raise the money for a coaching course. Even if that's the case, you should be sure to mention your efforts in any school or job application you file which is related to the test. Any selection committee with a heart is going to be impressed by the trouble you went to in trying to prepare for the test. A low score should not look as bad to a committee that knows the score reflects a lack of opportunity despite real desire, and the demonstrated initiative you took in trying to counter your problem should count for something.

Don't despair if you don't take a coaching course. Many students will do fine without that sort of specialized training because they've already absorbed the essentials one way or another. You can make it without a coaching course. If you want some preparation but aren't about to—or aren't able to—spend the kind of money coaching schools are asking for, there are less expensive substitutes that can help. Go to any major bookstore's education or testing section. There you will find row after row of books called *How to Take This Test,* and *How to Take That Test.* Most of these books cost around $10 or less, and should at least provide some test-taking drills. Drills are of limited value in test preparation, so don't rely exclusively on this type of studying. Look closely at books that explain the process of figuring out answers on standardized tests. Or if you can get help from a friend who is good at the tests and is willing to listen to you work through some sample test questions out loud, by all means take advantage of your friend's offer. In any event, I strongly recommend that you buy or borrow from the library a copy of a book by Bernard Feder called *The Complete Guide to Taking Tests* which was published by Prentice-Hall, Inc. in 1979. It is a paperback and currently costs $4.95.

Feder's book covers essay examinations as well as standardized tests, so check for the chapters which are most relevant to your needs. Feder pulls no punches when he declares: "In the long run, the effort you apply to learning test-taking will pay off far more handsomely than the effort to learn most school subjects. Your future depends on your skill in taking tests. True reform in testing appears a long way off, and in the foreseeable future, truly skilled test-takers should be able to continue to beat the system."[5] While I don't vouch for everything in *The Complete Guide to Taking Tests,* it's a valuable and practical book which will provide you with detailed pointers on how to prepare yourself for a close encounter with standardized tests. There are other good books and pamphlets on the topic, so don't hesitate to explore the shelves containing books on education and tests. Bear in mind that the sooner you start to get ready for a test the greater your gain can be. A steady program of learning about the tests and of studying for the one you have to take is surely better than frantic efforts at the last minute. Whether you take a coaching course or teach yourself, you will gain the most if you do this *before* you take a test for the first time, rather than waiting until it is time for a retest. There are two reasons for this. One, some testers (such as ETS) may challenge the second, higher score as the product of cheating if it matches certain patterns on their computer programs. As we know, it could be that the initial, lower score was the inaccurate result, so why run the risk of having to "prove" yourself all over again to some test publisher? The delay caused by score verification could make you miss some application deadlines. Two, many institutions average test scores whenever a candidate reports two or more.

For example, say you are going to have to take the SAT before applying to college. If you take the test to see how you do and then decide to prepare for it the second time around, even if your preparation bears fruit, it won't be as sweet as if you had picked the time before the first SAT to work. Let's say you got a 470 on the SAT-V and then studied for a retest and you succeeded in pushing that score up to 550 the next time. A college may average those two scores and arrive at a composite SAT-V score for you of 510. This is better than if you did nothing after receiving the first score. But if you had put all your effort into preparing for the first SAT and earned a 550, then you would have received full credit for that score in the deliberations of a college admissions committee. Maybe you wouldn't have been able to prepare as effectively without having taken the SAT once, so that a program of preparation would only yield a 520. That 520 still looks better than an average of 510. In fact, a single SAT score of 510 is probably more beneficial to you than an average SAT score of 510. This is because someone may look at the averaged scores of 470 and 550 and wonder if the 470 wasn't the more accurate of the two. With a single score of 510, the question doesn't come up. The moral, then, is to do your homework before you take a test for the first time. If you get a satisfactory score that way, you don't have to worry about it being dragged down by an earlier and lower test score. And you only have to take the test once as opposed to twice or more. Further, if you get a low score the first time, you still have the opportunity to come back for another try and aren't any worse off than if you had taken the test without preparation. Should you have reason to be unhappy with a test score, by all means feel free to take it again after some extra work to get ready for it. If you improve, it will reflect favorably on you. Yet if it is at all possible for you to channel that energy into being in shape the first time you take on the test, you'll be ahead of the game.

What does it mean to have "reason" to be unhappy with a test score? Two factors are involved. First, what could you reasonably expect to score? Second, how high a score do you need to meet the standards of the school or job you are applying for? Your personal expectations should be based on your past dealings with tests and your performance in school and other academic pursuits. If you're a B+ student and have done well on the standardized tests you've taken before, and suddenly your SAT comes back as a 330, then something is amiss. You should be able to improve that score. The other side of the coin is knowing when to leave well enough alone. If you've always done poorly on standardized tests and have a very low GPA and your SAT comes back with a 770, don't take it again to see if you can go up to an 800. In fact, even if you have a great track record with these tests and a 4.0 GPA, don't retake a 770. While you might be able to go up a few points, you could also go down a lot. That 770 is impressive enough that taking the risk of improving on it is not a smart bet. This is where the second factor comes into play. If you know with some degree of assurance what kind of score it takes to be selected, you will avoid gambling for a few points more when you are already over the score requirement. The decision of whether to retake a test has to be yours alone depending on the facts in your case. However, remember that if you are rejected even though you have a 770, it is probably for reasons other than your test score—the odds are that you would not have been admitted even with an 800. And if you have a 770, but retake the test and get a 650 (which by itself is still an excellent score), you are going to be most unhappy with your decision.

There are a few simple rules to follow whenever you show up to take a standardized test. The mechanical rules are: bring extra number 2 pencils, bring your admission ticket, bring a watch, and bring candy and/or something to drink to keep you awake during the test (unless food and drink are forbidden, as is sometimes the case). The extra pencils are in case the test proctors run out of them. The watch is so that you can keep track of your progress under time pressure in case the room doesn't have a wall clock. The food and drink are for bursts of energy which you may find necessary as the test wears on. Eat a good meal before taking the test. In some ways a standardized test is a test of physical endurance, so why handicap yourself by drooping in the middle of the morning because you're low on food? In the same vein, unless you are chained to your chair, or the proctors are surly, stand up and move around a little at some point during the test to get the blood flowing again. Try to go to the bathroom a few minutes before the test starts so you won't have to squander any of those precious minutes on functions not related to math (assuming you're allowed out of the room at all once the test is in progress). If you think you'll be tested on some complex formulas or the conjugation of irregular verbs in a foreign language that you're desperately trying to remember, write them down on a piece of scratch paper (*if* scratch paper is allowed) the instant the test begins.[6] You can't write this information down ahead of time and bring it in—that's cheating. But once the test starts you're not cheating if you scribble down a few key details so that you won't forget them before you get to the section covering that material. That way you can concentrate fully on each question as it comes up, rather than trying to keep the formulas in your mind at the same time you're working on a different subject. Take extra time to read the instructions on the test twice, just to be careful. If you misunderstand what you're being asked to do, you aren't going to excel on the test. And if you should discover that you've misnumbered your answers or something of that sort—and it's too late to correct it yourself— bring it to the proctor's attention and insist that a note be made of your complaint. This way the test publisher may be more understanding when you raise the problem in a letter to them as soon as you get home. The same approach should be followed if you think a lot of your answers were smudged in erasing. If you were sick during the test, call or write the test publisher immediately to see about getting your test cancelled and taking it over later when you're healthy.

After you receive your test score, there are still a few options open to you. If you think there must have been a mistake in the scoring of the test, you can request that it be rescored by hand. At least some test publishers will honor this request, although there may be a fee of several dollars for the work involved. If the publisher of your test makes copies of the questions and answers on the test available to test-takers for a nominal charge, you should seriously consider asking for that information. A review of your reasoning compared with the designated answers should be informative and may be of help to you in the future in thinking like a test writer on another test. If you continue to get low scores despite your best efforts while also doing well in school or on the job, be sure to mention that fact in filling out your application. A demonstrated record of good performance and poor test scores may be enough to persuade a selection committee to downplay the test scores in their evaluation. You may be reluctant to do this for fear that you will be drawing attention to something you'd rather have overlooked, but if your scores are low enough, they are unlikely to go unnoticed whether you say anything or not. If you bring the issue up, at least you have a chance to explain why the test scores are not particularly meaningful in this instance. You may not be able to persuade the committee of the justice of your argument, but you will have had a chance at bat. Otherwise, the test scores may strike you out without even a decent swing on your part. Don't overdo this—don't poormouth your scores if they really are good. But if you have a legitimate gripe about the tests, don't let it slide without saying anything. No committee can read your mind, so speak up. Ideally you will want to cite specifically why the test did a bad job of measuring *your* skills as opposed to reciting abstract arguments about the inadequacy of tests in general. If you can get some people who are aware of the shortcomings of the test in reflecting your potential to write extra letters of recommendation, your claim may find a more receptive audience.

Finally, once you have done the best you can in getting ready for, and taking, a test, and have supplied any meaningful supplemental information to the appropriate people, don't dwell on the results forever. Whether your score was superb or below par, it doesn't prove anything about you unless you let it. However, if you are concerned about the fairness and accuracy of the general system using these standardized tests, there is much you can—and should—do as part of the test reform movement. Chapter 14 discusses a reform proposal that would help nudge tests in the right direction. Once you have faced the short-term problem of surviving a test, you may want to become involved in a more long-range effort to reduce the level of test abuse.

CHAPTER FOURTEEN

Opening
the Industry

Many of the ills of testing are caused by the virus of excessive secrecy. Secrecy prevents test-takers from reviewing the questions and answers which have been used to evaluate their academic skills. Secrecy prevents outside researchers from freely examining the quality of these tests and making their findings known to the public. Secrecy preserves an aura of mystery around the tests, an aura which—like shimmering hot air—distorts the true image of test imperfections and strengths alike. Secrecy precludes a better understanding by the public of the construction, use, and abuse of tests. Secrecy protects the testing industry from the constant scrutiny so necessary for test accountability and improvement. One of the vital first steps in turning around our overreliance on tests is to open up the industry to the light of day, to the inspection of interested students and parents. The mere act of ordering disclosure of essential information about the tests won't reform them or prevent possible future shenanigans. But it will make the publishers more responsible for the worth of their tests, and it will provide a measure of fairness in the lives of those who lose out on their goals because of poor test scores.

This is what open testing is all about. Open testing, which is also called truth-in-testing, would require that all test questions and answers actually used in arriving at the raw score for an individual be released to the public at the same time, or shortly after, the test scores are reported. This fairly modest proposal has engendered heated controversy and often bitter opposition from some quarters of the testing community. Why is this? Open testing is not a regulatory law. It does not say that from now on test publishers will have to meet certain standards of test quality before tests can be brought to the marketplace. It does not say that admissions committees and others who use these instruments in great quantities have to pass a test of their own to show they understand the theory and limits of the tools they are employing. It does not say when and how such tests may be used in selection decisions. All open testing calls for is disclosure. Let us see the tests. Let us judge for ourselves what kind of a job they are doing. Let us exercise our right to know in this area that affects us and our children so deeply. If the tests are so good, then surely release of this information will only serve to enhance their reputation in the long run. If the tests are bad, hiding them doesn't make them any better and may forestall the kind of pressure that could force the industry to redesign them.

The most significant open testing law now on the books is in New York State. That law requires full disclosure of questions and answers used in computing scores for postsecondary and professional school admission tests within thirty days of the reporting of scores to students. In addition, the New York law also forces publishers to release special statistical reports about test validity and to provide certain background information about the tests to all prospective examinees. An impressive array of organizations backed the passage of the New York legislation. Included in this group were the local chapters of the PTA, the National Education Association, the NAACP, the Puerto Rican Legal Defense and Education Fund, and the New York Public Interest Research Group.[1] Unsung volunteers and interested testing experts banded together under the leadership of several concerned legislators and their staffs to withstand the onslaught of the professional testers and their allies. In the end, Governor Hugh Carey signed the bill into law on July 14, 1979[2] which also happened to be Bastille Day. This coincidence was appropriate. At least in New York, test-takers will now be free to view the tests which have formerly been confined behind the closed walls of secrecy. As David White wrote, "No longer will it be necessary to launch an uncertain lawsuit to examine the tests."[3] The *Boston Globe* praised the event in an editorial: "We live in the world's most test-oriented society. And while colleges and graduate schools may claim that test results are but one measure they employ in admissions, they do clearly matter. Students have a right to confirm, if only to satisfy themselves, that the scores that shape their lives are accurate. Further, the whole notion of education in our society revolves, or should revolve, around an open exchange of ideas and the accumulation of skills and ideas that can lead to wisdom. The administering of tests for which the 'correct' answers are never revealed and the students' work never returned tends to convert education into a frantic scramble up the greasy pole. It is fundamentally at odds with what the whole process of education ought to be about."[4]

The frenzied opposition of the testing industry following the signing of the New York law raised the prospect of a test boycott of the state. Some publishers were threatening to isolate the state from the standard forms of the national tests or levy substantial cost surcharges in retaliation. These tactics didn't sit well with a number of state residents. The *New York Times* warned in an editorial, "The intemperate responses of some academic testers to New York's Truth-in-Testing law are certain to damage their cause more than the law itself . . . their complaints are overstated. In fact the law is welcome; it's time to take the mystery out of college testing."[5] The *Times* went on to point out that open testing was little more than an extension of commonly accepted principles from other areas into the realm of standardized testing: "There is the matter of elementary fairness. These academic tests help to shape the course of people's lives—their schooling, their careers, the very sense of their own abilities. Students deserve to know how they are being rated and judged. There are freedom-of-information laws, truth-in-lending laws, truth-in-packaging laws. Why not truth-in-testing as well?"[6] Why not truth-in-testing indeed? The fact that the industry which would be affected by public inspection of its product is unhappy with that possibility is hardly a convincing reason to defer action. What is needed is a national counterpart of the New York law so that the benefits of open testing will be available throughout the country while the costs are distributed over a larger base of people, thus reducing even further any potential additional cost per test-taker.

The arguments for the passage of open testing laws, whether they be efforts to extend the New York law to more states or a national resolution to insure uniformity in practice, fall under three main headings. One, there is a need to open up the testing industry so that normal tenets of accountability can operate in that cloistered world. Two, there is a need to open up these tests so that those whose lives are most directly affected can have some assurances of fairness in fact as well as in industry rhetoric. Three, there is a need to open up the research and data banks of the industry so that an informed public discussion of testing can restore perspective and help mold future policy. So far, the drive for open testing laws has been spearheaded by people most pre-occupied with the problems of testing for selection at the high school level and up. This is understandable since dramatic and visible consequences attach to tests at that level. But the plight of younger children should not be overlooked since they are the ones least equipped to appeal the summary judgment of the tests; some pioneering efforts in Massachusetts by state education offi-cials and school principals, among others, indicate that the spe-cial needs of elementary school children will not be overlooked by the test reform movement. For now, let's look a little more closely at the three central reasons for enactment of open testing laws.

"Accountability" is a rallying cry that can be overdone; however, when it comes to tests, it is hardly done at all. Even though these tests have been adopted as a means of determining the quality and quantity of education that many of us will receive and as a guide for decisions on job licensing and hiring, the in-dustry resents the intrusion of public demands on its fiefdom. We are told to go away and focus on some other aspects of American life because we can rest assured that the tests operate in our best interests and the testers are all above reproach. This is not a unique reaction from an industry which is used to having its own way without any backtalk. Should it deter us from taking steps to ensure that tests reflect the needs of society as well as the convenience of the industry? Layton Olson of the National Stu-dent Education Fund had this message for the New York legisla-tors who considered the truth-in-testing bill: "Mass process standardized tests . . . have substantial potential for good use and misuse; [but] testing services are currently outside the normal channels of accountability to the public . . . [they are] in effect, educational public utilities acting as near monopolies under delegations of public powers in providing public services all of which are financed by test-takers."[7] Pat Rooney of the Golden Rule Insurance Company put it a bit more bluntly: "It seems to me that if this piece of legislation . . . dealt with the insurance industry or with other profit making ventures, there'd be no question at all of its passage. It would pass, and I don't think anybody today is going to successfully uphold the issue of secrecy in commerce."[8] We've already seen that the label "nonprofit" doesn't confer perfection on an organization. Neither should it be an all-purpose shield from legislation aimed at the abuses which can take place in tests, whether they are sold for profit or not.

Plato is credited with the statement, "The life which is unexamined is not worth living." The same may be said of standardized tests: the test which is unexamined is not worth giving. Some publishers have countered that they are already supplying all the information the public could ask for, and then some.[9] But who are they to be the sole judges of what information the public wants and is entitled to? Wouldn't it be better to provide unfettered access and let the public decide what is important and what is not? Rosalyn Herman of the Division of Research and Educational Services of the New York State United Teachers testified in Albany about the importance of open testing to a careful review of standardized tests. She said, "The aura of mystery needs to be dispelled. What we need is something that defines the limits of test use but also defends what they are good for. The Truth-in-Testing bill would insure that tests are properly used and that test result information would be made available to the test-taker."[10] The cleansing effects of open testing were cited by Paul Jacobs in his testimony. "It *will* allow a student to gain an indepth understanding of what goes into the test. It will also permit the entire academic community to scrutinize the tests that now are so routinely accepted, and this, in turn, would expose any cultural or ethnic biases on the test."[11] This in itself would be reason enough to support open testing legislation.

The dearth of crucial information about tests has been repeatedly bemoaned by experts in the field. Since the experts outside the testing industry complain of lack of access to the facts, you can imagine how little of this material is ultimately filtering down to the general public. Ellen Schultz of the New York State Personnel and Guidance Association went on the record with a criticism of this information gap. She testified, "It has been our experience in the past that many major tests have not provided adequate information to the test-taker and as a matter of fact [have] been detrimental both as an interpretive instrument and psychologically. . . . The lack of preliminary information is one of the key abuses in the present testing system."[12] Oscar Buros, former publisher of the *Mental Measurements Yearbook,* gave a speech several years ago in which he noted that the information publishers revealed about their "secure" (or secret) tests fell short of what was needed to reach a responsible conclusion about them. "Since the tests themselves can be examined only under highly restricted conditions, if at all, it becomes of greatest importance that detailed information be provided for secure tests. . . . Yet far less information is available on these secure tests and, to make matters worse, much of the information which the publisher does possess is considered to be confidential—for in-house use only. If detailed information were made available simultaneously with the publication of tests, not only would educators and testing specialists be in a better position to evaluate the tests and to interpret the results more intelligently, but the publishers would be impelled to construct tests, pointing out their strengths and weaknesses."[13] Test publishers have had decades to open their books for analysis voluntarily; their obstinacy in refusing to do so is in large measure the catalyst for disclosure laws.

Industry insensitivity to concerns about the tests has been another source of energy for the movement. This behavior sometimes verges on arrogance and is by no means a relic of the past. During hearings on an open testing bill in 1979, one representative of a testing company attacked a provision which would have required test publishers to provide a specific statistic. The official said, "The type of reporting called for, namely, the extent to which test scores improve prediction of grade point average, expressed as a percentage, is a virtually meaningless statistic, as well as one that would be scarcely comprehensible to most candidates."[14] You can pick yourself up off the floor after reading that one. The ability of tests to improve prediction of grade point average *is* important. If tests aren't making any improvement in this prediction when used with previous grades, recommendations, and so forth, then what is their purpose? This "virtually meaningless statistic" is the bedrock (or quicksand) underpinning the argument for the use of standardized tests in the first place. It is the claim of test publishers that their tests improve these predictions which has served as their strongest selling point for years. And now members of the industry are fighting requirements that the magnitude of this improvement be expressed as a percentage and distributed to the public? Note also the condescension dripping from the remark that this information "would be scarcely comprehensible to most candidates." This information would be far more comprehensible to most candidates than the rising impatience with industry patronizing is to at least some test publishers.

This same official also dismissed the proposed requirement that publishers compile figures to show what relation—if any—high test scores have to actual career achievement. He said, "Such information is almost never available, in large part owing to the extreme difficulty of defining and measuring career success. Moreover, most tests used for admissions purposes purport only to predict success in training programs or, where used for certification and licensure purposes, to measure only the knowledge requirement and none of the other attributes that make for career success."[15] All the more reason to require the widespread dissemination of this admission that standardized tests at their very best try only to measure knowledge or predict success in training programs. If more people realized how limited the value of tests is in forecasting career success, which is what we should care about most, then maybe some of the symptoms of test overreliance could be alleviated. Test publishers are often very candid in discussion about the limitations of their tests. But they will sometimes turn around and fight tooth and nail against any provisions which would help get this information to a much larger group of people.

"Fairness" is a theme which permeates the speech of those

pushing for the enactment of open testing laws. This isn't hard to understand. It is asking too much of people that they should submit to the dictates of a test which is written in secret, administered under great time pressure, and then graded in secret. In American courtrooms you have a constitutional right to confront your accuser. On American standardized tests, all too often the only right you have is to pay to take the test again, unless you want to be written off on the basis of your present score. Steve Solomon, a leader of the battle for the New York law while with the New York Public Interest Research Group, explained the motivation for forcing tests into the open: "A basic tenet of fairness dictates that people have the right to review the criteria used to evaluate their ability. Standardized admissions tests are also major instruments of public policy. They influence decisions about who is admitted to colleges, graduate schools, law, medical, and other professional schools. It is essential that such instruments of public policy be available for public discussion and review."[16] Even if the tests were absolutely perfect, as they most assuredly are not, it would be unacceptable to keep them locked away from sight so that people were dependent on the good intentions and competency of the testers. We long ago rejected the notion of government rule by secrecy, except in matters of total national security; surely what is forbidden to the FBI is not fair game for the testing industry. Fairness does not encompass test sleight-of-hand.

Dr. Walter Haney, a testing expert with the Huron Institute, a research group concerned with educational policy, thinks "the main argument in favor of open testing is the proposition that, as a matter of simple justice, individual test-takers have a right to know the basis on which they're judged, specifically the details of the assessments on which their life chances both in terms of educational opportunities and other employment opportunities might be affected."[17] Another aspect of the fairness question involves the unequal access to coaching schools for test preparation. If you don't have a lot of money, a test preparation course could be out of your reach. And to the extent that these courses are able to help students score higher, those who are kept outside suffer an additional disadvantage in the competition for scarce positions. Abby Helfer of the Syracuse University Student Association asked the rhetorical question: "Is the student who can afford a $200 course a smarter student?"[18] The answer, of course, is intended to be "no," but you wouldn't always come to that conclusion if you relied on the results of the tests. One way to reduce this unfairness is to release test questions across the board, rather than allowing them to be hoarded by the test courses which compile lists of the information that is released in pieces. As New York State Senator Donald Halperin put it, "One reason for disclosing the questions is to put everyone on equal footing since really the questions are not as secret as some would be led to believe."[19] If the test questions become part of the public domain, then students who can't afford to buy access to test questions and facsimiles at coaching courses at least will have a wealth of general information to draw on. That won't end all the unfairness associated with tests, but it should lessen it, if only a little.

It's not always easy to tell where the fairness argument leaves off and the secrecy argument begins. One way of thinking is that fairness is a matter of treating individuals properly, while secrecy concerns society as a whole being deprived of the information it needs to decide how to use tests. As David Stratman said, "Due to the mask of 'security,' the public has been unable to evaluate dispassionately the claims of test makers, the uses by public school systems and institutes of higher learning, or the many reported abuses. Information about the tests and the testing process is minimal."[20] Vito Perrone sees the enactment of open testing laws as a way to start evolving a more comprehensive vision of individual capabilities. "Would we have more commitment to broader definitions of talent—to alternative means of presenting competences and accomplishments—if tests such as the SAT and ACT were more accessible . . . ? Would students and counselors alike benefit from item by item review? Again, I believe so."[21] Neither tests nor test publishers are unabashed villains in this saga, but the intoxication with secrecy only serves to emphasize whatever sinister impressions people initially have about the system. One official of a highly regarded test company tried to deflect the open testing surge in this fashion. He testified with candor that, "Tests indeed are imperfect. There is bias in testing that is both tenacious and yet to succumb to vigorous research. Test results are sometimes misused. Use of tests is growing and sometimes perhaps without adequate reason. ACT has addressed these issues."[22] No doubt ACT has addressed and will continue to address these issues. Yet that overlooks the fundamental point: we must all address these issues. ACT has done some superb work in this area, and will continue to do so in the future. But no testing organization, not even the entire testing industry, can do this job in solitude. Public confidence, if it is to be restored, demands public involvement in setting the ends and selecting the means of standardized testing.

Even if testing were entering the last part of this century with a clean slate, the times would not permit a few companies to exercise unlimited discretion in so vital an area. As it is, with a history of test injustices that stretches back to the start of this century, the tremendous reservoir of trust from all segments of society that would be needed to sustain secrecy has gone bone dry. Testers will have to supply vast amounts of information to students and parents if they ever hope to refill that reservoir. Some observers are pessimistic that the testers are up to the task. Paul Pottinger told Congress, "Testing companies, concerned about the financial impact of selling their products to people who would no longer be in the dark about the value of these tests, will argue against this law. . . . The testing companies should fear loss of credibility and revenue if the truth gets out about tests. This is a legitimate fear based on their own knowledge that the tests we are talking about fail to be fair or competence-based."[23] But Urbain DeWinter, an associate dean and director of Arts and Sciences Admissions at Cornell University, takes a more optimistic tack. In his opinion, "Disclosing the tests . . . would add to our knowledge of the tests and demystify the secret contents that promote misunderstanding of the tests among students, parents, and admissions officials. . . . Disclosure would lead to a more realistic appraisal of the strengths as well as the limitations of a test; ultimately, it will strengthen the credibility of tests, for they will be examined by a wide variety of educators who are interested in maintaining their high quality."[24] The performance of the testing industry in the years to come will finally resolve the dispute over whether pessimism or optimism is called for. The steadfast opposition to change demonstrated by the bulk of the testers, even when they make cosmetic alterations in the hope of diverting wrath, is not an encouraging sign.

Opponents of open testing have tried to assail the proposal on technical points rather than by taking an untenable position against openness as such. They claim that open testing will cost too much or that it will invalidate tests or that it's superfluous because so much information is already in circulation. These arguments are like the waves of an ocean crashing on the beach. Both are strong and apparently moving in just one direction. But both also can conceal deep and powerful currents that would carry anyone caught up in them out the other way. Take the arguments about cost for example. Certainly open testing would require writing more test questions, although exactly how many is the subject of another controversy. But the industry expenditure on test writing as a percentage of the charge to the consumer is small, at least if the figures reported for ETS are any indication. Prior to enactment of the New York law, test publishers were claiming they would have to raise test charges in the state anywhere from $4 to $25 per test-taker.[25] But ETS critic Allan Nairn has asserted that ETS only spends 5 to 10 percent of test revenues from their biggest tests for question writing.[26] Nairn cited an internal ETS document, the "Activity Analysis" for 1970–71, in support of his statement. This document backs up Nairn's conclusion, and to my knowledge ETS has never challenged its authenticity. In fact, an official of ETS confirmed to me that a figure of 5 to 7 percent for test development cost is correct.[27] That official pointed out that the particular percentage is subject to change if either the number of tests or candidate volume varies.

Yet the basic fact remains that the current development cost is so low that it could be multiplied many times before it became a substantial consideration. The 1970–71 development cost of $.32 for the SAT,[28] for example, would have to be multiplied more than twelve times to reach the minimal $4 price increase that the College Board claimed was in the cards.[29] After the law was enacted, the College Board raised the price of taking the SAT in New York from $8.25 to $10—an increase of $1.75 per test. The Board also set a fee of $4.65 for providing an individual with a duplicate set of her answers on an SAT form.[30] What's more, there is the question of "excess revenues" earned by some test publishers on some tests, even though they are nonprofit organizations. New York State Senator LaValle raised this point in his testimony before Congress. Referring to an ETS estimate that SAT development costs would balloon by more than a million dollars in New York, LaValle said, "Even if ETS's figure is accepted, despite our conflicting data, it still amounts to less than one-third of the surplus taken by ETS and College Board on the SAT. Between 1975–76 and 1976–77 the earned surplus ranged from $3,000,000 to $3,541,000. Upon learning of the extremely profitable nature of this industry, many legislators asked, 'Why don't we legislate a decrease in the cost of these exams?' "[31] The cost figures cannot be more exact because the testing industry hasn't invited outside challengers to go over their financial records. In these circumstances, as Dr. Haney wrote, "It is impossible to judge this issue until test publishers provide us with a detailed accounting of what current test development, administration, and scoring costs are."[32] If test publishers have this detailed information which would establish conclusively the mammoth costs of open testing, why aren't they providing us with it? You wouldn't expect businesses to dispense such information freely, but then neither would you expect nonprofit outfits to be so guarded. Unless and until there is a full accounting, common sense and the cost figures that have leaked out both suggest that the incremental cost of open testing would be manageable.

At bottom, though, in the words of David White, "It's pretty clear that cost isn't the only issue. If it were, we'd decide who should succeed and fail in this society with the flip of a coin. We're also interested in validity."[33] Despite the wails of doom for test validity emanating from the camp of the testers, no such outcome is the inevitable consequence of open testing. Test publishers have raised all sorts of possible problems if the status quo gives way. But Dr. Haney has testified, "If one accepts the validity of the proposition that individual test-takers have a right to know the basis on which they are judged in detail, and personally I give considerable credence to that proposition, then issues of test development and technical quality need not stand in the way of open testing policies designed to implement that right."[34] So far the industry has displayed a failure of imagination and resolve in facing up to the conditions of open testing. They are so busy repeating the phrase, "It can't be done," that they haven't given full attention to how to do it. As to the cry of impossibility, Vito Perrone said, "There is absolutely no basis for such a claim. The most critical qualities of validity and reliability should not be affected at all if the test publishers bring to the task of openness the same degree of knowledge and commitment they bring to the promotion of secure tests."[35] The task is made even less arduous for the testers by the care that drafters of open testing legislation have displayed in exempting from disclosure requirements questions used solely for pretesting or equating. Thus testers can still protect certain questions, as long as they use them for keeping the test scale constant rather than for scoring purposes, a procedure currently followed on at least some of the major standardized tests.

The "abundance of current information" argument has been advanced by ETS in the following form: "But for all that, the tests are not secret. . . . All programs with which we are familiar will make sample questions and directions available. In addition, actual tests for virtually all national testing programs are available for professional scrutiny and have been for many years. The *Mental Measurement Yearbook* is probably the most famous example of such external professional review, which typically includes scrutiny of test questions against specifications and statistical reports."[36] But this boast rings hollow when the acoustics are provided by the structure of Oscar Buros's thoughts. This former editor of the *Mental Measurements Yearbook*, the very work cited above as "the most famous example of such external professional review," declared in March 1977, "The information available to permit an adequate assessment to be made of these secure tests is quite unsatisfactory. . . . I would like to repeat a statement which I made forty-two years ago: today it is practically impossible for a competent test technician or test consumer to make a thorough appraisal of the construction, validation, and use of most standardized tests being published because of the limited amount of trustworthy information supplied by test publishers and authors. . . . Unfortunately, although some progress has been made, my 1935 complaint is equally applicable today to the majority of existing tests, and especially so for secure tests."[37] If this is the conclusion of an expert called to the stand by the testing industry in its own defense, how many more witnesses need to be produced by the opposing side? How could anyone be confident that the present practice of partial release of test information is sufficient to assure test validity and reliability?

I spent approximately a year researching and writing a report about the virtues and vices of open tests as opposed to secure (secret) tests.[38] The report examines the issues in open testing in much greater detail than I have done here. There are conflicting arguments on the issue of open testing, of course. On balance, however, the arguments pointed to the conclusion that, in the public interest, the current status of secure testing needs to be changed. To begin with, open testing would help us move closer to the goals of fairness for individuals and accountability for the test industry. I subscribe to the view expressed by Dr. Walter Haney that in our society the burden of proof for security—or secrecy, as it might be put—in public practices must rest with those who advocate security or secrecy.[39] This burden of proof has not been met. Statements that invalidity must result from disclosure, and that present disclosure is adequate, do not hold water. Costs may increase somewhat under open testing, but estimates made by opponents of open testing seem greatly inflated in light of the skimpy supporting data available. Finally, although I don't believe open testing will eliminate all the problems associated with test coaching, neither do I believe that open testing is likely to make the existing state of affairs significantly worse.

Expanding on the report, in my judgment open testing would be a net plus for the educational community and the public as a whole. But open testing is not a panacea. It will not cure all the infirmities of testing. In fact, it is a relatively minor, a relatively innocuous reform in and of itself. Yet open testing has a symbolic power to those who see it as a wedge for prying society loose from its adherence to standardized testing. Some opponents of open testing fear that exposure of test questions will inevitably lead to the abolition of all tests. You can't disprove the possibility, but this exaggerated fear is reminiscent of the story of a backpacker who slipped off a cliff. On the way down he desperately grabbed out and caught hold of a branch jutting from the side of the mountain. After a while, he realized that he could not climb back up—he had fallen too far—and he didn't dare look down to see if there was a safe ledge just underneath him that he could drop to. So he looked to the skies above and hollered: "Is anybody up there?" And a voice answered, "Do you believe?" The person hanging from the branch joyfully responded, "Yes, I do." "Then . . . let go with one hand." The hiker did. The voice, whose source was unclear to the hiker, asked, "Do you still believe?" "Oh, for sure." "Then . . . let go with the other hand." There was a pause, a long moment of indecision, before the hiker anxiously scanned the sky and shouted, "Is anybody *else* up there?"[40]

Test publishers who cling so tightly to the branch of secrecy are a lot like that hiker. The industry has fallen off the cliff of total public confidence and is terrified that the fate in store for it is a further plunge into the unknown. Testers dread what may happen to them if they shift their position ever so slightly, so they embrace a course of maintaining the status quo. This can last for a while. But they will never be able to make it back up the cliff if they rigidly insist on hanging on to that thin limb of secrecy. If testers really have faith in the value of the questions they ask and the procedures they follow, they ought to be willing to take the chance and let go. If the publishers are correct in their assessment of the worth of standardized testing, then that quality will give them the strength to make the arduous climb back up the mountainside. Perhaps they will fall some after they release the branch and public criticism mounts. Yet if the tests are sound at bottom, they will rest on a ledge of support. Once on that ledge, the industry will have a better vantage of alternate routes to regain the heights. Moreover, publishers should ponder the risk they run by staying immobile for too long. They may so weaken the health of the testing community through a process of attrition that vigorous efforts in rescaling the cliff become impossible. To phrase it differently, test secrecy is not even in the best interests of the industry. Secrecy is like a security blanket: it gives the illusion of safety from attack, but it also reveals an unwillingness to face reality.

The industry must be responsible for meeting its obligations under the New York Truth-in-Testing law. As long as they have to comply with that law, they could voluntarily grant the same benefits of increased access to test instruments nationwide, which should cost them no more than what the New York law entails.

This would change the focus of the debate from their fascination with secrecy to the substantive issues of test improvement. In fact, the sponsors of the Law School Admission Test, the Graduate Management Admission Test, and the Graduate Record Examination deserve credit for deciding on their own to meet the disclosure requirements nationally rather than just in New York.[41] On the other hand, the industry could continue its current policy of giving ground grudgingly and only when forced by legislation or public opinion. The latter rearguard approach to reform is unlikely to win any new friends for the industry and may well backfire with the passage of new and stricter laws. As Allan Nairn testified in Albany, "The forms written to comply with truth-in-testing can be used for the entire country, just as ETS currently writes a single set of forms for the entire country. There is no psychometric or economic justification for making up a different set for the rest of the country."[42] As of now, the testers are issuing conflicting signals as to their intentions. They sometimes make conciliatory gestures as though they were resigned to open testing. But then a close reading of their announcements shows these moves may be little more than tactical ploys to stall for time in order to continue the fight to maintain secrecy. Paul Pottinger has testified about the industry's "elaborate and extensive lobbying effort to defeat the New York bill. They are now working with equal vigor to rescind this bill which they publicly praise."[43] Test reformers have been forced to the conclusion that a national open testing law must be passed because the industry cannot be counted on to honor its principles when the heat is off.

The testers have shown they will play as rough as possible to thwart these legislative initiatives. State Senator LaValle said of the debate in New York, "Most of the opposition offered was based on fear—fear instilled by unsupportable threats of dire circumstances made by the major testing agencies."[44] These fears can be overcome by painstaking presentations and an aroused citizenry. Unfortunately, time to rebut last minute fears is often in short supply in the furious scramble of a legislature. Further, the testers enjoy a substantial financial advantage that dwarfs the resources available to groups pressing for change. Still, the imperative behind open testing is a potent force in itself. Once the fears are responded to, the threats lose power. In the words of Vito Perrone, "There is some degree of intimidation in all this that is unacceptable. There is little evidence that any of the dire circumstances need to prevail unless, again, the testing industry refuses to bring already existing knowledge and fresh commitment to bear on the new circumstances."[45] The final irony is that the testing industry is being dragged kicking and screaming into a method of operating which could actually lead to more understanding of their product and a more appreciative public once the facade of perfection has been stripped away.

The charge has been made by an opponent of open testing legislation that "on balance, this legislation appears to be a child only of those with a hidden agenda, the destruction of all testing as we know it."[46] If that's the agenda of the preponderance of open testers, it is pretty well hidden indeed. Listen to the PTA: "The PTA's support for this legislation is not to be construed as opposition to testing, but rather viewed as a concern that the public be better informed of the nature, purposes, uses, and limitations of standardized testing."[47] That doesn't sound as though the more than 6,500,000 members of the PTA are out to pull down the pillars of the testing temple. Steve Solomon of NYPIRG testified that the purpose of those who advocate open testing laws is "not necessarily to just look at these tests and see what they can find wrong with them, but to help improve the quality of these tests. Independent review should be welcome for this reason."[48] Is that a call for test abolition? Vito Perrone's most drastic vision of the consequences of open testing is that it might help to restore standardized tests to the functions publishers claim they favor. Perrone testified: "The greatest social policy gain to be derived from more openness is that tests may become less powerful in selection and more useful for advisement and placement. Such a direction has the potential for encouraging alternatives to our existing structures that might be more effective in assuring access to the best resources of higher education for *all* who deserve and can benefit from such resources."[49] If competition for tests and alternatives to supplement their inadequacies is equivalent to "the destruction of all testing as we know it," then we ought to endorse the dawn of a new era of testing. The fact is that the current state of the testing art leaves a lot of space on the canvas for additions which enhance the picture rather than obscure it.

If you want to join the struggle for open testing, there are several things you can do. Contact the members of the education committees in your state legislature and tell them you want action. Contact the offices of U.S. Representatives Ted Weiss and Shirley Chisholm of New York and George Miller of California. They have introduced a national open testing bill (the Educational Testing Act of 1979; H.R. 4949) which needs your support to be enacted. Contact the state chapter or national headquarters of the PTA or the National Education Association or the NAACP or the Public Interest Research Group or the National Center for the Study of the Professions to see what you can do to help. Any of these organizations should be able to direct you to further contacts who are engaged in open testing efforts and are located near you. Start your own group, if one doesn't already exist. You will be amazed to discover how many people have been touched by standardized tests and feel deeply that something should be done to bring them under control. New York demonstrated that the testing industry can be beaten in a legislature, but only when the open testing forces are dedicated and well organized. Similar efforts in many states are building a head of steam. At last count, open testing bills have been introduced in some twenty states, "with nine [of the bills] given a chance of survival."[50] But they won't go anywhere if we all count on the other person to do our work for us. If you're tempted to stay out of the fray because you don't have enough at stake to make the labor worthwhile, think again. Tests won't turn around 180 degrees of their own volition. Unless you and your children are planning on foregoing the educational and vocational fields in which standardized tests are rife, your action or inaction will have important consequences for you in the years to come.

To borrow from the report for the National Consortium on Testing (NCT) on open testing, we must answer two crucial questions in the coming decade: "What purposes and whose interests are to be served by standardized testing either in the schools or for postsecondary admissions and selection? If publicly mandated standardized testing is to serve the interests of those tested, on what grounds are we to argue that test-takers should be denied access to the corrected results of the tests they are required to take?"[51] Open testing is an important part of the answer that is evolving to these questions in the 1980s. Yet open testing is still just part of the answer. In the next chapter we will discuss some other answers that have been offered in response to these concerns. It won't be easy, but we can extricate ourselves from the testing trap that has ensnared us if only we can muster the will for a sustained effort.

CHAPTER FIFTEEN

Escaping
the Trap

After the shock of blundering into a trap wears off, a rational person considers alternative escape plans and tries to break free. This is how we should deal with our entanglement with standardized tests. The ideas presented in this chapter are moves we could take to get out of the testing trap. Unlike the multiple-choice test, there is no single "right" answer here. Most of these ideas are not original with me, but have been advanced by conscientious women and men who have spent years studying these tests. You may have better suggestions, in which case you should join the public debate and speak up in whatever forum you think would give your points a fair hearing. Once we get all the possibilities spelled out we can decide which direction looks most promising. If there is to be real test reform, this is the time to act. Attention directed to the problems of testing in the past few years provides an opportunity which should not be squandered. This attention may become riveted elsewhere while the memory of test abuse fades. An exchange in *Through the Looking-Glass* carries the message. "The horror of that moment," the King went on, "I shall never, never forget!" "You will, though," the Queen said, "if you don't make a memorandum of it." We must collectively make a memorandum of our determination that tests should serve the purposes of education and not vice versa.

The ideas for test reform in this chapter have been organized into three broad categories: symbolic, substantive, and systemic. The symbolic changes are steps which are small and not about to spring us from the trap overnight. But despite their modest dimensions, they are at least a start. And they could be accomplished without any great expenditure by the testing industry. The substantive changes go to the basics of the current use of tests, with the hope that the construction and use of tests can be improved. The systemic changes are more daring, for they require a reexamination of the fundamental assumptions about standardized tests and the selection system based on them. We should not be afraid to let our imaginations loose in an effort to design a process that meets our highest standards of efficiency and equity. The way things are today cannot be the outer boundary of our thoughts for tomorrow. As Walter Haney has declared, we should recognize that "current practices are by no means the standard by which we ought to limit our vision of the future."[1] With that in mind, let's explore some visions of the future.

Symbolic. One reason tests are overrelied on is their meticulous appearance of precision. A test score of three digits measuring such impressive attributes as "verbal aptitude" or "reasoning ability" packs a wallop with the folks who see it. Why not use scores that will more accurately convey the fact that these standardized tests are capable only of predicting within some mighty wide ranges? Test publishers admit their tests don't have pinpoint accuracy, but the form of the scores fosters the impression that the tests can distinguish between a 461 student and a 462 student. So change the form. Let's have test scores released as two-digit spreads. If our test has a standard error of 30 points each way on a three-digit scale, let's convert those 461 and 462 scores into something a little more realistic. Have the testers report that these students scored "between a 43 and a 49." That sounds a little less precise than the labels "461" and "462," which is the way it should be. We haven't lost any predictive power on the test itself, we're just giving scores that are a closer approximation of the true statistical imprecision of the test. You might say this is a pretty silly thing to do, although harmless enough, because everyone's going to divide the range in two and assign scores that are the average. That will probably happen, but what of it? We will have forced the averagers to do this dubious division rather than serving up the single score on a computer printout platter. And maybe this will make an impression on some people who otherwise would not have considered the way standard error and the like can rumple the otherwise impeccable clothes covering testing assumptions. It's hard to take the whispered warnings of test publishers that their tests have a built-in error too seriously when the trappings of the score report present more precise figures than Peggy Fleming ever cut on ice.

While we're at it, why not insist on some warnings in plain English of the shortcomings of these tests? Since one of the problems with tests is the unfamiliarity of many people with their limitations, let's make some changes that will bring the point home. Is it too much to ask at least of the nonprofit test companies that they highlight these blemishes until the public is well acquainted with them? A representative of one of the New York teachers' unions testified in Albany that test companies should "be required to display prominently on tests and test scores that the scores are only approximations. Students are usually not aware that scores are only accurate within 60 points, which is part of the inevitable margin of error."[2] After all, as noted by Professor Sylvia Johnson, "we are dealing with probabilities, not certainties."[3] As Scrooge might have said in *A Christmas Carol,* these tests are like the ghost of Christmas Future: they are but shadows of what *might* be, not what will be. If an ornery character like Scrooge was able to wheedle that information out of the ghost, do our children deserve any less information when visions of their future are projected? These symbolic actions on the part of the test industry won't put a stop to test abuse, but they would make such abuse at least a shade less likely without depriving us of the information we obtain from test scores. We require plastic caps on aspirin bottles to make it harder for someone to swallow pills by mistake. We should require tight warnings on tests to make it harder for someone to swallow exaggerated claims of test infallibility by mistake.

Renaming some of the tests so that they don't promise more than they convey is another symbolic move that could pay off. If we called tests by their right names instead of their grand titles, it would be easier to remember what it is these tests are—and are not—capable of doing. We have already discussed how the term "intelligence test" is a misnomer. Maybe if they went under a less exalted handle, they would have less potential to shatter a child's education before it has even begun. The same could be said (at different stages of life) for terms like "aptitude" and "competency." If they are tossed around with abandon they can do damage far out of proportion to any powers of assessment they have exhibited. They could more properly be named "tests of developed ability in certain fields," or something of the sort. The new names would have less glamor than the old ones, but they would give a more accurate impression of the work tests do. Nomenclature is a small thing in itself, but it has the power to shape a debate by the assumptions implied. If a mood of diligence were afoot, we could even start in on the use of statistical terms such as "objective" and "reliable," which can mean something quite different than their meaning in everyday usage. There is nothing earth-shaking in this fussing with language, but a tightening up on our testing vocabulary would leave less room for misinterpretation of test results.

Substantive. The very first thing that should be done is to treat tests like any other product and demand that the officials responsible for buying them be intelligent consumers. You don't buy a house, a car, or a TV without shopping around, and neither should our educational authorities spend money buying tests without inspecting the goods and looking for value. If the test purchasers become tough customers for the tests, then only those tests which can live up to the more exacting standards will survive the competition. If you have a role in test acquisition, read the reports on the contending tests that can be found in Buros's *Mental Measurements Yearbook* and in testing journals. Inform yourself of the track record of these tests and determine if they are up to your specifications. Check to see how well the items emphasized on a given test match the objectives that are stressed in your curriculum. Don't assume that the presence of statistical trimming in the publisher's brochure, especially in tandem with a distinct lack of comprehensible sentences, is any guarantee of test quality. Get an interpreter if you have to, but be aware of what you are buying.

J. Parker Damon has written an exemplary article called, "Questions You Should Ask About Your Testing Program."[4] This is a common sense guide to what is entailed by standardized testing. Parents would find this article especially helpful in formulating a checklist of things to find out about the tests used in their children's schools. Here are some of the questions Damon recommends asking *before* the tests are given. How does the proposed standardized test supplement other forms of assessment and evaluation already in use? How much time will administering the test involve? How much will it cost? How will the test results be used and kept? How else might the same information be acquired? Why is the test being given? You can find this article reprinted in a book entitled *The Myth of Measurability*.

The men and women who work most intimately with standardized tests on a daily basis will obviously have much to do with whether, and how, tests are reshaped to better serve the needs of the public. Teachers, guidance counselors, admissions personnel, and test sponsors should all receive training in the theory and practice of standardized tests as part of their professional preparation. Familiarity may breed contempt, as the saying goes, but a lack of familiarity with test instruments almost surely produces an unjustified awe of the scientific nature of the tests. The people we rely on to interpret tests for us and for our children should maintain a healthy skepticism of test results. We need interpreters who know the nuances of the testing language, not spokesmen for the positions of the testing companies. Teachers have a direct interest in the proper use of standardized tests. More and more school districts are requiring a form of standardized licensing test for teachers. So access to the teaching profession may soon be controlled by tests. And the certified teacher must face a kind of testing double jeopardy, for the rise of minimum competency tests means a teacher's work in the classroom may come to be evaluated on the basis of the performance of his pupils on tests. Clearly teachers have a need to know about tests. Teachers can also be effective in devising alternatives to standardized tests which can do as good a job as the tests, or better, without some of their drawbacks. Amity Buxton has spoken of a successful teacher-inspired program in Oakland, California, which is used as a substitute for some tests and which seems to work better for the children concerned.[5] In one effort, the teachers at the kindergarten level developed checklists of specific student behaviors which they use for assessment and as self-reminders of what skills to concentrate on.

Test publishers have an obligation to see to it that the people who use their tests have at least a rudimentary understanding of proper test use. Certainly it is beyond the capacity of the testing industry to police all the uses of their tests. But it is not too much to ask them to redouble their efforts on consumer education through workshop seminars and more explicit instructional pamphlets. At the same time, those institutions which invest tests with more authority than they rightfully possess should not be let off scot-free. The temptation to save staff time and payroll money by overrelying on tests may be strong, but such behavior is reprehensible nevertheless. The test industry has enough criticism to face without being blamed for irresponsible actions by parties over whom they have no control. But the industry could help itself by condemning this sort of abuse whenever it is encountered and by suspending test sales to any institutions which persist in using test scores in blatant disregard of the standards established by appropriate industry, academic, and professional organizations. By the same token, the test-sponsoring organizations could show more diligence in fulfilling their duty to supervise test publishers. It would be easier to accept these sponsoring bodies as independent of the testing industry if at least the occasional criticisms that even the most satisfied of customers has about any product were to surface in public. Evidence that sponsors have complaints about tests and are prepared to switch test companies if they are not corrected would be a far more convincing indication of test accountability than the sponsor-issued defenses of the industry.

An ambition more difficult to achieve would be to make the tests go through a rebalancing, a restandardizing process so that the cultural diversity of the American people is more fully reflected in the test scores. This would be something akin to what happened in the 1930s when tests were adjusted so that they would yield results showing males and females to be of approximately equal intelligence. This was done by changing the ratio of questions so that more questions which women tended to do well on ended up on the test, while some questions which had favored men were dropped.[6] Isn't it at least *possible* that tests need to be inspected to see if a repetition of this process is merited for other groups which have long been unfairly stigmatized as less capable than the rest of society? James Fallows has asked: "Is it so outrageous to contemplate additional test items on which able poor or black children would excel?"[7] This is a tricky business because any modifications made would have to remedy those score differences which are merely artifacts of class while keeping public trust that standards of real life competency are not lowered. This can be done—no one today argues that women are improperly boosted on their test scores—but it requires an all-out commitment on the part of the industry that seems lacking so far.

In the meantime, the controversy over whether tests are just humble mirrors of society or magnifiers of social disadvantage will roar on. David Stratman maintains that "standardized entrance examinations are not 'mirrors of society' in the sense that they reflect the skills and knowledge of students from different backgrounds. They are mirrors only in the sense that they reflect and enforce historical patterns of social hierarchy."[8] To the extent that this is so, one could simply assert that life is unfair across the board and tests are not exempt from that pattern. But that begs the question. What we need to decide is whether we will strive to lessen that unfairness to the level our abilities permit, or whether we will refuse this task and leave the essential inequities unhindered as they claim the inevitable victims. Those content with the second course should remember that this educational victimization starts at a very young age. As a representative of the NAACP protested, "If tests used in elementary school already begin to put our children in a disadvantageous position, how can we reasonably expect them to be competitive on postsecondary education tests?"[9] There is something else involved here, too. Unlike the usual procedure for handicapping most contests, the early use of standardized tests handicaps the expected *losers* of the race. Anyone who starts out behind is liable to be subjected to labeling which can serve only to keep that individual well back of the pack.

One approach to the pains of selection is to point out the flaws in the system even as we seek to eliminate them. Fallows has written, "The proper challenge to testing is to accept a higher modesty, one that begins with the understanding that this 'merit' system pretends to more fairness than it delivers. All systems of selection are unfair; all are tempted to claim too much justice for their results. We recognize this about previous systems, but are reluctant to face it in our own. Once that fact is recognized, it may be possible to think again about the proper building blocks for a meritocracy—measures that do not seal fate at an early age, that emphasize performance in specific areas, that expand the pool of talent in more than a hit-or-miss way, and whose limits are always visible to us, so that we are not again deluded into thinking we have found a scientific basis for the order of lords, vassals, and serfs."[10] There is always the danger of unintended consequences, of course, even when enforcing something as restrained as a higher modesty. It would be ironic if all the streamlining of standardized tests brought on as a result of reform pressures served to further increase the reliance on tests without any complete overhaul of the internal machinery.

Finally, something needs to be done about the glaring disparities in access to test preparation, whether that preparation is part of the normal curriculum of a good school or is received under the auspices of a commercial test review course. The catch is that it is not entirely clear what that "something" should be. We could come up with a "test coaching voucher plan" which would guarantee every student admission to some review course. But aside from the obvious cost of such a plan, it would tend to further enshrine standardized tests as the final arbiter of academic ability when we know tests are unworthy of such a task. If we put facsimiles of these courses in our public schools, we may cut back on the cost, but we would still be dancing to the tune of the tests and taking precious resources away from other subjects. So, there may be some dead ends in the region of substantive test reforms. That's why we must be ready to entertain thoughts of more comprehensive actions which would alter the system rather than just patch it up.

Systemic. Possibly the most important thing we can do outside of devising alternative and improved forms of tests is to give greater weight in selection to what an applicant has actually done in contrast to what a test says she might do. A demonstrated ability to perform the feats we consider important is worth a whole lot of "potential" as detected on a test which is restricted to searching for surrogate skills. Of course, potential should count for something, and tests can be useful in making this estimate. Yet we know that there are times when testing is to true skill as Russian is to roulette. As Professor McClelland has written, "The testing movement is in grave danger of perpetuating a mythological meritocracy in which none of the measures of merit bears significant demonstrable validity with respect to any measures outside of the charmed circle."[11] In other words, if someone tests well, all we know is that he tests well, not whether he can do the job we want (unless that job is taking tests for a living). We also know that the best guide to future performance is past performance, whether the field consists of physical, academic, or professional endeavors. As a society we have got it backward anytime we value accomplishment on a predictive test over accomplishment in life.

How can we gather the information needed to base judgments on proven ability without bogging down in a morass of detail? There is no question that work remains to be done in this area. But enough has been done already to hold open the hope that performance can return to its rightful position of preeminence in selection. Studies have been performed based on self-prediction, self-reporting, and peer-prediction which indicate these methods can be as useful as standardized tests. To be sure, there are bugs which must be worked out, but the simplicity of the idea is appealing. If you want a better selection process, ask the applicants how they think they will do if selected and what they have done in the past that gives them this impression. Some people will lie and overestimate (and some will even falsely underestimate), so safeguards must be built to protect against fraud. Yet, when asked, it seems that most people are remarkably honest in their assessments of themselves and their contemporaries. What's more, any time an applicant can document outstanding personal achievement which wouldn't normally register on standardized tests and school grades, you have some very worthwhile information indeed. Experimentation is needed here and should be given priority.[12]

The point is that test scores are not the only "hard" data which should figure in our decisions. Tests are only meant to add to our knowledge of an individual, not to paint the entire picture. The more that is known about the important characteristics of an individual, the less we need to lean on the crutch of standardized tests. Vito Perrone hit this nail square on the head in testimony submitted to Congress. He discussed the implications of the work of Cliff Wing and Michael Wallach and others with regard to our values in selection. According to Perrone, "Wing and Wallach give particular credence to what they call accomplishment characteristics—political leadership, work experience, acting, writing, painting—behaviors which are ends in and of themselves. They conclude, as have others, that such factors act quite independently from grades and test scores. . . . When Wing and Wallach applied to Duke's application pool a preference to nonacademic accomplishment, with minimum SAT scores set at the 50th percentile and with high school grades falling among the upper two-thirds of a class, they ended up with a selected population radically different—broader in every respect —than the population actually selected by a formula which weighted only SAT and high school grades. This suggests, I believe, a reasonable case for seeking in greater detail what have tended to be nontraditional data and to use that data in our academic selection procedures. That we have tended to place more emphasis on test scores and grades than seems justified is becoming more clear and the need to retreat from such an emphasis is gaining adherents."[13] Paying serious attention to these nontraditional data may prove to be an advance in the way we parcel out opportunities.

What about the tests themselves? How can we make them better? One way is to focus on what Professor McClelland has written about so persuasively, namely that the best kind of test involves what is called criterion sampling.[14] This means you look directly at the behavior you want to measure rather than looking through the prism of some proxy behavior. If you want to know if someone can drive a car, you watch them drive a car; you don't give them a standardized test on the theory of manual transmissions and the history of automobile manufacturing. Anytime you are able to write a test so that an applicant can pass it only if he demonstrates the skills that will be needed on the job or at school you've written a good test. Of course the difficulty comes when the logistics of administering such a test become cumbersome.

One way of seeing if high school seniors can do the work at old Alma Mater U. is to have them take some courses and look at their marks. That is impractical on a large scale, so we have to depend on past performance, which in most cases will mean high school grades and any individual intellectual distinctions. Standardized tests will play their part as well, but it should be strictly in the supporting performance category. And maybe it wouldn't be such a bad thing if students who are determined to make it at a particular college were given a trial run to show their ability despite any indications to the contrary by tests and high school grades. Would it be such a strain to allow open registration in a few selected entry courses at a college with the promise of admission to those who show by their work that they have what it takes?

Some alternatives to the prevalent norm-referenced standardized tests do exist. One variant is called the criterion-referenced test, and it can be an improved form of testing when properly used. The criterion-referenced test uses performance standards rather than the bell-shaped curve to arrive at a test score. Thus, a student has to demonstrate mastery at a predetermined level before a criterion-referenced test will pass him to the next stage. So an entire class could be found ready or wanting on a particular subject, unlike the norm-referenced test which tends to spread out the distribution of scores. However, the criterion-referenced tests depend entirely on the wisdom of the test writers in deciding what those required levels of performance are, and what questions will be asked to probe a person's proficiency. Other test innovations include a renewed concentration on testing for diagnostic purposes and an exploration of the variety in testing made possible by the advent of advanced computer technology. Good tests are needed just as much, if not more, to spot areas of learning difficulty. With the spread of computers it should be possible to create huge test item banks which would be placed at the disposal of teachers and administrators. These people could punch in their requirements for certain kinds of questions to test specific knowledge and have an array of questions printed out for them in minutes. Teachers could then have the flexibility to tailor test questions of proven validity into a package to meet the needs of their classes. Jerrold Zacharias has been an advocate of such a technique, and new technology may turn his idea into reality.[15]

In the meantime, we would be well advised to readjust the operation of standardized tests so that they more closely parallel the real life talents we want to measure. For instance, why not start using some partial credit in scoring multiple-choice tests to help cope with the ambiguity which lurks in the questions? If test publishers don't hesitate to denote one alternative as the "correct" one, they probably wouldn't shy away from picking out the second-best alternative. Hasn't the student who has been able to reason her way to the second-best choice shown more skill than the student who picks one of the other alternatives? Rather than all or nothing on the tests, a "correct" answer could be worth two points while the "almost as correct" answer would earn one point. Maybe scoring patterns would change, and maybe that would be a good thing. What would definitely be a good thing is the rejection of the attitude that old assumptions about tests need never be challenged. It has been suggested after all, that the ability to eliminate wrong alternatives is worth some recognition, even when the process doesn't lead to the one "right" answer. In Pennsylvania, the Liacouras committee on the state bar examination followed this philosophy in an early 1970's report recommending the minimum passing score for this exam.[16] We should also look to see whether test formats couldn't be changed to be more in accord with everyday practice. Since a large part of a lawyer's work involves finding legal precedents, distilling them, and then using them, why not make part of the MBE an open-book exercise? Ask some questions that require research skill to balance all the others which call for snap judgment and regurgitation of memorized rules soon to be consigned to oblivion.

Resort to more thorough test reforms is always a possibility, if the industry adamantly refuses to accept its responsibility to put the testing house in order, or if it is just not possible to improve standardized, norm-referenced, multiple-choice tests much beyond their present level for one reason or another. It is not enough to rely on the testing industry for self-policing since the consequences of test abuse have become more significant with the growing complexity of American life. We need more competition among testers and among forms of tests to stimulate creative approaches to the collection of information about individual competence. We need more protection for the rights of students and job-seekers not to have their talents denigrated and their advancement blocked because of erroneous judgments based on test scores. And we need to learn more about what standardized tests do and what they are doing to us. As Paul Pottinger testified, "We must learn if tests are contributing to the loss of our ability to think, analyze, understand, and write. . . . We must know if we are decreasing the intellectual nourishment of our youth by seducing them into memorizing facts or using phony analytical skills on trivial multiple-choice problems."[17] The long-range impact on society of unquestioned dominance by standardized tests could be more adverse than anyone would have dreamed a few years ago. If we allow the rewards of higher education and prime employment to be handed out on the basis of tests which are geared to passive responses and superficial thought, then we as a society will suffer. If we fail to recognize lasting brilliance of character and determination because they are lost in the glare of test scores, then we have only ourselves to blame if those qualities are no longer considered quite so alluring. If we are not careful, our values may be usurped and our children reshaped in the image of the tests without our knowledge or consent.

These worries are common to many who have looked closely at standardized tests. School principal Arthur Laughland has written, "I read recently that our children's lives are far too precious to entrust them to professional educators. How much more foolish to entrust our judgments about quality education to the cheap panacea of easily administered tests."[18] Congresswoman Shirley Chisholm, a former teacher, has declared, "For too long, test development and content, and testing procedures and uses, have remained shrouded in ambiguity and an aura of omnipotence. I am convinced that the current atmosphere and mystique surrounding testing is not conducive to the educational interests of our children."[19] Professor Banesh Hoffmann has written of the seriousness of being caught in the testing trap: "Testing is no game. It is in deadly earnest. If tests are misused, the consequences can be far from trifling. Lives can be warped and careers ruined—as much by unwarranted promotions as by misguided guidance and lack of recognition of ability. . . . The strength and vitality of a nation may be jeopardized."[20]

Yet for all the importance of testing practices, the public has still not been fully informed. As an official of the National PTA said, "From early childhood through entry into professional schools or jobs, standardized tests make significant judgments about our children. Yet no portion of the public school system is less understood than the facts about standardized tests, their assets and their limitations."[21] If you want to find out more about standardized tests, there are several sources which I recommend highly. This is not an exclusive list; I'm sure I've inadvertently left out some fine works. But if you check the writings mentioned here you will run across additional references.

Books: 1) *The Tyranny of Testing*, by Banesh Hoffmann (Collier Books, 1962); 2) *The Myth of Measurability*, edited by Paul Houts (Hart Publishing Company, 1977); 3) *The IQ Controversy*, edited by N. J. Block and Gerald Dworkin (Pantheon Books, 1976); 4) *The Complete Guide to Taking Tests*, by Bernard Feder (Prentice-Hall, 1979); 5) *The Reign of ETS*, by Allan Nairn and Associates (released in draft form on January 14, 1980, and due for publication in book form at an unspecified time); 6) *Hurdles: The Admissions Dilemma in American Higher Education*, by Herbert Sacks et al. (Atheneum, 1978); and 7) *Data Analysis for Politics and Policy*, by Edward Tufte (Prentice-Hall, 1974). This book is not about testing, but is a fine introduction to the theory of regression analysis which is applicable to the more technical aspects of standardized tests.

Pamphlets and articles: 1) "How Fair Are the College Boards?" by James Fallows in the *Atlantic Monthly*, February 1980; 2) *The Measurement Mystique* by Sylvia Johnson (a paper of the Institute for the Study of Educational Policy, Howard University–Dunbarton Campus, 2935 Upton St., N.W., Washington, D.C. 20008); 3) *The Test Information Packet*, Leslie Law, Project Manager, published by the *Department of Instructional Services*, Virginia Beach Public Schools, P.O. Box 6038, Virginia Beach, Va. 23456; 4) *The Testing Maze*, by the National PTA

(700 North Rush Street, Chicago, Illinois 60611); 5) Just about anything written on the subject appearing in the pages of the *New Republic* and the *Washington Monthly*, both of which have a long and honorable tradition of quizzing test claims; 6) Just about anything appearing in the *New York Times* with Edward Fiske's byline, among others, for fair and thorough reporting on tests; 7) National Consortium on Testing Staff Circulars, obtainable through the Huron Institute (123 Mount Auburn Street, Cambridge, Mass. 02138); and 8) David White, "Culturally Biased Testing and Predictive Invalidity," *Harvard Civil Rights–Civil Liberties Law Review,* Spring 1979.

We have covered a lot of ground on this march through the testing wilderness. There were many places worth further observation for background detail, but time would not permit that. You should know your way around well enough now so that you can go back and explore on your own. You may cross paths with people who are working to make the trek safer for all those who have to pass through this territory on their way to the schools and jobs that lie beyond. Your help in that venture would surely be appreciated.

Footnotes

Introduction

1. Walter Lippmann, "The Great Confusion," *New Republic*, January 3, 1923, p. 146.
2. Dr. David G. Stratman, Prepared Statement on the Educational Testing Act of 1979 (H.R. 4949), before the Subcommittee on Elementary, Secondary, and Vocational Education of the House Education and Labor Committee, October 20, 1979, p. 9.
   Note: Because the report of the hearings conducted on H.R. 4949 had not yet been published when this book was being written, I have relied for extracts of testimony upon the prepared statements distributed by the speakers and made available to me by an aide of one of the bill's sponsors. All such material will be cited as "D.C. Testimony" and page references will be to the prepared statements, not to the committee report.
3. N. J. Block and Gerald Dworkin (eds.), *The IQ Controversy* (New York: Pantheon Books, 1976), pp. xii–xiii.
4. Jacques Barzun, Foreword to Banesh Hoffmann, *The Tyranny of Testing* (New York: Collier Books, 1962), p. 8.

Chapter One

1. "Aptitude-Test Scores: Grumbling Gets Louder," *U.S. News & World Report*, May 14, 1979, p. 76.
2. Joanne Omang, "Making the Grade: Standardized Tests Are Under Attack," *Washington Post*, December 26, 1979, p. A10.
3. See note 1.
4. Dr. Frank Snyder, D.C. Testimony on behalf of the Association of American Publishers, September 10, 1979, p. 7.
5. Barbara Demick, "The Kindergarten Rat Race," *New Republic*, September 29, 1979, p. 25.
6. This quotation is found in the opinion of Chief United States District Judge for the Northern District of California Robert F. Peckham in the case of *Larry P.* v. *Riles*, issued on October 11, 1979, on p. 112. Further references

to this opinion will be cited as "Peckham." Judge Peckham attributes this string of quotes to Carl Brigham's book, *A Study of American Intelligence* (Princeton, N.J.: Princeton University Press, 1923). Peckham notes the Brigham quote can be found in *The Science and Politics of IQ* (Potomac, Md.: Lawrence Erlbaum Associates, Publishers, 1974) by Professor Leon Kamin on p. 21.

7. Peckham, p. 113, quoted in Kamin, *The Science and Politics of IQ,* p. 21.
8. Peckham, p. 113, quoted in Kamin, p. 22.
9. Kamin, p. 16.
10. Quoted in Daniel J. Boorstin, *The Americans: The Democratic Experience* (New York: Vintage Books, 1958), p. 222.
11. "In Classroom and On Campus: The Test Dethroned," *New York Times,* July 3, 1932.
12. *Ibid.*
13. Peckham, p. 123.
14. *Ibid.,* p. 41.
15. Walter Lippmann, "A Future for Tests," *New Republic,* November 29, 1922, p. 10.
16. Dr. James W. Loewen, D.C. Testimony, August 15, 1979, pp. 11–12.
17. Oscar K. Buros, "Fifty Years in Testing: Some Reminiscences, Criticisms, and Suggestions," *Educational Researcher,* July–August, 1977, p. 9.
18. Quoted in Sherwood Davidson Kohn, "The Numbers Game," published in *The Myth of Measurability,* Paul L. Houts (ed.), (New York: Hart Publishing Co., 1977), p. 177.
19. Bernard Feder, *The Complete Guide to Taking Tests* (Englewood Cliffs, New Jersey: Prentice-Hall, Inc., 1979), p .73.
20. Maxwell Gould, "MCAT Scores Fall from Past Level, Prompt Regrading," *Harvard Crimson,* May 19, 1978, p. 1. See also *Boston Globe,* May 23, 1978.
21. J. Wyatt Emmerick, "Error in GMAT Scores Affects 200 Applications," *Harvard Crimson,* January 18, 1978, p. 1.
22. Carey Winfrey, "Revised Law School Test Leads to a Dispute," *New York Times,* April 28, 1978, p. A23; Steven Brill, "Law Boards Scandal," *Esquire,* April 25, 1978, p. 22; Peter R. Melnick, "Changes in Law School Admission Test Increase Number of High Test Scores," *Harvard Crimson,* April 13, 1978, p. 1.
23. Kim Masters, "ETS's Star Chamber," *New Republic,* February 5, 1977, pp. 13–14.
24. Arthur MacDonnell, untitled, *Boston Globe,* July 3, 1979.
25. Phone conversations with legal counsel in February 1980 and later.
26. Josh Barbanel, "Computer Slows 1980's Selection for Law Schools," *New York Times,* January 19, 1980, p. 27.
27. *Ibid.*

Chapter Two

1. New York State Senator Donald Halperin, D.C. Testimony, August 1, 1979, pp. 1–2.
2. See James Fallows, "How Fair Are the College Boards?" *Atlantic Monthly,* February, 1980, p. 38.
3. "Aptitude-Test Scores: Grumbling Gets Louder," *U.S. News & World Report,* May 14, 1979, p. 76.
4. Herndon's remarks came during the course of a discussion of truth-in-testing legislation on the MacNeil/Lehrer Report broadcast on November 2, 1979.
5. Peckham, p. 104. The discussion of the E.M.R. program is based on Judge Peckham's decision.

6. *Ibid.*, p. 23.
7. *Ibid.*, p. 24.
8. *Ibid.*, p. 18.
9. *Ibid.*, p. 85.
10. *Ibid.*, p. 33.
11. *Ibid.*, pp. 27–28.
12. *Ibid.*, p. 28.
13. See *Hobson* v. *Hansen*, 269 F. Supp. 401 (D.D.C. 1967) at 489, *affirmed, sub.nom. Smuck* v. *Hobson*, 408 F. 2d 175 (D.C. Cir. 1969).
14. Peckham, p. 110.
15. "Hispanic Pupils Held Hampered in Tests Tied to English Ability," *New York Times,* September 16, 1979, p. 1.
16. "Macchiarola Challenges Grades on Some Tests," *New York Times,* May 15, 1979, p. B3.
17. "Students to Retake City Reading Tests," *New York Times,* May 24, 1979, p. B4.
18. See note 16.
19. *Ibid.* (See also Walter Haney and Eugene Radwin, Summary of the Fall 1979 Conference of the NCT, available from the Huron Institute, p. 71).
20. See the passage on Ann Cook's talk in the Summary of the Fall 1979 NCT Conference, p. 32.
21. Both Ann Cook and Deborah Meier spelled out some of these points during the course of the NCT meeting, as well as in a draft paper entitled, "New York Students Show Spectacular Rise in Reading/New York City Students' Scores Indicate Steady Decline in Reading," which was distributed at the conference.
22. Deborah Meier discussed this point with the author on November 6, 1979.
23. Eugene L. Meyer, "Improprieties Found in School Testing; Principal Resigns," *Washington Post,* September 29, 1978, p. B1.
24. *Ibid.*
25. Vivian Dawn Rigdon, " 'Obsession with test scores' blamed for teachers' blunder," *Prince Georges' Sentinel,* March 30, 1978, p. A1.
26. *Ibid.*, p. A9.
27. *Ibid.*, p. A1.
28. *Ibid.*, p. A9.
29. *Debra P.* v. *Turlington*, 474 F. Supp. 244 (M.D. Fla. 1979). Of course, the ultimate outcome of this case and some of the other cases cited in this book (such as *Larry P.* v. *Riles,* for example) is potentially subject to change in subsequent litigation. Further, different courts may reach different conclusions in similar circumstances. Nonetheless, even if these decisions were to be overturned on appeal, the initial findings of fact in these cases are disturbing. They indicate that the methods of using standardized tests are matters of concern in educational policy regardless of whether the courts finally conclude that reform is legally compelled.
30. Jean Seligman, "A Really Final Exam," *Newsweek,* May 28, 1979, p. 97.
31. *Debra P.* v. *Turlington*, pp. 250–252.
32. Nancy Rubin, "Test-Coaching: Is It Worth It?" *New York Times,* September 9, 1979, section 12, p. 1.
33. R. Jeffrey Smith, " 'Truth-in-Testing' Attracts Diverse Support," *Science,* September 14, 1979, p. 1114.
34. New York State Senator Donald Halperin, Comments During a Joint Public Hearing of the Senate and Assembly Standing Committees on Higher Education, May 9, 1979, pp. 23–24.

> *Note:* Because the report of the hearings conducted on the New York Truth-in-Testing bill was not yet available when this book was being written, I have relied upon the minutes of those proceedings as supplied by an

aide to one of the bill's sponsors. All such material will be cited as "Albany Testimony," and page references will be to these minutes.

35. See note 33.
36. *Ibid.*
37. FTC News Release, November 2, 1976, pp. 1–2.
38. See the remarks of Arthur Levine in Walter Haney and Andrew Strenio, Summary of the Spring 1979 Conference of the NCT, available from the Huron Institute, pp. 15–17.
39. See note 33 and Gene Maeroff, "Pick One: S.A.T. Coaching Is (Is Not) Fair to Students," *New York Times,* May 6, 1979, p. E11; Maeroff, "Agency Finds Coaching Can Raise S.A.T. Scores," *New York Times,* May 30, 1979, p. A10; Maeroff, " 'Coaching' Findings May Change S.A.T.," *New York Times,* June 5, 1979, p. C5; Diane Shah, "SAT Cramming: Does It Work?" *Newsweek,* June 11, 1979, p. 113; "Coaching Daze," *Time,* June 11, 1979, p. 57; Mitchell Lynch, "Probe of Coaching for Scholastic Tests Raises Issues About Exams Themselves," *Wall Street Journal,* December 4, 1978, p. 31; "Cram Courses May Lift Aptitude Test Scores of Some, Study Finds," *Wall Street Journal,* May 30, 1979, p. 10; and William McKibben, "FTC Study Backs Coaching for Tests," *Harvard Crimson,* November 17, 1978, p. 1.
40. "Effects of Coaching on Standardized Admission Examinations," Revised Statistical Analyses of Data Gathered by Boston Regional Office of the Federal Trade Commission, issued by the Federal Trade Commission, Bureau of Consumer Protection, March 1979, Executive Summary, p. 1.
41. Gene Maeroff, "Agency Finds Coaching Can Raise S.A.T. Scores," *New York Times,* May 30, 1979, p. A10.
42. See note 40, pp. 8–9.
43. The College Entrance Examination Board, *College Bound Seniors, 1973–1974,* p. 27.
44. See note 2, p. 47.
45. David C. McClelland, "Testing for Competence Rather Than for 'Intelligence,' " *American Psychologist,* January, 1973, p. 10.
46. Author's notes from discussion on November 6, 1979.
47. James Meade, "Dyslexia and discrimination," *Boston Globe,* January 21, 1979, p. A18.
48. Thomas C. Wheeler, "The American Way of Testing," *New York Times Magazine,* September 2, 1979, p. 40; adapted from his book, *The Great American Writing Block* (New York: Viking Press, 1979).
49. *Ibid.,* p. 42.
50. *Ibid.*
51. "The Great S.A.T. Debate," *New York Times Magazine,* October 14, 1979, p. 139.
52. Quoted in Hoffmann, *The Tyranny of Testing,* pp. 121–122.

Chapter Three

1. "Aptitude-Test Scores: Grumbling Gets Louder," *U.S. News & World Report,* May 14, 1979, p. 76.
2. *Ibid.*
3. *Ibid.*
4. Don Cameron, Assistant Executive Director of the National Education Association, D.C. Testimony, October 10, 1979, p. 2.
5. Steven Rattner, "In Business Terms, Testing Is a Success," *New York Times,* May 1, 1977, section 12, p. 16.
6. Feder, *The Complete Guide to Taking Tests,* pp. 4–5.

7. See Houts (ed.) *The Myth of Measurability*, p. 16; Hoffmann, *The Tyranny of Testing*, pp. 37–38; and note 1.

8. Feder, *The Complete Guide to Taking Tests*, p. 4.

9. Joanne Omang, "Making the Grade: Standardized Tests Are Under Attack," *Washington Post*, December 26, 1979, p. A10.

10. Oscar Buros, *Tests in Print II* (Highland Park, N.J.: Gryphon Press, 1974), p. xxxiv.

11. Sherwood Davidson Kohn, "The Numbers Game," published in *The Myth of Measurability*, p. 164.

12. Jon Haber, D.C. Testimony on behalf of the United States Student Association, August 1, 1979, p. 4.

13. *Ibid.*

14. Gil Sewall, "Tests: How Good? How Fair?" *Newsweek*, February 18, 1980, p. 100. Copyright 1980, by Newsweek, Inc. All rights reserved. Reprinted by permission.

15. See note 14 and Edward Fiske, "Student Testing Unit's Expansion Leads to Debate," *New York Times*, November 14, 1979, pp. A1 and A27.

16. Fiske, p. A1.

17. *Ibid.*, p. A27.

18. Allan Nairn, Albany Testimony, p. 135.

19. See note 14.

20. "Getting Testy," *Time*, November 26, 1979, pp. 114–115. Quotation verified and supplemented by John Richard of Ralph Nader's staff and reprinted by permission.

21. ETS Press Release, July 31, 1979, p. 3.

22. R. Jeffrey Smith, " 'Truth-in-Testing' Attracts Diverse Support," *Science*, September 14, 1979, p. 1110.

23. Chuck Stone, Albany Testimony, p. 89.

24. Robert Solomon, Albany Testimony on behalf of ETS, p. 112.

25. Fiske, op. cit. p. A27.

26. Jerry Schechter, Albany Testimony, p. 270.

27. Fiske, op. cit. p. A27.

28. Martin Mayer, *The Schools* (Garden City, N.Y.: Doubleday & Company, Inc., Anchor Books, 1963), p. 420.

29. Dr. Barbara Lerner, "The War on Testing: *Detroit Edison* in Perspective," published by Educational Testing Service, 1979, p. 4.

30. *Ibid.*, p. 3.

31. "Less Than an 'A' for the S.A.T.," *New York Times*, January 21, 1980, p. A22.

32. See note 14.

33. Hoffmann, *The Tyranny of Testing*, p. 209.

34. Robert Solomon, D.C. Testimony on behalf of ETS, July 31, 1979, p. 5.

35. Dean Fred Hargadon, D.C. Testimony on behalf of CEEB, July 31, 1979, pp. 2–3.

36. Dr. Philip Rever, Albany Testimony on behalf of ACT, p. 70.

37. See note 12.

38. Fiske, op. cit. p. A27.

39. Dr. Frank Snyder, D.C. Testimony, September 10, 1979, p. 1; and see note 11, p. 159.

40. Dr. Roger Lennon, D.C. Testimony on behalf of HBJ, August 1, 1979, pp. 1–2; and see note 11, p. 173.

41. See note 39, p. 10.

42. Address by Terry Herndon of the NEA to the National Conference on Testing Reform in Washington D.C., November 7, 1979.

43. Barbara Demick, "Evening the Score," *New Republic*, August 25, 1979, p. 9.

44. Feder, *The Complete Guide to Taking Tests,* p. 6.
45. Professors John Rothney, Paul Danielson, and Robert Heimann, *Measurement for Guidance* (New York: Harper, 1959), p. 323.
46. Dr. Paul Pottinger in D.C. Testimony on September 10, 1979, p. 10, stated: "More valid and less discriminatory technology is available. It simply is not being used. The testing companies are locked into their old techniques."
47. George Hanford, executive vice-president of the College Board, in a talk at the summer conference held at the Harvard School of Education, June 28, 1979.
48. See note 46, p. 8.
49. William Turnbull, "Public and Professional Attitudes Toward Testing and ETS," Memorandum dated August 14, 1978, p. 6.
50. *Ibid.,* p. 3.
51. *Ibid.,* p. 7.
52. *Ibid.*
53. *Ibid.,* p. 17.
54. Hoffmann, *The Tyranny of Testing,* p. 212.
55. *Ibid.,* p. 214.

Chapter Four

1. Robert Solomon, D.C. Testimony on behalf of ETS, July 31, 1979, p. 13.
2. Dr. Philip Rever, Albany Testimony on behalf of ACT, p. 79.
3. Banesh Hoffman suggested in *The Tyranny of Testing* on p. 61 that the term "objective" test could be replaced by the terms "child-gradable" or "machine-graded."
4. Albert Shanker, D.C. Testimony, October 10, 1979, p. 2.
5. Jacques Barzun, Foreword to Hoffmann, *The Tyranny of Testing,* p. 10.
6. Peckham, p. 37.
7. Hoffmann, *The Tyranny of Testing,* p. 108.
8. Christopher Jencks and Mary Jo Bane, "Five Myths About Your IQ," *Harper's,* February 1973, pp. 28, 32.
9. Hoffmann, *The Tyranny of Testing,* p. 109.
10. See the Spring 1979 NCT Conference Summary, pp. 13–14.
11. Dean Hargadon, D.C. Testimony, July 31, 1979, p. 8.
12. Marion Epstein, quoted in "Aptitude-Test Scores: Grumbling Gets Louder," *U.S. News & World Report,* May 14, 1979, p. 78.
13. Donald McNeil, Jr., "State Is Rejecting Tests Given Nurses Throughout Nation," *New York Times,* September 16, 1979, p. 1.
14. Richard Meislin, "Education Chief Validates Controversial Nursing Test," *New York Times,* October 27, 1979, p. 23.
15. Banesh Hoffmann raised this point at the Fall 1979 NCT Conference. See the Summary, pp. 62–63.
16. See, for example, *New York Times,* February 10, 1980, p. E11.
17. Spring 1979 NCT Conference Summary, p. 17.
18. Kim Masters, "ETS Wins Copyright Suit for Misuse of SAT Questions," *Education Daily,* March 19, 1979, p. 2.
19. Dr. Philip Rever, D.C. Testimony, September 10, 1979, p. 20.
20. New York State Senator Donald Halperin, D.C. Testimony, August 1, 1979, p. 3.
21. Dr. Paul Jacobs, Albany Testimony, p. 217B.
22. James Fallows, "How Fair Are the College Boards?" *Atlantic Monthly,* February, 1980, p. 45.
23. Hoffmann, *The Tyranny of Testing,* p. 20.
24. *Ibid.,* p. 66.
25. Judah Schwartz, "The Illogic of IQ Tests," published in Houts (ed.), *The Myth of Measurability,* p. 95.

26. Hoffmann, *The Tyranny of Testing*, p. 85.
27. *Ibid.*, pp. 91–92.
28. Author's notes of NCT discussion on November 5, 1979.
29. Philip Morrison, "The Bell Shaped Pitfall," published in *The Myth of Measurability*, p. 88.
30. Francine Patterson, "Conversations with a Gorilla," *National Geographic*, October, 1978, p. 454.

Chapter Five

1. Virginia Sparling, D.C. Testimony on behalf of the National Congress of Parents and Teachers, September 10, 1979, p. 7.
2. Robert Ebel, "The Social Consequences of Educational Testing," published in Anne Anastasi (ed.), *Testing Problems in Perspective* (Washington, D.C.: American Council on Education, 1966), pp. 25–26.
3. "Standardized" is being used in its broadest sense to include not only the elaborate statistical procedures involved in selecting a standardization group and the questions to be asked under controlled conditions, but the norming function as well. You can have a standardized test without norming—the written portion of a driver's license exam is an example. That test is standardized in the sense of asking individuals the same or similar questions under nearly identical testing conditions, but without knowing whether test scores are comparable over time.
4. See Feder, *The Complete Guide to Taking Tests*, p. 24.
5. See Hoffmann, *The Tyranny of Testing*, p. 139.
6. Althea Simmons, D.C. Testimony on behalf of the NAACP, September 24, 1979, p. 12.
7. New York State Senator Kenneth LaValle, D.C. Testimony, August 1, 1979, p. 6.

Chapter Six

1. Paul Houts, "Introduction: Standardized Testing in America," published in Houts (ed.), *The Myth of Measurability*, p. 13.
2. Gil Sewall, "Tests: How Good? How Fair?" *Newsweek*, February 18, 1980, p. 97.
3. Sherwood Davidson Kohn, "The Numbers Game," published in *The Myth of Measurability*, p. 166.
4. See note 1, p. 16.
5. Edward Fiske, "Student Testing Unit's Expansion Leads to Debate," *New York Times*, November 14, 1979, p. A27.
6. See note 3, p. 168.
7. Barbara Demick, "The Kindergarten Rat Race," *New Republic*, September 29, 1979, p. 25.
8. *Ibid.*, p. 21.
9. Virginia Sparling, D.C. Testimony on behalf of the National Congress of Parents and Teachers, September 10, 1979, p. 3.
10. Dr. Ralph Tyler mentioned this story during the course of his address entitled, "The Advantages and Disadvantages of Standardized Testing," delivered during the Spring Forum of the University of Massachusetts School of Education on March 27, 1979.
11. William Corbett, "Two Principals Look at Standardized Tests," published in *The Myth of Measurability*, p. 335.
12. Rosalyn Herman, Albany Testimony on behalf of the New York State United Teachers and its president, Thomas Hobart, p. 227C.
13. Summary of the Fall 1979 NCT Conference, p. 49.

14. Arthur Laughland, "Two Principals Look at Standardized Tests," published in *The Myth of Measurability*, p. 332.
15. See note 9, p. 2.
16. Hoffmann, *The Tyranny of Testing*, p. 121.
17. See note 9, p. 5.
18. Fall 1979 NCT Conference Summary, p. 34.
19. Ann Cook and Deborah Meier, "New York Students Show Spectacular Rise in Reading/New York City Students' Scores Indicate Steady Decline in Reading," unpublished paper distributed at the Fall 1979 NCT Conference.
20. Hoffmann, *The Tyranny of Testing*, p. 107.
21. *Ibid.*, p. 106.
22. Martin Mayer, *The Schools*, pp. 408–409.
23. *Ibid.*, p. 419.
24. Walter Lippmann, "The Abuse of the Tests," *New Republic*, November 15, 1922, p. 297.
25. Walter Lippmann, "The Reliability of Intelligence Tests," *New Republic*, November 8, 1922, p. 277.
26. Feder, *The Complete Guide to Taking Tests*, p. 2.
27. Lee Cronbach, "Five Decades of Public Controversy Over Mental Testing," *American Psychologist*, January 1975, pp. 6–7.
28. David Harman, "Reading Tests," published in *The Myth of Measurability*, p. 314.
29. Quoted in Feder, *The Complete Guide to Taking Tests*, p. 14.
30. *Ibid.*, p. 152.
31. Dr. Vito Perrone, "On Standardized Testing and Evaluation," published in *The Myth of Measurability*, p. 366.
32. *Hobson* v. *Hansen*, 269 F. Supp. 401 (D.D.C., 1967), at 515.
33. Edwin Taylor, "The Snares of Secrecy," *Education Development Center News*, Winter 1978, p. 1.
34. Edwin Taylor, "Damaging Secrecy," London *Times* Educational Supplement, November 16, 1979, p. 24.
35. Jerrold Zacharias, "The Trouble with IQ Tests," published in *The Myth of Measurability*, p. 75.
36. Paul Houts, "The Score Against IQ," in *The Myth of Measurability*, pp. 100, 102, and 103.
37. Hoffmann, *The Tyranny of Testing*, p. 100.
38. Fall 1979 NCT Conference Summary, p. 48. See also "Bombs Rain on New York!" *Education USA*, November 12, 1979, p. 84.
39. Edwin Taylor, "Science Tests," published in *The Myth of Measurability*, p. 291.
40. *Ibid.*, pp. 298, 301, and 302.
41. See note 9, p. 6.
42. See note 22, p. 419.
43. Fall 1979 NCT Conference Summary, p. 43.
44. See note 35, p. 66.
45. See note 14, pp. 332 and 334.
46. Thomas Cottle, "Going Up, Going Down," published in *The Myth of Measurability*, p. 144.

Chapter Seven

1. Judith Weitzman, "SAT cramming: Dead end or road to success?" *Boston Globe*, March 16, 1978, p. 3.
2. Marian Schlesinger, *Snatched from Oblivion* (Boston: Little, Brown & Co., 1979), p. 113.

3. "The First 75 Years," brochure published by the College Entrance Examination Board, 1975, p. S7. See also Michael Schudson, "Organizing the 'Meritocracy': A History of the College Entrance Examination Board," *Harvard Educational Review,* February 1972.
4. From phone conversations with John Smith, ETS press officer, on January 30 and February 8, 1978.
5. *Ibid.*
6. Gil Sewall, *et al.,* "Tests: How Good? How Fair?" *Newsweek,* February 18, 1980, p. 97.
7. Michael Schudson, "Organizing the 'Meritocracy': A History of the College Entrance Examination Board," *Harvard Educational Review,* February 1972, p. 55.
8. Feder, *The Complete Guide to Taking Tests,* p. 80.
9. *Ibid.,* p. 75.
10. Dr. Vito Perrone, D.C. Testimony, September 10, 1979, p. 10.
11. Dean Fred Hargadon, D.C. Testimony on behalf of the College Board, July 31, 1979, p. 6.
12. Hargadon's remarks came during the course of a discussion of truth-in-testing legislation on the MacNeil/Lehrer Report broadcast on November 2, 1979.
13. *College Guide to the 1978 Summary Reports,* Admissions Testing Program of the College Board, p. 19.
14. Jon Haber, D.C. Testimony on behalf of the United States Student Association, August 1, 1979, p. 4.
15. *Ibid.* On p. 5, Haber conducted a similar analysis of the number of student test-takers whose scores would vary by 60 or more points from their true score.
16. Patricia McCormack, UPI education editor, "Colleges Reduce SAT Emphasis," The *State* (Columbia, South Carolina), November 1, 1979, p. 12C.
17. Edward Fiske, "Student Testing Unit's Expansion Leads to Debate," *New York Times,* November 14, 1979, p. A27.
18. See note 10, p. 6.
19. Cliff Wing, Jr., and Michael Wallach, *College Admissions and the Psychology of Talent* (New York: Holt, Rinehart and Winston, Inc., 1971).
20. See, for example, "Aptitude-Test Scores: Grumbling Gets Louder," *U.S. News & World Report,* May 14, 1979, p. 79.
21. Banesh Hoffman noted this correlation figure decades ago in *The Tyranny of Testing,* p. 140.
22. See note 10, p. 7.
23. *Ibid.,* p. 5.
24. *Ibid.,* p. 6.
25. Althea Simmons, D.C. Testimony on behalf of the NAACP, September 24, 1979, p. 11.
26. Peter Wells, "Applying to College: Bulldog Bibs and Potency Myths," published in Herbert Sacks and Associates, *Hurdles: The Admissions Dilemma in American Higher Education* (New York: Atheneum, 1978), p. 65.
27. "Less Than an 'A' for the S.A.T.," *New York Times,* January 21, 1980, p. A22.
28. Chuck Stone, Albany Testimony, p. 86.
29. *Ibid.,* pp. 86–87.
30. Mayer, *The Schools,* pp. 417–418.
31. David White, Albany Testimony, p. 191.
32. *Ibid.*
33. Hoffmann, *The Tyranny of Testing,* p. 136.

34. David McClelland, "Testing for Competence Rather Than for 'Intelligence,'" *American Psychologist,* January 1973, p. 6.
35. Professor E. W. Kelly, Albany Testimony, p. 163.
36. See, for example, Don Hoyt, "The Relationship Between College Grades and Adult Achievement: A Review of the Literature," American College Testing Program Report No. 7, September, 1965.
37. See note 35, p. 2.

Chapter Eight

1. Millard Ruud, D.C. Testimony on behalf of the Association of American Law Schools, August 1, 1979, p. 5.
2. James Thomas, "Heavy Traffic on the Purple Brick Road," published in Sacks *et al., Hurdles,* p. 216.
3. Gene Maeroff, "More College Seniors Found Putting Off Graduate Work," *New York Times,* June 28, 1978, p. 1.
4. *Ibid.,* p. 217.
5. Lansing Lamont, *Campus Shock* (New York: E. P. Dutton, 1979), p. 58.
6. "Questioning the Bar Exams," *Time,* February 25, 1980, p. 44.
7. William Schendel and Paul Silver, *Law and Law-Related Fields* (Braintree, Mass.: Semline, Inc., 1974), prepared for use by the Office of Career Services and Off-Campus Learning at Harvard University, p. 11.
8. *Ibid.*
9. *Ibid.*
10. Joel Seligman, "Selecting the Chosen Few," *Student Lawyer,* February 1978, p. 45. See also Joel Seligman, *The High Citadel: The Influence of Harvard Law School* (Boston: Houghton Mifflin Company, 1978).
11. Peter Liacouras, "Adding Up the LSATs," *Student Lawyer,* March, 1975, pp. 34–35.
12. Howard Zaharoff, "Does LSAT Measure Legal Aptitude," *Harvard Law School Record,* March 3, 1978, p. 6.
13. See note 11, p. 36.
14. See note 7, p. 58.
15. See note 11, p. 36.
16. See note 10, p. 46.
17. See note 5, p. 61.
18. See note 2, p. 223.
19. "The Law School Admission Test," *Occupational Outlook Quarterly,* Fall 1975, p. 7.
20. See note 11, p. 35.
21. A. M. Minehart, "ETS: No 'Multiple Choice' For the Law School Applicant," *The National Pre-Law Newsletter,* June 1976, p. 2.
22. Steven Brill, "The Secrecy Behind the College Boards," *New York,* October 7, 1974, p. 74.
23. *Ibid.*
24. See note 19.
25. See note 22.
26. Prelaw Advisor Kit 1976, p. 11.
27. Dedra Hauser, "What's ETS Worth?" *Juris Doctor,* March 1976, p. 13.
28. See note 10, p. 47.
29. See note 12.
30. *Ibid.*
31. Dr. Harold Hodgkinson, speech to the Conference of the Bureau of National Affairs of the American Bar Association, June 20, 1975. (Quoted in the American Personnel and Guidance Association *Guidepost,* September 11, 1975.)

32. Edward Bronson, "Trial By Numbers: The LSAT and Cultural Bias," *The National Lawyers Guild Practitioner,* Spring 1977, pp. 38–39.
33. Bruce Zimmer, executive director of the Law School Admission Council (LSAC), Albany Testimony on behalf of the LSAC, p. 151.
34. Professor Jerry Schechter, paper submitted as Albany Testimony, pp. 8–9 (pp. 277–278 of the unofficial record).
35. *Ibid.,* p. 9 (p. 278 of the unofficial record).
36. David White, Albany Testimony, p. 190.
37. See note 33, p. 152.
38. See note 36, p. 192.
39. *Ibid.,* p. 193.
40. See note 11, p. 36.
41. Dean Craig Christensen of the Syracuse University College of Law and a member of the Legal Affairs Committee of the LSAC, Albany Testimony, p. 266.
42. Morton Levitt, "That Bouillabaisse: Medical School Admissions," published in Sacks *et al., Hurdles,* p. 240.
43. "Med School Applications Decline Here, Nationally," *Harvard Crimson,* April 7, 1978, p. 1.
44. Gene Maeroff, "She Has Better Chance Than He of Getting into Med School," *New York Times,* March 16, 1977, p. B4.
45. Carlos Pestana, *The Rejected Medical School Applicant: Options and Alternatives* (San Antonio, Texas: self-published, 1978), p. 62.
46. See note 5, p. 60.
47. Alfred Gellhorn, "Prescription for Premed Students," *Change,* October 1976, p. 7.
48. Jeremy Main, "Careers for the 80's: 10 of the Best—and 10 of the Worst," *Money,* November 1977, pp. 62ff.
49. Richard Lyons, "Gifts from Parents to 'Buy' Places in Professional Schools on the Rise," *New York Times,* April 23, 1978, p. 20.
50. See note 45, p. 6.
51. See Chapter 3 of *Medical School Admission Requirements 1979–80,* published by the Association of American Medical Colleges (Dupont Circle, Washington, D.C. 20036).
52. Sanford Brown, M.D., *Getting Into Medical School* (Woodbury, New York: Barron's Educational Series, Inc., 1975), p. 35.
53. "What's News?" *Wall Street Journal,* December 27, 1977, p. 1.
54. See note 5, p. 59.
55. See note 45, p. 40.
56. Martha P. Leape, *A Guide for Pre-Medical Students.* President and Fellows of Harvard College, 1976, revised 1977, p. 32.
57. See note 45, p. 17.
58. See note 51.
59. Drs. John Rhoads, Johnnie Gallemore, Daniel Gianturco, and Suydam Osterhout, "Motivation, Medical School Admissions, and Student Performance," *Journal of Medical Education,* December 1974, p. 1119.
60. See note 42, p. 239.
61. See note 5, p. 97.
62. *Ibid.*
63. Dr. Howard Hiatt, speech delivered at the 86th Annual Meeting of the Association of American Colleges, November 1975, reprinted by the Center for the Analysis of Health Practices, Harvard School of Public Health, p. 16.
64. H. Jack Geiger and Victor W. Sidel, "M.D.'s for Everyone," *New York Times,* August 9, 1976, p. 23.
65. *Ibid.*

66. See note 5, p. 96.
67. *Ibid.*
68. See note 64.
69. See note 59.
70. *Ibid.*, p. 1121.
71. *Ibid.*, p. 1125.
72. John J. Conger and Reginald H. Fitz, "Prediction of Success in Medical School," *Journal of Medical Education*, November, 1963, pp. 943–948.
73. Hilliard Jason, "The Admissions Process in Medicine," *Journal of Medical Education*, August, 1972, p. 663.
74. See note 47.
75. Robert Turner, "Enrollment Prospects in Graduate Schools of Business in the Next Ten Years," a paper presented at the Annual Meeting of the Graduate Management Admission Council, May 13, 1977, p. 5.
76. Michael Jensen, "Students Are Bullish about the M.B.A.," *New York Times*, April 30, 1978, section 12, p. 8.
77. Michael Knight, "Harvard MBA: A Golden Passport," *New York Times*, May 23, 1978, p. D1.
78. Robert Turner, "Enrollment Prospects for Collegiate Schools of Business," *Business Horizons*, October, 1976, p. 62.
79. Dena Rakoff, *A Guide to Graduate Schools of Management* (Prepared for the Office of Career Services and Off-Campus Learning, Harvard University, 1977), p. 2.
80. Elizabeth Fowler, "Restudying Curriculum for MBA," *New York Times*, July 5, 1978, p. D8.
81. See note 48, p. 63.
82. See note 79, p. 6.
83. ETS Annual Reports, 1976 and 1977.
84. Roger Ricklefs, "Glutted Professions Put Students in Job Market at Corporations Again," *Wall Street Journal*, January 14, 1976, p. 1.
85. *Ibid.*
86. See note 79, p. 14.
87. Detlev Vagts, "The Other Case Method: Education for Counting House and Court House Compared," *Journal of Legal Education*, Vol. 28, 1977, pp. 403–422.
88. Lois Crooks, "Personal Factors Related to Careers of MBAs," *ETS Findings*, vol. iv, no. 1, 1977, p. 4.
89. J. Sterling Livingston, "The Myth of the Well-Educated Manager," *Harvard Business Review*, January–February 1971, p. 79.
90. ETS Annual Report, 1978.
91. Feder, *The Complete Guide to Taking Tests*, p. 76.
92. *Ibid.*, p. 77.
93. See note 5, p. 48.
94. *Ibid.*
95. See note 12, p. 7.
96. See note 2, p. 221.
97. See note 12, pp. 6–7.
98. See note 11, p. 35.
99. See note 2, pp. 226–228.
100. *Ibid.*, p. 227.
101. See note 22 from Chapter 1.
102. James Fallows, "The American Class System and How to End It," *Washington Monthly*, February 1978, p. 20.
103. See note 47.
104. See note 5, p. 60.
105. *Ibid.*

Chapter Nine

1. Edward Fiske, "Student Testing Unit's Expansion Leads to Debate," *New York Times,* November 14, 1979, p. A27.
2. George Hanford, executive vice-president of the College Board, in a talk at the summer conference held at the Harvard School of Education, June 28, 1979.
3. Dr. Paul Pottinger, D.C. Testimony, September 10, 1979, p. 1.
4. "Aptitude-Test Scores: Grumbling Gets Louder," *U.S. News & World Report,* May 14, 1979, p. 80.
5. "FTC Drops LSAT," *The Testing Digest,* Summer 1979, p. 10.
6. *Ibid.*
7. "Tests on Trial in Florida," *Time,* July 30, 1979, p. 66.
8. Patricia West, "Chicago Principals' Exam in Dispute," *The Measuring Cup,* September–October 1979, p. 4.
9. David White, Albany Testimony, p. 194.
10. John Feinstein and Jackson Diehl, "Question on P.G. Police Test Proves Difficult to Answer," *Washington Post,* December 29, 1978, p. B1.
11. David McClelland, "Testing for Competence Rather Than for 'Intelligence,'" *American Psychologist,* January 1973, p. 4.
12. "Multistate Bar Examination—Bulletin of Information for Applicants," February 28 and July 25, 1979, published by the National Conference of Bar Examiners and ETS; and Victor Schwartz, *Barron's How to Prepare for the Multistate Bar Examination* (Woodbury, New York: Barron's Educational Series, Inc., 1977).
13. See Schwartz, note 12, p. ix.
14. "Questioning the Bar Exam," *Time,* February 25, 1980, p. 44.
15. *Ibid.*
16. *Ibid.*
17. Jon Haber, D.C. Testimony on behalf of the United States Student Association, August 1, 1979, pp. 15–16.
18. See Schwartz, note 12, p. 11.
19. See note 14.
20. David White, "Truth:Testing::Justice:Law," *The Measuring Cup,* Special Supplement, November–December 1979, p. 2.
21. See note 14.
22. Dr. Paul Pottinger, D.C. Testimony on behalf of the National Center for the Study of Professions, September 10, 1979, p. 6.

Chapter Ten

1. For background reading detailing the origins and development of the IQ tests, relied on in this account, see Leon Kamin, *The Science and Politics of I.Q.;* Jeffrey Blum, *Pseudoscience and Mental Ability* (New York: Monthly Review Press, 1978); and Lee Cronbach, "Five Decades of Public Controversy Over Mental Testing," *American Psychologist,* January 1975.
2. Testimony of Professor L. Kamin, cited in Peckham, p. 8.
3. Peckham, p. 8. See also Lewis Terman, *The Measurement of Intelligence* (Boston: Houghton Mifflin, 1916), p. 6.
4. See Terman, note 3, p. 91.
5. Daniel Boorstin, *The Americans: The Democratic Experience,* p. 223.
6. See Kamin, note 1, pp. 176–177, and Carl Brigham, *A Study of American Intelligence* (Princeton, N.J.: Princeton University Press, 1923), p. 29.
7. See Jeffrey Blum, *Pseudoscience and Mental Ability* (New York: Monthly Review Press, 1978).

8. Peckham, p. 38.
9. *Ibid.*
10. See Walter Lippmann, "A Future for the Tests," *New Republic,* November 29, 1922, p. 9.
11. *Ibid.*
12. Peckham, p. 31.
13. David McClelland, "Testing for Competence Rather Than for 'Intelligence,'" *American Psychologist,* January 1973, p. 6.
14. *Ibid.*
15. Walter Lippmann, "The Reliability of Intelligence Tests," *New Republic,* November 8, 1922, p. 276.
16. Judah Schwartz, "The Illogic of IQ Tests," published in Houts (ed.), *The Myth of Measurability,* p. 91.
17. Arthur Laughland, "Two Principals Look at Standardized Tests," published in *The Myth of Measurability,* p. 331.
18. Thomas Cottle, "Going Up, Going Down," published in *The Myth of Measurability,* p. 142.
19. Paul Jacobs, Albany Testimony, p. 217A.
20. Oscar Buros, *Mental Measurements Yearbook,* sixth edition (Highland Park, N.J.: Gryphon Press, 1965), p. xxiv.
21. *Ibid.*
22. James Fallows, "How Fair Are the College Boards?" *Atlantic Monthly,* February 1980, p. 47.
23. *Ibid.,* p. 46.
24. James Fallows, "The American Class System and How to End It," *Washington Monthly,* February 1978, p. 14.
25. *Ibid.,* p. 18.
26. *Ibid.,* pp. 14–15.
27. The story is entitled, "Extract From Captain Stormfield's Visit to Heaven."

Chapter Eleven

1. Dr. James Loewen, D.C. Testimony, August 15, 1979, p. 11.
2. *Ibid.,* p. 10.
3. *Ibid.*
4. Peckham, p. 71.
5. *Ibid.,* p. 72.
6. Leon Kamin, *The Science and Politics of I.Q.,* p. 30.
7. Peckham, p. 43.
8. Sylvia Johnson, "The 'Measurement Mystique'—Issues in Selection for Professional Schools and Employment," a paper published by the Institute for the Study of Educational Policy, 1979, Number 02.
9. Testimony of Professor Leon Kamin, cited in Peckham, p. 122.
10. Peckham, pp. 46, 122.
11. *Ibid.,* pp. 45–46.
12. James Loewen, D.C. Testimony, September 24, 1979, p. 5.
13. James Fallows, "How Fair Are the College Boards?" *Atlantic Monthly,* February 1980, p. 48.
14. David White, Albany Testimony, pp. 199–200.
15. Edwin Taylor, "Damaging Secrecy," London *Times* Educational Supplement, November 16, 1979, p. 24.
16. Dr. David Perham, Albany Testimony, p. 168.
17. *Ibid.,* p. 169.
18. *Ibid.,* pp. 172–173.
19. Edwin Taylor, "Science Tests," published in Houts (ed.), *The Myth of Measurability,* pp. 293–294. Taylor cites, in connection with this passage,

Mary Jo Bane, *Tests and Testing* (McLean, Va.: National Council for the Advancement of Education Writing, 1974).

20. David McClelland, "Testing for Competence Rather Than for 'Intelligence,' " *American Psychologist,* January 1973, p. 3.
21. Dean Fred Hargadon, D.C. Testimony on behalf of the College Board, July 31, 1979, p. 5.
22. Dr. Vito Perrone, D.C. Testimony, September 10, 1979, p. 6.
23. See note 1, p. 3.
24. *Ibid.*
25. Chuck Stone, Albany Testimony, pp. 85–87.
26. See note 1, p. 12.
27. *Regents of the University of California* v. *Bakke,* 438 U.S. 265 (1978).
28. See note 22, p. 8.
29. See note 8, p. 13.
30. *Ibid.*, p. 1.
31. *Ibid.*, p. 27.
32. Dr. Ralph Tyler used these figures during his address entitled "The Advantages and Disadvantages of Standardized Testing," delivered during the Spring Forum of the University of Massachusetts School of Education on March 27, 1979.
33. Professor George Madaus of Boston College mentioned this nickname during his talk to the NCT Fall 1979 Conference on November 5, 1979.
34. Diana Pullin of the Harvard Center for Law and Education cited these figures during her talk at the NCT Fall 1979 Conference. See the Fall 1979 NCT Conference Summary, p. 12.
35. See note 33, p. 19, where Professor Madaus made much the same point, i.e., that given the severe sanctions, eventually what is emphasized on the test will become part of the curriculum and test scores will go up.

Chapter Twelve

1. Edward Fiske, "Student Testing Unit's Expansion Leads to Debate," *New York Times,* November 14, 1979, p. A27.
2. *Ibid.*
3. Layton Olson, Albany Testimony on behalf of the National Student Education Fund, p. 234B.
4. *Ibid.*
5. *Report of the Commission on Tests: Righting the Balance* (New York: College Entrance Examination Board, 1970), p. xv.
6. *Ibid.*, p. 57.
7. Jerry Adler, "Wide-Open Admissions," *Newsweek,* April 21, 1980, p. 111. Copyright 1980, by Newsweek, Inc. All rights reserved. Reprinted by permission.
8. *Ibid.*
9. Dr. Vito Perrone, D.C. Testimony, September 10, 1979, p. 1.
10. Allan Nairn, Albany Testimony, p. 136.
11. Feder, *The Complete Guide to Taking Tests,* p. 29.
12. Sherwood Davidson Kohn, "The Numbers Game," published in Houts (ed.), *The Myth of Measurability,* p. 177.
13. Robert Solomon, executive vice-president of ETS, D.C. Testimony on behalf of ETS, July 31, 1979, p. 11.
14. *Ibid.*, p. 12.
15. David White, Albany Testimony, p. 189.
16. *Ibid.*, pp. 189–190.
17. *Ibid.*, p. 190.
18. Hoffmann, *The Tyranny of Testing,* p. 183.

19. *Ibid.*
20. Dr. Lewis Pike, Albany Testimony, pp. 179–180.
21. *Ibid.*, p. 180.
22. *Ibid.*, pp. 185–186.
23. See note 13, pp. 14 and 15.
24. Dr. Paul Pottinger, D.C. Testimony on behalf of the National Center for the Study of the Professions, September 10, 1979, p. 9.
25. Jon Haber, D.C. Testimony on behalf of the United States Student Association, August 1, 1979, p. 10.
26. See note 15, pp. 195 and 196.
27. *Ibid.*, p. 196.
28. *Ibid.*
29. See note 24, p. 12.
30. Abby Helfer, Albany Testimony on behalf of the Student Association of Syracuse University, p. 240.
31. James Stern, Albany Testimony, p. 254.
32. Dr. Paul Jacobs, Albany Testimony, p. 218.
33. Mayer, *The Schools*, p. 420.
34. See note 12, p. 162.
35. See note 18, p. 135.
36. *Ibid.*, p. 144.
37. See note 11, p. 155.
38. Professor E. W. Kelly, Albany Testimony, p. 164.

Chapter Thirteen

1. Feder, *The Complete Guide to Taking Tests*, p. 77.
2. *Ibid.*, p. 21.
3. Dr. Philip Rever, D.C. Testimony on behalf of the American College Testing program, September 10, 1979, p. 20.
4. *Ibid.*, pp. 20–21.
5. See note 1, p. 156.
6. Suggested by Lisa Healy in a phone conversation with the author, April 22, 1980.

Chapter Fourteen

1. R. Jeffrey Smith, " 'Truth-in-Testing' Attracts Diverse Support," *Science*, September 14, 1979, p. 1110.
2. For background reading on the event, see Lawrence Altman, "Citing New Law, Medical Schools to Bar Entry Tests in New York," *New York Times*, July 18, 1979, p. 1; Edward Fiske, "Scholastic Testing Industry Facing Regulation by State," *New York Times*, July 5, 1979, p. D6; Edward Fiske, "Resolve the Testing Dilemma, Go to the Head of the Class," *New York Times*, October 14, 1979, p. E6; and John Weiss, "Truth-in-Testing," *The Testing Digest*, Fall 1979, p. 1.
3. David White, "Truth:Testing :: Justice:Law," *The Measuring Cup*, Special Supplement, November–December 1979, p. 2.
4. "Testing the test-makers," *Boston Globe*, July 19, 1979, p. 12.
5. "Truth in Testing," *New York Times*, July 24, 1979, p. A14.
6. *Ibid.*
7. Layton Olson, Albany Testimony on behalf of the National Student Education Fund, p. 234C.
8. Pat Rooney, Albany Testimony, p. 53.
9. See, for example, Robert Solomon, Albany Testimony on behalf of ETS, pp. 97–98.

10. Rosalyn Herman, Albany Testimony on behalf of the New York State United Teachers and its President, Thomas Hobart, p. 227D.
11. Dr. Paul Jacobs, Albany Testimony, p. 217B.
12. Ellen Schultz, Albany Testimony, pp. 175A–175AA.
13. Oscar Buros, "Fifty Years in Testing: Some Reminiscences, Criticisms, and Suggestions," *Educational Researcher,* July–August 1977, p. 14.
14. Dr. Roger T. Lennon, D.C. Testimony on behalf of Harcourt Brace Jovanovich, Inc., August 1, 1979, p. 7.
15. *Ibid.,* pp. 6–7.
16. Steve Solomon, Albany Testimony on behalf of the New York Public Interest Research Group, p. 33.
17. Dr. Walter Haney, Albany Testimony, pp. 155–156.
18. Abby Helfer, Albany Testimony on behalf of the Student Association of Syracuse University, p. 240.
19. New York State Senator Donald Halperin, Remarks during Albany Hearing, pp. 24–25.
20. Dr. David Stratman, D.C. Testimony on behalf of the Campaign for the Future, October 20, 1979, p. 8.
21. Dr. Vito Perrone, D.C. Testimony, September 10, 1979, p. 11.
22. Dr. Philip Rever, Albany Testimony on behalf of the American College Testing program, p. 78.
23. Dr. Paul Pottinger, D.C. Testimony, September 10, 1979, p. 8.
24. Dr. Urbain DeWinter, D.C. Testimony, September 24, 1979, p. 8.
25. See, for example, the Associated Medical Schools of New York, "Memorandum in Opposition [to the New York proposal]," April 25, 1978, p. 2.
26. Allan Nairn, Albany Testimony, pp. 125–129.
27. Robert Moulthrop, director, Information Division, ETS, letter to author of November 30, 1979.
28. See note 26, pp. 127–129.
29. The College Entrance Examination Board, "Memorandum in Opposition to Senate 5845–B by Mr. LaValle," not dated, but prepared for use in connection with the debate over the New York bill, p. 4.
30. Ralph Blumenthal, "Test-Makers Face New Test," *New York Times,* April 20, 1980, Section 12, p. 25.
31. New York State Senator Kenneth LaValle, D.C. Testimony, August 1, 1979, p. 4.
32. Dr. Walter Haney, letter to Stephen Solomon, January 18, 1979, p. 2.
33. David White, Albany Testimony, p. 189.
34. See note 17, p. 160.
35. Dr. Vito Perrone, Albany Testimony, p. 257.
36. Educational Testing Service, "Memorandum of Opposition [to the New York bill]," not dated, but prepared for use in connection with the debate over the New York bill, p. 2.
37. See note 13, p. 14.
38. This report was written at the Huron Institute in Cambridge, Mass., where I worked with Dr. Walter Haney and others studying the implications of testing policy. The Huron Institute provides staff support for the National Consortium on Testing, which is an umbrella organization composed of all types of associations interested in tests. The NCT membership spans the chasm between test critics and supporters, with bodies such as ETS, CEEB, NYPIRG, the National Education Association, and the PTA all represented. The views I expressed in the report don't necessarily reflect the convictions of the people in the NCT, or those at the Huron Institute, since neither organization has taken an official position on this matter. A copy of the 71-page report, called NCT Staff Circular No. 6, "The Debate Over Open Versus Secure Testing: A Critical Re-

view," can be obtained from the Institute (123 Mount Auburn Street, Cambridge, Mass. 02138) for a nominal charge. The report summarizes the cases made for and against open testing and then analyzes these cases before proceeding to the conclusions.

39. See note 32, p. 2.
40. This story was first told to me by Greg Conderacci on November 6, 1979.
41. See note 30, p. 1.
42. See note 26, p. 141.
43. See note 23, p. 9.
44. See note 31, p. 2.
45. See note 35.
46. Frank Erwin, D.C. Testimony on behalf of the American Society for Personnel Administration, October 10, 1979, p. 13.
47. Virginia Sparling, D.C. Testimony on behalf of the National Congress of Parents and Teachers, September 10, 1979, p. 1.
48. See note 16, pp. 33–34.
49. See note 35, p. 258.
50. See note 30, p. 1.
51. See note 38, p. 62.

Chapter Fifteen

1. Dr. Walter Haney, Albany Testimony, p. 160.
2. Rosalyn Herman, Albany Testimony on behalf of the New York State United Teachers and its president, Thomas Hobart, p. 228.
3. Professor Sylvia Johnson, "The 'Measurement Mystique'—Issues in Selection for Professional Schools and Employment," a paper published by the Institute for the Study of Educational Policy, 1979, Number 02, p. 42.
4. J. Parker Damon, "Questions You Should Ask About Your Testing Program," published in Houts (ed.), *The Myth of Measurability*, pp. 348–363.
5. Summary of the Fall 1979 NCT Conference, pp. 43–45.
6. See James Fallows, "How Fair Are the College Boards?" *Atlantic Monthly*, February 1980, p. 48.
7. *Ibid.*
8. Dr. David Stratman, D.C. Testimony, October 20, 1979, p. 5.
9. Althea Simmons, D.C. Testimony on behalf of the NAACP, September 24, 1979, p. 8.
10. See note 6.
11. Professor David McClelland, "Testing for Competence Rather Than for 'Intelligence,'" *American Psychologist*, January 1973, p. 2.
12. As suggested by Dr. Vito Perrone, D.C. Testimony, September 10, 1979, p. 10.
13. *Ibid.*, pp. 8–9.
14. See note 11, p. 7, and the Summary of the Spring 1979 NCT Conference, pp. 50–54.
15. See the Summary of the Spring 1979 NCT Conference, pp. 47–49.
16. See John Antonides, "Minorities and the Bar Exam: Color Them Angry," *Juris Doctor*, August/September 1978, pp. 58–59.
17. Dr. Paul Pottinger, D.C. Testimony, September 10, 1979, pp. 13–14.
18. Arthur Laughland, "Two Principals Look at Standardized Tests," published in Houts (ed.), *The Myth of Measurability*, p. 335.
19. As quoted in *The Measuring Cup*, November–December 1979, p. 6.
20. Hoffmann, *The Tyranny of Testing*, p. 103.
21. Virginia Sparling, D.C. Testimony on behalf of the National Congress of Parents and Teachers, September 10, 1979, p. 1.

Index

315